The Constant Conversation

To Diana,

with best regards—

Joe Crowley

March 2002

Joseph N. Crowley

~

The Constant Conversation: A Chronicle of Campus Life

Foreword by
James W. Hulse

The Black Rock Press
University of Nevada, Reno
2000

Printed in the United States of America

ISBN   1-891033-18-2

The Black Rock Press
University Library/322
University of Nevada, Reno
Reno, NV 89557-0044

775.784-6500 ext.317
blackrock@unr.edu
www.library.unr.edu/blackrock/

The quote by A. Bartlett Giamatti is from his book, *A Free and
Ordered Space; The Real World of the University*. New York: W.W.
Norton, 1988, pp 24-25.

The university ... is still a constant conversation between young and old, between students, among faculty; between faculty and students; a conversation between past and present, a conversation the culture has with itself, on behalf of the country ... Perhaps it is the sound of all those voices ... giving and taking, that is finally the music of civilization, the sound of human beings shaping and sharing, mooring ideals to reality, making the world, for all its pain, work.

A. Bartlett Giamatti,
former president of Yale University and
the late Commissioner of Baseball

For Benjamin, Colleen, Ryan, Chase, Gracie, and Annie

Contents

Foreword

FOR THOSE WHO WANT TO EXPLORE THE CONUNDRUM of how and why Joe Crowley survived for more than twenty-two years as president of the University of Nevada in Reno, this volume should be Exhibit A. Between these covers Joe has given us, as a parting keepsake upon his departure from office, various revealing reminders about his style, attitude, and philosophy of life.

Even those who have found Joe garrulous and tedious in his public presentations from the platform (the annual State of the University address has been regarded as a form of water torture by not-a-few faculty members) will adjudge these essays to be insightful and indeed refreshing. There are fifty or so of them plus assorted letters and pieces of whimsy, but they are short—bite-sized samples of his wit and wisdom. He testifies that he kissed the Blarney stone twice; here is the proof.

The playful, light-hearted, self-effacing tone that enriches these pieces reflects a stoicism that formed a shield against the slings and arrows that are inevitably directed at the office and the person of a university president. More important, these articles reveals his competence in what Thomas Aquinas called the *disputatio,* the art of careful listening, reflecting, and writing or speaking—of communicating—which is the hallmark of university life. It is characteristic of Crowley that he includes some exchanges with his most caustic critics.

Friends of Joe and of the University will probably want to ingest these morsels over time. Many will be familiar to regular readers of the *University Times* or the *Silver & Blue.* This book is a laudable companion to Crowley's two previous contributions to the literature on the university presidency — the volumes entitled *Notes From the President's Chair: Reflections on Life in a University* (1988) and *No Equal in the World: An Interpretation of the Academic Presidency,* (1994). In this instance we have a rich assortment of his thoughts during the university's most prosperous years.

At several points in the course of reading or re-reading these items, I thought I had found a piece particularly succulent, worthy of individual recommendation to prospective readers. Alas, there are too many. But one suggestion is pertinent. The reader who wants to rush through these pages quickly is strongly advised not to miss "The Last Word: A Brief Memoir."

So this reader's short explanation for Joe's long tenure and remarkable success at the helm of the University in a turbulent, challenging era is that he has been an effective, patient communicator over a long, long time. He has listened well, taken into account the counsel of his antagonists as well as his close associates, and represented the interests of higher education eloquently within and outside its walls.

James W. Hulse ('52)
Professor of History, Emeritus

⁓

Preface

I HAVE HAD A GOOD TIME PUTTING THIS BOOK TOGETHER. The experience brought back many memories, mostly good ones. It was something of an education, as well, as I relearned some lessons of two-plus decades as a university president. I wrote a lot during those years, about the president's life and that of the institution he served, about people and adventures and misadventures, about initiatives that succeeded and others that went astray. I wrote letters, too, thousands of them, usually responding to the thousands I received.

As my time in office neared its end, I was invited to select some of what I had written for publication in what has turned out to be a kind of farewell volume. I want to thank Bob Blesse, head of Special Collections at the university's Getchell Library and director of the Black Rock Press, for issuing that invitation. Thanks also to the John Ben Snow Foundation for underwriting the costs of publication.

An effort such as this one requires the help of many people. I am especially grateful to the following:

Mike Sion, executive editor of *Silver & Blue*, and Theresa Crowley, a teacher and writer (and my daughter), for reading and commenting on the manuscript. I asked them to be unsparing in their criticisms, corrections, and suggestions, and they were. They have made this book something much better than it was before they laid their hands and eyes on it.

Shannon Clopton, a secretary in my office, who typed the manuscript in several drafts, offered useful advice, and proposed for selection most of the letters included herein.

Shelba Gamble, the wonderful woman who has been my assistant for all of the years I have served as president, who not for the first time found me the time to put this volume together.

My colleague, friend, and sometime critic, Jim Hulse, for his generous foreword to the book.

My family—wife Joy and children Theresa, Neil, Margaret, and Tim. They shared the life, the adventures and misadventures, the highs and lows, and made sure that, through it all, I stayed a happy man. They are in this book in spirit, if not in name. So are my six grandchildren, college students of the future, to whom the book is dedicated.

There are hundreds more to thank—no, thousands—for providing the material from which the musings and letters that follow are forged. That would include the many who have so ably advised and assisted me down through the years, and my critics and correspondents, and the students, whose interests I have tried above all to serve, and the many others who joined me in a 23-year conversation. It would also include, of course, many members of the University and Community College System of Nevada Board of Regents, who gave me leadership, friendship, and support, and who persisted in periodically renewing my contract, allowing me thus to engage in that conversation.

Such mistakes and misjudgments as remain in the book, despite the efforts of readers to clear them away, are solely the author's responsibility.

∿

Part One

≈

MUSINGS

Musings

I HAVE HAD AN UNABASHED, though never unrequited, love affair with words since I was a youngster in knickers and knee socks. I'm not sure how I got smitten. Maybe some storytelling genes passed down the ancestral line from early Irish forebears, and landed in my pool. Maybe it was my mother, who insisted when I was around age 6 that I peruse the newspaper every day. Or my father, who at about the same time began to bring home to me (once a month or so) what was then one of the greatest treats a little boy could get: a novelty item known as the "big little book." And he would say to me, "Don't just look at the pictures, read the words!"

The big little book, I regret to say, is no more, having passed from the scene decades ago. But newspapers are still around, and I still read them—two or three of them—every day. And whatever the source of my word urge, I can't help myself. I am lexically inclined, a phraser of sorts, a neologist sometimes, a defender of the written manifestation of the mother tongue. I have indulged this consuming impulse through reading and writing, composing essays and letters and (every so often) books, taking leisurely voyages through dictionaries and thesauri, producing (for a limited audience) the occasional piece of doggerel, even jotting down at odd times the odd sentence that comes unbidden to mind and that may never find its way into a paragraph.

I have had the opportunity to express myself as well through a regular column in the university's alumni magazine, throughout the years I have served as president and encompassing periodic changes in the title of the magazine. This opportunity has also afforded me an avenue of contemplation, a road down which university presidents typically have little time to travel. Time for contemplation is a luxury not just for presidents but for all who make their way in a busy, stress-filled world. I have had the good fortune at least six times a year to find that time.

I have been dependent, in my efforts to fill the time wisely and efficiently, on a personal muse who sometimes resists my invitations to come perch upon my shoulder and advise me on how to get a boundary line around my thoughts and herd them thence onto a piece of paper. My muse can be busy elsewhere when I most need her, or she can be obstinate, or maybe just seized by the need to show who's boss. Nevertheless, I am grateful to her. My muse has also been generous. I have often found my contemplative labors to be most rewarding, even when I have been less than successful in discovering the words to describe the product of those labors.

When, in my case, the love of lexicon has met an opportunity for contemplation, the result has been a series of, well, of musings. Some of them are set forth in Part One, mostly in the form of columns I have written for the magazine. They deal with aspects of the president's job, with reflections on the American university generally (and one such institution in particular), with a subject—technology—that has long baffled and intrigued me, and with that *sine qua non* of academic life: people.

Chapter One

∼

The Job

EVERY YEAR, DURING NATIONAL READING WEEK, I am invited by one or two local elementary schools to come by and read to a class. I always accept if I'm in town. Most times, after a couple of books have been covered, the children and I have a little conversation. On every such occasion I can remember, at least one of the kids will pop the question: "OK, so what does a university president do?"

"Ahem," I respond. "Let's see ... um, well, there's , uh ..." The fact is that, although I have written a lot on the subject (one book, numerous articles) and discussed it over the years in many college classrooms and other venues, I am hard put to explain the position to second- or third-graders or anyone else expecting a reasonably concise answer. This chapter provides not one answer, but several, focusing mostly on specific duties and approaches and moving on to a more general set of appraisals toward the end.

The Four P's come first. When I speak to those college classes, I often use these P's (patience, persistence, perspective and pain) to communicate the fundamental requirements of the presidency. Additional P words could be deployed, no doubt. I am tempted to say I could explain the office in its entirety relying only on all the P's, including, among others, politics, persuasion, planning, personnel, partnerships and (some might add) purgation. And, of course, people. We will get to them (the people) later. Here, we begin with the fundamental four.

Planning is next, however, as an emphasis in the chapter's second article ("Dad Knows Best"). The broader consideration in this case is the need to balance good planning with a readiness to seize opportunities, noting even so that it would be best to get beyond a sense of the presidency as simply a balancing act and little more.

Commencement, presiding over which is the greatest privilege accorded the president, is taken up in three pieces. One ("Bird Watching") describes certain of the author's experiences, at several ceremonies. Another ("Weather Watching") deals with the 24 hour period surrounding a particular ceremony and, in the process, takes up the delicate issue of speaking duties. This issue is further explored in a third segment "Entrée News" which gives Commencement a seasonal context and offers reflections also on the popularity of chicken as *the* seasonal banquet fare.

Two responsibilities demanding a large share of the president's time are legislative participation and international travel. These worthy causes are given some attention in this chapter ("A Summer Summary"). There is much more that could be said on both topics.

So, too, with athletics, dealing with which can consume far more presidential energy than the priority of sport in the overall university scheme of things. But nothing an American university does is more consistently visible, with more potential to build the institutional name—for good or ill—than athletics. In my own case, though I did not plan it this way, the athletics responsibility led to a national commitment during a decade of reform. That commitment is taken up in "Manual Labor, Shoe Views, and the Reform Agenda," which covers also what needed reforming (and what still does).

Two other pieces discuss aspects of the position that the literature on the presidency has largely ignored, perhaps with good reason. One ("Sign of the Times") is a lament of sorts about the increasingly burdensome business of affixing one's signature. The other explores the less dignified side of the president's routine ("Chip Shot").

Next come efforts to assess the office from the vantage points offered by the passage of years—13 of them in one instance ("A Constant Conversation"), 20 in another ("Thorns, Thistles, and Humble Pie"). Here can be found some discussion of the role of controversy, of the hard reality of criticism, the gripes of those who hold the office, and the metaphors (some nice, some nasty) that a century-and-a-half of writing about the position have yielded. The chapter concludes with a look at what's involved in leaving the job on your own momentum ("Moving On").

∾

Four P's, If You Please

S EVERAL TIMES A YEAR, a colleague will take pity on me and offer me a chance to do a little teaching. I am reminded then that this was once to be my life's work. That was before a perverse fate intervened and shuffled me off to presidential duties. I have been trying to keep my head above the administrative waters ever since. It is a relief to take occasional leave of these exertions and get back to the classroom, where I can recharge the pedagogical batteries and learn again on whose behalf I hang out at the president's office.

Sometimes I teach, or co-teach, a course. More often, these days, I spend a few hours in somebody else's course, usually discussing leadership. I had that opportunity this semester, in a graduate seminar, and one of the things I talked about (although I didn't dwell on it) was pain.

That subject seemed to interest the students, maybe because they had not heard leadership described in quite that way before. I was only trying to communicate a sense of what is required to do a leader's job, and so gave them a few minutes each on the four P's. That would be patience, persistence, perspective and pain. You have to master those P's, I opined, to get the work ably done.

Pain comes in two parts, or so I told them: You have to be able to both endure it and inflict it. Difficult decisions can bring pain to the lives of the people affected, and the decision-maker can expect, as a result, to catch some coming from the other direction. It's no big deal, nothing to get exercised about as long as you toss in compassion on the inflicting side and a tough hide when it's time to endure.

People often ask how you can put up with all the criticism you receive in a job like mine, especially the virulent kind where your ancestry gets questioned, your integrity impugned and your suitability for pursuing an afterlife in the nether regions heartily endorsed. I respond rather like a coach might: those who pay the price of admission (as all kinds of people do where my job is concerned) have a right to speak their minds, however inelegant the speech may be and however small the mind.

When I was in my junior high days back at Sacred Heart School, I learned a coach's lesson. I was elected, for some forgotten reason, to be the captain and coach of the eighth grade no-helmet, no-pads tackle football team. Our only opponent was the seventh-grade team, led by a large fellow we can call Hot Dog Roberts (almost his real name). Hot Dog had failed school a couple of years and, when he had the ball, wise opponents (and that would include all of us) stayed out of his way. Despite the implementation of sophisticated game plans conceived by me, the seventh-graders beat the stuffings out of us. Twice. The eighth-grade girls began to question our mettle. One day, after school, the rest of the team had a secret meeting. They fired me, as I learned later. That was painful, the kind of pain coaches endure, and was pretty good training for a college president.

The following summer, I was playing first base in a sandlot game when Hot Dog came thundering down the line trying to beat out an infield hit. We didn't have umpires, so the guy playing the position got to make the call. We relied on the honor system. I called Hot Dog out, an honorable call. He took eloquent exception, and gave me an emphatic push, which led me to conjecture whether he might not have been safe after all. Instead, I bopped him on the nose, a prominent feature of his facial topography. He bled profusely. I rather enjoyed that. You don't always have to have compassion when inflicting pain.

The above tale, allowing for a certain amount of Irish windage, is mostly accurate. Maybe it is also slightly relevant. I don't mean to suggest that the battles of Nevada higher education were won on the playing fields of Sacred Heart School. But I learned some lessons there, about patience and persistence. I learned the value of perspective, too, and a little bit about pain. Getting fired when you're 13 years old, getting a chance to take the measure of Hot Dog Roberts ... well, those were instructive experiences.

So was the time, early in my grammar school career when I was invited, on a cold winter's day, to apply my tongue to a frozen metal bar on the playground. I accepted the invitation. I learned that frozen metal and human tongues, when joined, tend to develop intimate, lasting relationships.

A part of my anatomy still resides on that bar, on that playground, the same place where Hot Dog ran for those easy touchdowns. For all I know, Hot Dog himself may be there still, making life miserable for the eighth-graders.

∼

Dad Knows Best

I WAS 5 YEARS OLD when my father took me to my first baseball game. We were in St. Louis, visiting relatives, and Dad and I went to Sportsman's Park to watch the Browns play the Cleveland Indians. The Browns were a team that finished in last place, or close to it, practically every year. That explains why there weren't many fans in the stadium on that long-ago Sunday; there never were, which is why the Browns later moved to Baltimore and became the Orioles. Anyway, we had great seats, down close, between home plate and first base. I don't remember who won the game, but I distinctly recall the foul balls. They fell everywhere, several not far from where we were sitting. Kids were catching them, or chasing them. I wanted one badly, but Dad vetoed the idea. "When you're older," he said, "you'll have your chances." He told me that baseballs are hard objects and, when they come your way, you have to be ready.

Dad had played several years of second base for a team he described as the South St. Paul Saints. I hadn't played anything but catch with a tennis ball. So he was the voice of authority on the subject (any subject, actually) as far as I was concerned. This was the case even though, as I later learned, his playing days were with the town team in Maynard, Iowa (pop. 800), which was, indeed, located south of St. Paul (about 250 miles south).

I don't know how many games I've been to since that summer afternoon. My folks went to St. Louis often when I was growing up, and I got back to Sportsman's whenever we were in town. I've seen major league contests in stadiums across the country. I've been to spring training games in Phoenix and Tucson. I covered high school baseball for the *Fresno Bee* when Tom Seaver was mowing down the local hitters. I've been to countless outings at Peccole Park. Since that first game between the Browns and Indians, I wanted to catch—as a spectator, although it was hard enough for me to do as a player—a foul ball. Never had one come my way. However, I always remembered my father's advice. I have always been ready.

Well, almost always.

One day last spring, I pulled up to my usual parking place at Peccole when the game was already underway. I put my Wolf Pack cap on. I got out of the car. I walked three steps. Then the world came to an end. A meteorite, maybe another planet, seemed to have struck Earth, or at least to have struck me and sent me earthward. OK, so it wasn't a planet, or even a piece of one. But it was a spheroid, and it did hit me. Right behind the ear. When I recovered my balance, I saw that spheroid bouncing around the parking lot. It was a hard object, just like Dad said. It was a baseball! It was a foul ball! One had finally come my way, and I wasn't ready. Sorry, Dad.

Some would say I should have planned ahead, since you never know when you might get beaned by a baseball, or, for that matter, by another planet. Planning, though, isn't that easy. We do a lot of it around here, and we take it very seriously. Planning provides the guideposts for our future. But we plan ever mindful of the fact that we do not know what, exactly, the future will hold for us. We have projections. We have expectations. We have lots of data on which to base them. But we understand that the future is likely to unfold somewhat differently from the way we project it and expect it to. We understand that circumstances will change and opportunities will present themselves. We understand that we need to think about opportunities like my Dad thought about foul balls: We have to be ready for them. Opportunities can be hard objects too, and you have to catch them when you can.

There is a balance involved here, between the imperative of serious planning on the one hand and the necessity of an occasional change of course on the other. Surrounded as I am by differing agendas and priorities, by ideas in conflict and constituencies in competition, I have learned that finding balances is a big part of my job. I know of the work of one student of the academic presidency who considers that establishing a balance is *the* job of the men and women who hold the office. He thinks of the president as a cybernetic administrator, an automaton of sorts who maintains the balance of power in the university like Britain kept the balance of power (the famous *Pax Britannica*) in 19th century Europe. And that's about all. The president goes to work, checks on the power arrangements, punches a button or two, restores thus the university world to a kind of *Pax Cybernetica*, and then leaves the rest of the institution's business to others.

Folks, the president's life is rather more complicated than that. A whole lot more. So, I say a pox (sorry) on this particular view of presidential authority. But as for balances, yes, finding them is part of the job. It is a responsibility to be carried out within the context of that sense of direction and purpose that good planning provides. It is a task that requires a willingness to recognize and pounce upon unexpected, unprojected opportunities when they arise. There can be risk there, and usually is. Slings and arrows may come your way. Or tomatoes. Or hard objects. You never know.

After my encounter with the foul ball at Peccole Park, the baseball coach sent me a batting helmet, with advice to wear it to future games (at least when I was getting out of my car). I declined the advice. But I accepted the helmet. I wear it around the office sometimes, when things get out of balance, just in case, just (thanks Dad) to be ready.

~

Bird Watching

I WAS STANDING IN THE SUN FOR AN HOUR-AND-A-HALF, shaking a thousand hands. My knuckles were swollen. My feet hurt. My legs ached. My nose was burning. My shirt was stuck, sweatbound, to my body. It was my 18th annual Commencement ceremony as president, and I was loving every hot and painful minute of it.

The university knows no finer hours than the two we schedule on a mid-May Saturday morning each year, on the Quad, with 12,000 proud people in attendance. The event is the culmination of a month-long season filled with receptions, banquets, services, observances and ceremonies of sundry description, all toward the purpose of honoring achievement. The two days prior to Commencement Saturday are laid end to end with such functions: The Phi Kappa Phi honors society students receive their awards at a lunch; graduates of our own honors program receive their yellow cords at a chocolate cake social; Distinguished Nevadans, President's Medalists and honorary degree recipients are feted at an evening affair; the Friday Graduation Luncheon is followed by the commissioning ceremony for ROTC cadets, which is followed by the pinning of nurses at the Orvis honors convocation, which is followed by the hooding exercise for our newest MDs. It's exhausting. It's wonderful. It's the best season of the academic year.

Silver and Blue, July/August, 1995.

And commencement on the Quad sums it all up nicely.

Of course, things can go wrong. It can snow, for example, as once it did on Commencement morning. We had to move to Lawlor Events Center, and it just wasn't the same. Or streakers may arrive in all their garbless glory, as once they did, though, fortunately for them, it was not snowing that day. Pirates can show up as well. Two of them did, on one occasion, and dueled expertly in front of the graduates. Not to the death, I'm pleased to say; not even to a scratch. But they did sever the microphone cord on their way off-stage. Or the president may forget to remove the ring on his shaking hand, as once, and only once, he did, and grew in the process a larger hand than the one he had started with. And I won't forget a graduate who had plagued my office with visits and phone calls for four years, always complaining about one thing or another. He gave me a beatific smile as I congratulated him when he crossed the stage, and he pressed something into my hand. It felt like a graduation picture, and I thought, how nice of him to declare bygones to be bygones in that symbolic way. In truth, it was a graduation picture, which showed him in his cap and gown, and wearing that same beatific smile. Perhaps that was because also in the picture was one of his fingers, making an unpleasant gesture that could be described as having a birdlike quality.

So, Commencements hold many memories, especially when you have presided over 18 of them. The memories they inspire greatly outnumber those that you recall for other reasons. And on this May Saturday, at this 1995 spring ceremony, I was storing up some very pleasant ones. It seemed to me that our graduates this day symbolized the diverse kind of institution the university has become. They were on hand from all 17 Nevada counties, from most of the states of the union and many of the countries of the world. They represented a wide spectrum of age and ethnicity. There were more female engineers this year, and women were as numerous as men among the MD graduates. Jason Frierson was there, receiving his pre-med degree. Jason is an African-American who came to the university to play football, hurt his knee, and turned then to the intense competition offered by student government. He is the third of his race to serve as student body president in recent years. He will be going places. So will another Jason. That would be Jason Geddes, who received a Ph.D. in environmental science and health at this Commencement, and who was Jason Frierson's predecessor as ASUN president four years ago.

It was a treat to see Neil Humphrey, the first chancellor of Nevada's higher education system, receive an honorary doctorate; and June Whitley, a regent for 16 years, a President's Medal; and Ed Pine, a former vice president of the university, a Distinguished Nevadan award. Ed's history of Nevada Commencements goes back to 1935, when he earned his baccalaureate degree here. There were 159 students in his graduating class. The Class of 1995 had nearly 2,000.

I'll remember all the special people and special moments from this Commencement. I'll forget the sweat, the sunburn and the afflicted extremities. Summer is a good time to summon up memories. There will be time to reflect on 18 years worth of graduations, and to consider as well the adventure — a new academic year — that will begin in late August and will end next May (with no streakers, one hopes, no snow, no swordplay, no birdlike gestures, maybe even no sore feet) in the grand ceremony that reminds us why we're here.

∽

Weather Watching

THERE IS A 24-HOUR PERIOD EVERY YEAR WHEN ACTIVITY IS RELENTLESS, sleep is fleeting, and my life is pretty much a blur. This period runs from noon Friday to noon Saturday—with maybe an extra hour or so on either end—in the middle of May. It's Commencement weekend, of course. This year I took notes. I thought you might be interested.

Actually, it all begins this time with a meeting of our Foundation trustees on Friday morning. The entry next to my name on the agenda says "brief comments," which, more or less, are what I offer. I leave the meeting early to check on the weather. The meteorological gremlins have been out in force this week. Nature has launched a variety of assaults on our creature comforts. We are due to be out on the Quad 12,000 strong tomorrow morning. I need a nice forecast.

I get one, in a qualified kind of way. I get a bad one, too. Vice president Pat Miltenberger stops by to tell me there is a green spot over Nevada on the weather channel. That sounds good until I remember that, on this channel, green is mean. I encourage the Commencement planners to summon up all the prayers, incantations, beseechments,

Silver and Blue, July/August, 1996.

and cajolery at their disposal. Just get us outside in the morning.

I head for Lawlor Events Center, for the Graduation Celebration lunch that marks the official beginning of my 24 hours of constant motion. My job here is to make introductions. I also get to tell the students they can remove from their purses and pockets the Class of '96 wine glasses they found at their tables; no purloining necessary — they are souvenirs. I ask the attendees whether they want to be out on the Quad tomorrow in bad weather or nice and warm and dry in Lawlor. They vote overwhelmingly for the Quad, except for Table 34, which would rather be comfortable.

Commissioning is next. Gen. Martin Brantner is the main speaker. He and I attended midwestern universities back in the 1950s. He went on to three stars in the Marine Corps. I went on to three stripes in the Air Force. Today, we are interested in gold bars, those bestowed on the young second lieutenants who are the honored center of attention on this occasion. I give another brief speech and move on to the nursing convocation.

At this event, the nurses get their pins, placed on their gowns, typically, by family members. It's very touching, a time when kleenex supplies are being rapidly depleted.

I give yet another brief speech. The principal oration is offered by State Sen. Bernice Martin-Mathews. She is eloquent. It is the first speech I have seen delivered sideways: The graduates are in back of her, the audience in front. She manages, with great effect, to speak to both at once from her oblique vantage point.

The convocation over, I'm back at the office by 4:30, consulting weather watchers. This is a very freaky storm system, I am advised: could rain, could blow, could pass us by. I decide to postpone the decision until early tomorrow morning. Then I am off to the medical school hooding ceremony.

Electric feeling is always high in the hall for this event. Tonight is no exception. The dean tells the audience I will be making a couple of very brief, short, condensed, remarks. I comply. Fifty-five freshly minted M.D.s get their hoods, receive their hugs and take their bows. The tear-absorbing tissues are out in abundance again. I dash off at 9 p.m. to George Gund's dinner.

Mr. Gund is to receive an honorary doctorate in the morning. The dinner is to celebrate that award, and the honoree has rented an entire restaurant for the affair. I make a couple of weather calls: Hopes

are fading. I give Mr. Gund a gift, prefaced by—what else?—brief remarks. It is my sixth speech of the day. A few people at the dinner have
sat through all six. Why is it, I wonder, that they are now rolling their
eyes?

It rains hard on my way home. The skies make ominous sounds all
night long. I'm up at 5:30, watching the Weather Channel and listening to howling winds. I call my climatological gurus, who advise an
inside move. I decide at 5:45 that we'll go to Lawlor. Table 34 is
victorious.

On the way to campus, as is a tradition on graduation day, I place a
small bet on the Preakness: a little money on the horse that lost the
Kentucky Derby by a protruding lip, a little more money on a longer
shot named Louis Quatorze. I am a $2 bettor; the university treasury is
not at risk.

Commencement moves me, as it always does. I get in the groove
early when Evelyn de la Rosa sings an invocation, "He's got the Whole
World in His Hands." She's one of our famous graduates, and has
performed in opera houses around the world. If there are any wine
glasses left over in Lawlor from yesterday, she shatters them. The Class
of '96 loves her. Speeches follow, one by me, short and sweet as ever.

Janet Price comes forward to receive her husband's diploma. He died
in February, just short of his goal. A young woman led by a seeing-eye
dog gets her degree and gives me a warm smile. The two Matts, Exline
and Papez, both with strong family connections to the university, both
with 4.0 averages, share the Gold Medal Award. A statuesque young
woman in a mermaid costume, dressed to gill as it were, her feet replete
with flippers, paddles (sort of) across the stage and implants on a surprised but not ungrateful president a pelagic peck on the cheek. Commencement does have its rewards. (I dismiss expeditiously the notion
of offering her a Ph.D.) Running late, we're done by 1 p.m., and I
make my way to the Golden Reunion luncheon.

I tell the reunionees I am speeched out, engendering thereby wild
applause. I bid them welcome and farewell, and, more than 24 hours
after it all began, I go back home to watch the Preakness. Louis Quatorze wins easily and pays handsomely.

Outside, the winds are calm and the sun is shining.

≈

Entrée News

A H, CHICKEN! As the man says in the television commercial (though he has another entree in mind), "It's what's for dinner." This is especially the case during that time of abundant banquets we know around here as the Commencement Season. If you like your life to be predictably led—at least that part of it occurring when you sit to sup— this season will give you great comfort. You will know, as you make your way through the month of celebratory meals preceding gradua- tion day, that you will find on your plate each evening a piece (or more) of that familiar barnyard fowl. It is one of the three features of these evenings you come to count on.

I hasten to add that I have nothing against chicken. It has long had a place of honor among my prandial preferences. Henry IV of France was onto something when he desired for his subjects, and par- ticularly for the poor, "a chicken in [the] pot every Sunday." And was it not Herbert Hoover who, some four centuries later, expressed a simi- lar sentiment on behalf of the American people? I grew up looking forward to chicken dinner once a week, although I confess it was not done then the way it often gets done these days. It was not boiled or baked, stewed or sauteed, fricasseed or cordon bleued. It was *fried*, and served with mashed potatoes and a thick, fatty gravy. Around my house, even now, when the temptation to eat something that's bad for us gets the best of us, we will have ourselves just such a satisfying meal.

Anyway, in my job, during Commencement Season, I can be secure in the knowledge that chicken will be there for me on almost every banquet day. I resign myself to my gustatory fate, gear up my palate for the taste awaiting it, set my jaw resolutely, and, when dinner time arrives, I just, well, what can I say?, bite the pullet.

So, you ask, what are the other two reliable features of this wonder- ful season? One of them may have to be learned. By you. If you are the university president. You may think otherwise at first. You may believe that the multitudes assembled at these honors dinners have come to hear you speak. But you are wrong! The president's presence at these affairs is intended to be symbolic, not oratorical. The people in attendance are there to be honored, or to watch their students or friends or loved ones be honored. They did not come to honor you. So you say a few words, and you sit down.

Silver and Blue, July/August, 1997.

Lessons of humility abound in my job. One of them came to me some years ago, when I was on the program at a campus workshop, to give a welcome. The participants were asked to provide a written evaluation of all the workshop speakers, me included. I received a very good grade, indeed, an "A." As it happened, my schedule was interrupted that day. I did not make it to the workshop. I did not deliver a welcome. I did not say a single word. And the audience members accorded me, therefore, their highest rating. This is a lesson in humility. This is why, when I get up to speak at the banquets, brevity is my middle name. Pith on the platform is as predictable, on these occasions, as poultry on the plate.

We come, then, to the third feature of the season. It's the only one, really, that counts. It's the reason people come together to tolerate both the chicken and the warm-up speeches. It's the reason I love those weeks leading up to Commencement. It reminds us of why we are here. This is the season when, more than any time on the campus calendar, we salute achievement. We recognize at the banquets, and at the lunches and receptions and assorted programs, the academic and other accomplishments of our students. We reward, for lots of folks to see, the contributions of our faculty, staff and community supporters. The heart warms on these occasions, as the hands come gratefully together in applause. The future, even in a grim era, can seem somehow more hopeful.

So, bring on those Plymouth Rocks and Rhode Island Reds. Bake them to a fault and fricassee them to a faretheewell. Bring on (but rarely) windy oratory from the dean, the department chair, the visiting dignitary (but never from the president). The price is worth paying for the celebration of success that's sure to follow.

~

A Summer Summary

SOMEHOW, SUMMER SLIPPED BY ME UNNOTICED THIS YEAR. I find myself asking, was there a July this time around, and a first half of August? Or were those six weeks abandoned in the interest of getting from spring to fall faster than usual, so we could arrive at the blissful autumn evenings and the turning of leaves without the usual tough travel through the dog days?

I look out at my pitiful garden at this writing (early September), remember how parsimoniously it has bestowed its blessings this year (two ripe tomatoes and three petite yellow squash to date), and conclude that, no, we just skipped summer for some reason.

Sure, you are going to ask about June. Well, there was no June in 1995; not for me, anyway. I was at the Legislature most of the time after the May Commencement. People said it was June outside, but you could not have proved it by me, so taken up was I inside those hallowed halls and chambers by the budgetary agenda of higher education. I was there at the end (when it was held by some that July had indeed arrived), shepherding a bill known as SB204 through the tortures of the damned. The bill died a thousand deaths and still got reincarnated somehow so as to present itself in the waning hours as one of the 68th session's last pieces of legislation.

It passed unanimously. It was (and is) worth $5 million to the University and Community College System of Nevada. It cost me June, but it was worth it.

I remember now that I did spend two weeks between fall and spring traveling to Thailand and China. The university does business with universities in those two countries—faculty and student exchanges and program development, for example— and one of them, in Bangkok, was kind enough to pay my way. It was a fascinating trip.

I had not been to Thailand, and found the country, like so much of Asia these days, bursting with energy and activity. The people are warm and welcoming. Our university partner there is an institution not unlike our own, with a similar grouping of colleges and schools and a lovely campus. Bangkok is, well, busy. We got to participate in the decade's worst traffic jam, during a monsoon, four-and-a-half-hours (of waiting and wading) for what is normally a 30-minute ride. On another occasion, we were stopped in a jam in front of a pizza parlor. So we sent in for some, got it ordered, crafted, tossed, baked, boxed, delivered and consumed while moving less than a block. The Thais like their pizza with ketchup, which only reminded me how poorly my tomatoes were doing back home.

As for Beijing, it had changed remarkably since I was last there, in 1982. It's a bustling city, new wealth visible everywhere and the universities alive with purpose and progress I had not seen 13 years ago.

Did I mention food (besides the pizza, I mean)? Let me mention food, mounds of it, courses of it, hours of it. In China, and in Thailand, we were treated by gracious hosts to wonderful, expansive meals. Sometimes, we did not ask what we were eating. Sometimes, we were told anyway: tongue of goose, stomach of pork, cartilage of shark, legs of giant bullfrog, bird's-nest soup (the real thing!), eel (twice), vegetables and fruits I had never heard of, duck every which way (Peking being the best way). We dined well, and often, and welcomed the occasional walks through heat and humidity to work off the constantly accruing pounds.

When I flew back home from Bangkok, the time was at hand to get the old place ready for a new semester. Summer had just up and fled the scene as though if you blinked you missed it, and I blinked. Maybe it's age. Maybe it's the failure of my vegetable garden. Maybe it's because, with the player's strike, I gave up on major league baseball. Maybe it's too much time spent in such exotic places as Bangkok, Beijing and Carson City. Anyway, summer is gone, what there was of it, if any. We are back full-swing in the academic year routine. The new campus carillon—a pleasant sound in any season— has called us to our autumnal duties.

And you know what? In my 30th year here, this fall feels just as good, just as vital, just as full of promise, as the 29 that came before. Who needs summer, anyhow?

~

Manual Labor, Shoe Views
and The Reform Agenda

THE INVITATION WAS CLEAR. Use this *Las Vegas Sun* space as "a sounding board," I was told. I thought a lot about the advice and, stepping into territory angels tremble at traversing, decided to sound off favorably about the National Collegiate Athletic Association.

There is a kind of conventional wisdom that sees the NCAA as a dark monolith rising from the plains of Kansas, periodically dispensing obtuse rulings, regulatory thunderbolts and undeserved punish-

Las Vegas Sun, September, 1996.

ments to hapless lawbreakers. It is a distant bureaucracy, in this view, somehow empowered to conduct its affairs without reference to normal constraints or to the wishes of its members.

But wait a minute, members! We have met the enemy here and, as Pogo knew and we ought to honestly admit, it's us! The NCAA is a democratic organization. Those rules, those thunderbolts, those punishments emanate not from dark monoliths or distant bureaucrats but from the 900-plus colleges and universities that are, in fact, the NCAA. It is the members who democratically decide in this organization, on big issues and small issues alike.

I have a friend who has a copy of the 1949 *NCAA Manual*. It's pamphlet-sized and approximately 45 pages long. This year's folio-sized manual runs to 579 pages. It got to that length because the member institutions set out decades ago to establish that will-o'-the-wisp, the level playing field. When loopholes were found in the rules created to establish that field, new, releveling rules were put in place. Then came new loopholes, more new rules, and so on. That's how we arrived at 579 pages. That's how we got to debates about the number of colors allowable in a recruitment brochure. In this way, the members inflicted on themselves these excessive regulatory wounds, and the *NCAA Manual* became land fill for the level playing field.

A couple of years ago, when I was serving a term as NCAA president, the news show *60 Minutes* decided to do a segment on the shoe contracts of college basketball coaches. Through such contracts, with athletic apparel companies, major college coaches often enjoy large monetary benefits for equipping their teams with company gear. The *60 Minutes* folks made it clear in advance that they thought this a very bad practice, contributing egregiously to the growing commercialization of college athletics. The NCAA should have outlawed it, and shame on the organization for not doing so. That was to be the show's point of view.

Someone had to defend the association's position, which was (and is) that this is an issue that should be handled at the institutional level. I was the designated sacrificial lamb.

Leslie Stahl, a pleasant person and talented interviewer, came to campus to talk to me. She and I had a vigorous, hammer-and-tongs discussion through 80 minutes of taping. The shoe show aired on the Sunday night between semifinal and championship games of the Final Four of men's college basketball. My 80 minutes of taping were translated into 20 seconds of a 20 minute segment. These were not—how to put this delicately?—my finest seconds. The NCAA lost the argument on this segment, the winning side—the *60 Minutes* side—saying, in effect, "Solve this problem through centralized regulation." Add another page or two, more land fill, to the *NCAA Manual*.

60 Minutes is a CBS property. So, by the way, are the broadcasts of the Final Four. On the game nights before and after the shoe contract debate, the network — rather in the manner of the sports apparel companies — raked in gazillions of dollars from its association with college athletics. "Do as I say," said one voice from CBS; "not as I do," said another.

Well, there is more to the NCAA than regulations. It's a very effective service organization to the member institutions. It provides funding and other kinds of support for many worthwhile programs: academic and financial assistance to student-athletes, for example. Overwhelmingly, the association's revenue is returned to the membership. News being what it often is, bad news being weightier and juicier on the whole than good news, these elements of the organization get relatively little public attention.

I have been significantly involved in NCAA affairs for nearly a decade. I now chair a committee overseeing the transition to a substantially reorganized governance structure. I have seen the problematic elements, the underlying causes of a poor public image. I have seen that manual grow. I have watched the previous structure evolve into something impossible to explain.

On the other hand, the structure, complicated and convoluted as it was, did work. People made it work, the volunteers from the institutions and the very talented NCAA staff. I saw that structure gradually reform itself, as institutional presidents came increasingly to influence policies and behavior. Indeed, I saw reform become the organization's watchword, and a series of significant changes enacted as a consequence.

These are matters that, for the most part, do not command the attention of the press. But they are consequential. They have made the NCAA a better association and athletics a more positive and integral component of campus life.

There is much to be done. The commercialization of sport is a major issue. Likewise, sportsmanship, ethics and the rights of student-athletes. And there is still that pile of landfill to reduce. The reorganized association will be in place a year from now. The presidents will be clearly in charge. I'll be done with my involvement then, and pleased to move on to other pursuits. I will be pleased, as well, to leave behind a greatly changed organization whose reality is far better than its image.

~

Sign of the Times

A FEW YEARS AGO, AT A SPORTS BANQUET, I sat next to a famous baseball player who busied himself before dinner, between courses and after dessert, signing autographs for a long, long line of fans. During lulls, while exercising his aching fingers, he complained mildly about all the money this signing frenzy was costing him. He was out of the game now, and often invited to business promotions to sign his name at twenty bucks a pop. He earned a tidy retirement supplement that way. And these freeloading fans were depriving him of a bundle.

I did a little mental arithmetic that night. I wondered what my bank account might look like if I got $20, or $10, or even (bargain-basement rate) $1 every time I signed my name. Bill Gates, move over! Alas!, in the autograph marketplace, I am a mere whiffet. Best, I concluded, to keep, as they say, my day job. My day job, it happens, is also my night job, and my weekend job. And over the years—days, nights, and weekends—a significant portion of my time has been spent in affixing my signature to assorted pieces and piles of paper.

It's no news that technology has its dark side. It has made communication so much easier; that's the bright side. It has made communication so easy, in fact, that people now send you—thanks to phone, fax, airmail, express mail, e-mail, voice mail, and copying machine—stuff you didn't used to receive because it wasn't worth the effort to get it to you and it wasn't all that important anyway. That's the dark side.

The problem is, once the message finds you, you feel the obligation (or at least I do) to answer it. Unless it's anonymous, in which case it is by definition unanswerable. I take a certain pleasure, even so, in dispatching that type of communication to the trash container, often in

Silver and Blue, July/August, 2000.

the shape of a paper airplane.

My regular office mail goes through two people before it reaches me, and they are expert, conscientious, discriminating sifters of the daily freight. Their sifting is steadily interrupted by the phone calls (far more frequent in this cellular era) and the jingling of the facsimile transmitter. But the job gets done every day and, every day, an armful of correspondence arrives at my desk. Lately, I have devoted a good bit of my time on weekends, and on airplanes, to answering this correspondence. That's because, communication-wise, the workdays are now considerably devoted to the telephone messages and e-mails, and to that prodigy of modern information dissemination known as the "meeting." And the nights are largely for receptions and dinners, where the dominant forms of discourse are formal speeches and informal schmoozing, and writing is confined to the table napkins.

Well, the bottom line here is the bottom line: my signature. All that return correspondence (except for e-mail) has to be signed. So do the letters and memoranda initiated by me. So do written communications prepared in other offices to be sent out over my name. So do contracts, compacts, protocols, parchments and other documents of sundry description. This is not scintillating work. Some days, I long for an excellent forger. On occasion, pondering the sheer volume of mail that technology has brought to my attention, I think fond thoughts about carrier pigeons, or of the age when carbon paper was king. Every so often, when my pen wobbles or my hand aches, I offer silent tribute to the motile glories of the Pony Express.

I should remember too, at these moments, to be thankful. What if I had been one of those 19th century college presidents who insisted, as many did, on using three names? If one employed that appellation so affectedly to signal one's sense of self-importance, then one had better carry it over into the signature line. Or, worse, I might have been born to parents from an even earlier time who thought it safest, in the interest of salvation, to regard the naming of their children as an act of supreme piety. Thus did one suffering soul go through life having been christened (truly!) as "Through Much Trial And Tribulation He Shall Enter The Kingdom Of Heaven Lindloff." How did his mother call him in, I wonder, when he was out at play? ("*Through!*— time for dinner"?) How did he introduce himself to strangers? ("Just call me T.M.T.A.T.H.S.E.T.K.O.H.") What if he had become a college president? (Order up some extra-wide stationery!)

As often as I can get away with it, my signature just reads, "Joe." Sometimes, since my middle name is Neil, I'll just use the initials, "JNC." (Only once in those thousands — millions? — of signatures have I ever signed something other than a variation of my own name: In a moment of confusion or perhaps experimentation, I signed the name "James Baker." But those staff sifters of mine caught it, and I was asked, among many other things, to sign again — correctly.) So the signing life is not really as onerous as I make it out to be. And I do get paid for leading this life, even if not at the rate of $20 an autograph. If you have any suggestions about how I might improve in this area, I would be pleased to have them. Don't write, however. Or call. Or wire. Or fax. Or advertise on the internet. Let's just schedule a meeting.

~

Chip Shot

THERE WE WERE: Yours truly, bent over a bit, permitting no muscle to move, allowing neither tic nor twitch nor twinge, staring intently at the fate awaiting me three feet away; and my partner in this risky enterprise, wielding his weapon from that distance, increasing its velocity, sending it ever closer to its target. The target was this too, too fragile flesh of mine. I felt a sudden surge of empathy for William Tell's son, he who stood stock still while his father loosed an arrow at the apple atop his head.

I had no apple, and my partner no arrow. I had a poker chip balanced ever so delicately on the upper edge of my left ear. He had ... well, a yo-yo. The objective was to direct that menacing instrument, traveling at warp speed, to the poker chip, dislodging same without damage to my head and hearing. My partner had about a quarter-inch of chip to work with.

There was reason to trust him. He was, with that worrisomely whirring device of his, the reigning American champion. Indeed, he was the reigning world champion. He had just put on a dazzling display of yo-yo mastery for several hundred guests on hand for a pre-football game brunch. He was Joel Zink, 13-year-old son of our dean of libraries, Steve Zink. Steve had bet his next—and possibly last—paycheck

Silver and Blue, March/April, 2000.

that Joel would not miss on this day. All you have to do, Steve said to me, is lend an ear.

I hoped just now that Joel understood how much I loved that ear. I hoped also that I could fend off the fidget I suddenly felt creeping up my arm, and delay the act of sternutation that seemed to be gaining energy in the area just behind the nose where latent sneezes reside.

People are often curious about my job. They wonder how university presidents spend a typical day or week. I have some standard answers: solving problems, attending meetings, setting plans, attending meetings, building consensus, making decisions, greeting visitors, boarding airplanes, attending meetings, doing noble deeds. I seldom mention the deeds I am called upon to do that are less than noble, like standing squarely in the path of a rapidly advancing yo-yo.

Or like leading an audience of 400 people in performing the Macarena. Now, I am not a talented terpsichorean. When it comes to tripping the light fantastic, the emphasis, for me, has always been on tripping. When I was a lad of 6 or so, my mother somehow concluded that I might have a little musical ability, and so sent me off to piano lessons. A year later, after a miserable recital, incessant pleading by me, and a skill developed to the point that my best effort was a two-fingered rendition of *The Battle Hymn of the Republic*, Mom gave up. Almost. This time, she sent me to tap-dancing lessons. It took less than a year, and only modest embarrassment to the family, to end that chapter of my musical adventures. I had one more go at hoofing, when I was called upon in the fourth grade to dance a jig, in a school variety show, to the tune of *The Irish Washerwoman*. Ancestral genes saved the day on that occasion. I didn't miss a step. But I knew when to quit. Feetwise, at least, my career behind the footlights was over.

In the ballroom dancing days of my youth, I could handle a foxtrot, and, on exuberant evenings, was mildly adept at jitterbugging. But those days ended long ago, when the quaint idea took hold that it was no longer desirable for people to dance with each other. The Frug, Twist, Hustle, Monkey, Mashed Potato, Gator, Jerk, Limbo, Locomotion, assorted other disco rhythms and a variety of highly individualized wiggles and wobbles had left me in the dance floor dust for several decades. Thus, I was surprised when the planners of the annual Staff Employees Luncheon approached me a few years ago with the Macarena proposal.

I accepted, of course. How could I not? I practiced daily with two attractive and experienced Macarenaters. I studied the steps, I picked up the beat. I memorized the moves. I learned to shake a certain body part at appropriate junctures. I got myself ready for the big day. And when that day arrived, I was elsewhere, called to Carson City by a legislative alert. Otherwise, I would have been there, leading the choreodrama. It's my job.

That shakable body part was called upon recently to do a different kind of duty. We dedicated a new playground one morning last fall. The College of Education has a program for a group of first-, second- and third-graders from Sierra Vista School. Some generous folks had built the playground on campus for these kids, and donated the equipment. My role was to greet the audience, introduce dignitaries, thank the donors, describe the program, acknowledge the school kids, and—as it turned out—slide down a brand-new slide. It was one of those curvy models that takes you around a few twists and turns and then dumps you, somewhat unceremoniously, at the bottom. Speaking of which, I learned from the seat of my pants on the way down that it had rained the night before. So I was damp when I was dumped, but all for a worthy cause.

I could go on. I could describe my experience in milking a cow (from the wrong side), wearing a wig (reduced glare for those looking on), shooting basketballs blindfolded (improved my accuracy, actually), and—for the sake of a photo session—undergoing three hours of peculiar water torture while decked out in Nor'easter garb and toy glasses with working windshield wipers. But the point is made: While there is ample opportunity in this job to feel important, even powerful, and to think of yourself as someone perched providentially above the teeming, toiling masses, there are those times when humility (humiliation, too) comes calling and reminds you not to take yourself too seriously. What goes up comes down, after all, and the downward trip can happen in a hurry. I have long maintained that a sense of humor is essential to survival if you happen to be a university president. I expect that's true of every job. And a sense of humor can really only do its wonderful, load-lightening work if it includes the capacity to laugh at yourself.

But wait a minute! Was this surgical yo-yo strike really a laughing matter? What if it were Joel who at the critical moment was seized by a sneeze or a fidget? What if he just happened to be having a bad day? I could suffer a lobe blow, or something much worse. That yo-yo was looking more and more like a weapon. If it broke en route, would its errant voyage mar my visage? The audience, sensing blood maybe, was beginning to crowd up close for a better view of the action. Still, too late now, I said to myself. Let the chip fall where it may. In a stroke, it was over. Joel proved to be an artful dislodger. The chip fell well. I was unscathed. The audience applauded. We all had a good laugh.

I remembered at that moment a 19th century president who was fired for having too much dignity. From this perspective, it was clear that my job, with its assorted responsibilities, its meetings, its deeds noble and otherwise, was safe for another day.

~

A Constant Conversation

I RECENTLY COMPLETED 13 YEARS IN THIS JOB, a numerical milestone if nothing else. I became acting president during my 13th year at the university and the regents appointed me to the position for real after 13 months of acting service. At that point, I became this institution's 13th president.

Possibly in acknowledgment of my lengthy tenure, an anonymous flyer arrived in the mail near the anniversary date. It was entitled, "Joe Must Go," and was distributed around the campus, around the state, possibly around the world, and it listed 10 reasons for such an imperative. The flyer did not quite have the eloquence, say, of Wilson's 14 points, or Luther's 95 theses, or those tablets Moses brought down from Mount Sinai. Still, the student newspaper found it convincing enough to print verbatim as a front-page story and to use several of its claims as a basis for an editorial.

The editor was kind enough to conclude that, even though he thought the university's future was at stake here, the time had not yet come to ask for my head. The implication was that, just now, a few fingers would suffice; perhaps an ear.

Elsewhere on campus, debates were underway on a variety of topics. The Gulf War was one such, though it did not engender that much argument. In several of our colleges, intense and conflictual discus-

Silver and Blue, Spring/Summer, 1991.

sions focused on both programmatic and process issues. Our new core curriculum had also stirred up the passions a little, and sides were forming. The so-called "fighting words" doctrine—a possible limitation of freedom of speech—was a subject of attention as the university grew, a bit painfully, into a more heterogeneous community. Relatedly, the political correctness controversy now sweeping the nation seemed to be getting modestly launched here. Was this campus, or some part of it, to become, as others were presumed to have become, a place where certain things could not be said about certain groups or certain subjects, where the curriculum was to be properly reflective of a particular political orientation? There appeared to be no danger of absolute truth being discovered in this matter, or of the debate ending anytime soon. But dander was up on this topic, as it was on other issues.

I am a collector of sorts. I collect descriptions of the American university. This venerable institution has been referred to, variously, as a guild, a corporation, a department store, a jungle, a lotus land, a hazardous zone, an organized anarchy, a standing insurrection and—language only a social scientist could love—a holding company for a federation of quasiautonomous subunits. It has acquired lots of other labels, as well. My personal favorite was supplied by the late A. Bartlett Giamatti, former president of Yale and, at his death, commissioner of baseball. He called the university "a constant conversation."

And so it is. That is more or less what we have been having on campus recently. We've been conversing, dander up and dander down, sometimes heatedly, sometimes with hyperbole, always because that is why we are here. A university is a place where issues have to get an airing. Oxen can get gored in the process. Gnats' eyelashes can get dissected. Feelings can get hurt. Reason usually rules, but fanciful speculation occasionally has its way. We converse, and we debate, because we must. Our conversation may have been rather more constant than usual this spring.

I also collect descriptions of the position I hold. Across the country and over the years, it has attracted a lot of characterizations. Some of them are not very pleasant. The president has been depicted as a nuisance, villain, autocrat, menace, minion, drayhorse, scapegoat, turncoat, discomfited buffer, rotten character, supreme peril, captive squirrel in a revolving cage, and as an interchangeable lightbulb. On the other hand, it has been suggested that the office requires someone with "the physical charm of a Greek athlete, the cunning of Machiavelli, the wisdom of Solomon, the courage of a lion [and] the stomach of a goat."

I suspect the anonymous author of my anniversary flyer would have placed me in the rotten character school rather than the one where wisdom and courage are housed. Or in those sundry other schools that suggest the president should be bold, compassionate, intelligent, inspirational, energetic, optimistic, prudent, persistent, resilient, respective, tactful, trusting and trustworthy, to cite a few more descriptors from my very large collection. I don't know if all those qualities are necessary, or even possible. I do know that in a job such as this, one needs, especially needs, perspective. One needs the perspective born of understanding the necessarily controversial life of a university, born too of hard-won patience and a sense of humor. Perspective engenders a desire for solid criticism and a tolerance of that which is less than solid. It gets a person over the humps and up from the dumps and it wards off corrosion of the spirit.

It allows me, certainly, to appreciate the extraordinary privilege with which I have been blessed, the privilege to lead a great university, to see it move, to assist in the challenge of moving it, controversy and all, in a time of excitement and enthusiasm. I have had that privilege for 13 years. Given the proper perspective, 13 does seem to be my lucky number.

The university, by the way, is off Exit 13 from Interstate 80. But I am not planning to hit the road anytime soon.

~

Thorns, Thistles and Humble Pie

BY THE TIME THE NEW YEAR OF 1978 GOT UNDERWAY IN EARNEST, I was feeling very good about life. I was 44, blessed with a wonderful family, chairing the department (political science) that had been my professional home for 12 years, doing some interesting research, and enjoying the classroom more than ever. I was a university professor, which is what I had long wanted to be, and I was almost sublimely content.

Silver and Blue, January/February, 1998.

Then, in February, came a wild week at the end of which my life was a whole lot different. For one thing, it wasn't my own any more. Other people, a good many other people, had suddenly become its custodians. The regents had fired the university president and had charged a campus committee with the task of nominating his replacement. The committee, with 26 or so members representing every known institutional constituency, met in a room on campus, developed a list of candidates, interviewed them, and made a decision. I was on that list, though I did not take my candidacy seriously. The thought of serving as a campus president had never entered my mind. Indeed, I was working behind the scenes on behalf of another person. It came, thus, as a considerable shock when vice president Bob Gorrell—the committee chair—called to tell me I was the nominee. A few days later, after a bit of intrigue and maneuver had failed to alter the result, the regents appointed me. That was on Feb. 24.

To be sure, I was then the *acting* president. It is a convention of the academy that acting presidents don't count for much. They do not show up on the historical rolls, except maybe by way of footnote. They are apparently considered to be folks who just kind of hold the place together—caretakers, by and large—until the *real* presidents come along. I was acting for 13 months before I became real, and so there will be those who will say my period of service dates from 1979, not 1978. I can tell you, though, that those acting days felt real enough to me: full of challenge, adventure, difficult decisions, and a formidable learning process. So I think of myself as having begun this job in February 1978. That means, to get at long last to the point, that I am about to celebrate (there must be a better word) 20 years in this challenging, adventuresome, difficult and formidable position.

Who would have thought it possible? Not I, certainly. Six years, it seemed, possibly eight, would be all a person could survive, and that would number you among the world's foremost optimists. I remember encountering two statistics very early on. One showed the average tenure of a running back in the National Football League. The other described the average tenure in office of a college president. The number was the same for both: four-and-half-years.

The literature on the college presidency tells you that this is a very tough position. The presidents themselves will tell you the same thing. You can learn from these sources that, should you take such a position, you will be expected to perform as a catalyst, communicator, cooperator, coordinator, compromiser, counselor, crisis manager, quarterback, cheerleader, enchanter, evocator, entrepreneur, moderator, mediator, negotiator, regulator, healer, preacher, planner, persuader, and politician, among your many other roles. You will need to have, it is said, courage, judgement and fortitude. You will have to be energetic, inspirational, patient, persistent, resilient, self-confident, stylish, stoical and tolerant. You should also be a good listener, with good manners and a good sense of humor, in a good family situation. You should have nerves like sewer pipes. You should be able to raise grapes from thorns and figs from thistles. You should have white hair for that look of experience and hemorrhoids for that look of concern.

The job just asks too much of you. That's what the literature says. That's what the presidents (who write some of the literature) say. Of course, the presidents are known to be chronic complainers. They have talked and written so much about how hard the position is that conventional wisdom now sees it as very nearly impossible. The newspapers and news magazines are full of such comment, and one suspects the general public perception is much the same.

Let me say a word here about my presidential colleagues, past and present. Actually, let me borrow the word from one of those colleagues, a wise man named Frederic Ness. Fred wrote that college presidents, when they gather at their annual meetings, are like a "convocation of morticians" assembled at a "wailing wall." He also said, and this is true, that what they are really doing is just letting off their ample reservoirs of steam.

Well, I got beyond those four-and-half-years, and beyond the six or eight I had imagined at the outside as well. I have spent my share of time at wailing wall convocations and done my share of complaining. I do not begin to possess all those qualities the pundits write about. Somehow, I will soon have served in this office for two full decades. I am grateful to have had the opportunity.

I don't begrudge a single day of these 20 years, not even those (and there have been plenty of them) when I have taken my lumps, not even those occasions when I have been served up healthy portions of humble pie, not even the times when I have said to myself, "What the hell am I still doing here?"

I know others also ask that question, as well they should. However, I'm still enjoying myself, relishing the challenge, welcoming the adventure, a commodity still in plentiful supply. I still don't understand exactly what happened back there in February 1978, but I'm happy it did and I hope to stick around here a while longer.

I don't own that head of that white hair yet, after all, although sometimes, I confess, I do have that look of concern.

∼

Moving On

WAS IT PURE COINCIDENCE THAT DURING THE SAME MONTH I officially became a presidential lame duck, the university hired its first webmaster? Or, was it that invisible hand (or foot) of fate that arranged things this way, or perhaps Dame Fortune issuing a decree? No matter, really. It seems somehow appropriate that the institution made a distinctly 21st century appointment in concert with the departure announcement by its leader, who has occasionally described himself as a 19th century man.

That announcement was hard duty. I have watched a number of retirement speeches in my time—from fellow presidents, political leaders, coaches, professional athletes and others. Emotion (a tear, a sob, a break in the voice) has usually been part of the proceedings. I had resolved that it wouldn't happen to me, that I would exercise iron self-control, treat the occasion as just another ordinary media briefing, and be calm, cool and composed. So I entered the Clark Room at Morrill Hall with a smile on my face, strode purposefully to the microphone, gazed serenely out on the crowd, set my jaw, opened my mouth, and . . . lost it completely.

Leaving a job that you have loved, which I will do at the end of December, is never easy. When the final day arrives, I will have held the position for nearly 23 years. Your life falls into a certain pattern in that space of time, even though unpredictable occurrences, unexpected challenges and improbable experiences are constant companions. You get accustomed to the pattern, derive some comfort from it, and further, when you are privileged to have the job that I have, there is an ineffable sense of satisfaction that it imparts. You know you are in for major changes when you are about to be no more what you have been for so long: the president. And my goodness, a day later, some-

Silver and Blue, September/October, 2000.

body is doing *your* job!

I wrestled with these thoughts for the better part of a year. Some days, I knew I wanted to stay, maybe forever. On others, the evidence seemed compelling that I should go. Would the decision come down, I wondered, to two mental falls out of three, or five of nine, or what? In the end, I listened to that familiar voice that speaks to us from the visceral region. It was saying to me, rather in the manner of the British publican from an earlier era, announcing the cessation of drinking hours: "It's time, gentlemen, time!"

Hard as the announcement was, troubling as was the year preceding it, I woke up the next morning —June 1—feeling mighty fine. I had seven months left to serve, tasks to get done, obligations to fulfill, problems yet to solve, promises still to keep.

And rounds to make. That would be a test as well, doing certain duties, attending certain functions, for the last time, like the retiring ball player on his final tour of the stadiums in which he has performed for years. There would be the banquets, of course: the traditional Governor's Dinner for our athletics program (coeducational now, and much less rowdy than once it had been); the Foundation Dinner in the fall (my 19th, I believe, and I had been at the first one, when former president Gerald Ford was the speaker); the Senior Scholar Banquet in December (an always-touching event, a product of the alumni association, and I have attended all of them). And the annual Holiday Party, sponsored by my office, offering the people of the campus a chance to say hello to each other in a festive setting. It has always been a treat for Joy and me to greet hundreds of cheerful souls at this event, and shake hundreds of hands. This time, there would be hundreds of hugs as well.

There would be those occasions that mark the movement of the autumn calendar: a reception for new faculty members; the State of the University address (I think, for a change, I'll make this a short one); the President's Concert; the home football games and the brunches that precede them; Homecoming; a series of last meetings—with staff, with the Faculty Senate and Student Senate, with the Board of Regents (about 250 meetings of that group since it all began); and, one last time, Commencement, the 31st over which I will have had the honor to preside. Probably, someone will want to throw a party or two for me, to test my roastability. (I should pass that test handily.)

I have this picture in my mind of Willie McCovey, my favorite baseball player; Willie, who played the game in four different decades, hit 521 home runs, made 17,567 putouts, had the sweetest swing you ever saw, was traded to San Diego when his legs began to show their age, but came back to San Francisco for his last season (1980), made his farewell rounds as a Giant and, in his last at bat, hit a double to the fence at Candlestick Park. I hope I can make my rounds as gracefully as Willie did, and I pray that, in my last at bat come December, I won't strike out.

It will be a trial for me, saying those good-byes.

But, you know what? I'm feeling pretty good about all this. I'm still enjoying the charge and challenge of the job. I am going to savor this final tour of the campus territory I know so well. Whatever the state of my allegiance to the 19th century, I intend to put in some hours with our institutional media people, learning how to teach with the modern technology. I will probably go pay my respects to our new webmaster (and let me add that we haven't been without web mastery before his appointment; we have simply been doing it, in the noble tradition of the academy, through a committee).

So, the lame duck life is not such a bad one. It will keep me busy. I know my colleagues will be tolerant as I make my way through—and please forgive me for fowling up the metaphor—a prolonged swan song. One day soon, that song will be over (although doubtless—dare I say it?—the mallardy will linger on). Things could be worse, you know: What if I had been the president of Drake?

You can tell that my visceral voice was right. It really is time I was moving on.

∿

Chapter Two

~

The University

THINK AGAIN ABOUT FORMER YALE PRESIDENT and baseball commissioner Bart Giamatti's idea of the "constant conversation," and of those other images of the institution its critics have proposed: jungle, lotus land, department store, organized anarchy. These rather contrary descriptors derive in part, perhaps, from the circumstance that universities are not places where life proceeds in a predictable, measured manner. I once suggested that the institution, "if it is doing what it ought to be doing, is by definition disorderly." There are, of course, more appealing depictions. One of Harvard's famous presidents (James Bryant Conant) thought of the university as "hallowed ground." And, a century earlier, Sir Benjamin Disraeli, the famed British political leader, portrayed it as "a place of light, of liberty, of learning."

We have something here that is hard to get your hands around, a multiform organization, a complex and versatile entity, a many splendored, many splintered thing. It's difficult to get to know such an enterprise.

I have had an opportunity to become intimately acquainted with this enterprise, both the one I serve in particular, and—through decades of reading, experience, discussion, reflection and occasional frustration—the university in a general sense. This chapter provides an assortment of impressions born of that acquaintanceship, as well as some samples of history drawn from the institution I know especially well. The chapter begins with an essay, ("Sync or Swim") written early in my tenure in office on a key lesson about the institution, painfully learned. I had understood it from my years in the faculty trenches, but I developed a greater grasp when (as Mr. Disraeli put it upon becoming prime minister) I got to the top of the greasy pole. From that vantage point, I could see better that, however disorderly a university is or ought to be, the grip of habitual behavior remains strong. There is no time to savor it, but the university's standing as at once a most liberal and a most conservative institution presents both a delicious irony and, because there is wisdom here, as well, a guide to presidential action.

Following that essay are excerpts ("A Matter of Definition") from a State of the University address I delivered as the University of Nevada moved from the 1980s into the 1990s, and related observations ("Home Sweet Home" and "Patience Pays") stemming from a sabbatical leave I took in fall 1989. Some developments of particular consequence are given attention next: the establishment and growth of the university foundation ("An Arduous Voyage"); a growing focus on written communication ("The Write Stuff"); and the witness we began to give again to the tradition and importance of campus aesthetics ("The Most Beautiful Campus in the World").

The growth of new types of higher education institutions in the last half of the 20th century changed the way universities understood, and dealt with, their students. At the same time, this growth offered testimony once more to the continuing vitality of that most consequential metaphor of American education—the open door. A personal appreciation of these matters is conveyed in two pieces written 16 years apart ("Who Should Come to College?" and, "The Eight-Year Degree"). A more broadly historical interpretation is advanced in "Reinventing the Wheel," and the need for public acknowledgment of and investment in higher education's growth potential is put forward in "By the Numbers."

The chapter concludes with articles that (1) look back (and forward, too) on a time-honored university ritual ("Homecoming!"); (2) consider the stresses (and, as it happens, the tresses) of decision-making ("Hobson's Choice"); and (3) contemplate the strains of student growth in the century ahead ("The Class of 2015").

A couple of my grandchildren are likely to be members of that class. I expect them to be participants in the campus conversation, to know the beauty of the place, to experience it at its hallowed and disorderly best, and to finish their baccalaureate degrees in less than the eight years required by their grandfather.

∾

Sync or Swim

HERE WE ARE AT THE OUTSET OF A NEW SCHOOL YEAR and this middle-aged man's fancy turns to . . . traffic signals. To one in particular, near the campus at Ninth and Sierra, which I encounter often and have for a decade.

This stoplight and I have faced one another on a thousand occasions. Never in all that time have I found the light on green, or even yellow. It has always been red on my arrival. Always, it seemed, that light was out of sync.

This bothered me for many years. I developed a passionate antipathy toward this crafty, stubborn machine that refused to yield to my determination to get from here to there expeditiously. I devised a variety of strategies to beat the thing —changing speeds, changing cars, calling forth maledictions from the gods, employing stealth and cunning, donning disguises, scrunching down in the seat so that stoplight could not see me, approaching it at different hours. All to no avail.

At length it occurred to me that it was not the stoplight that was out of sync; it was yours truly. I was swimming upstream and I was not a pregnant salmon. I came to understand that the stoplight sensed my frustration like a dog senses fear in the postman. I resolved not to care anymore. For the most part, I have retained that resolve. The time I spend waiting at the stoplight is now put to productive purposes — pondering decisions, glancing at the newspaper, making a few notes, counting my blessings. I feel no more frustration. I am swimming with the current. A kind of security, a feeling of stability, envelopes me at the intersection in question. It even seems possible that, one day soon, I will meet with green when I come upon that signal.

You could say I have seen the light.

Not to stretch the parallel too far, but this little saga is akin to certain experiences I have had at the university. You can come up against some ever-glowing red lights here. You can launch ambitious initiatives, develop brilliant strategies to advance them, marshal your forces carefully, and move them down the road. And you can find yourself waiting, waiting, waiting at an intersection. You may see red for an eon. At the least, it can take a long time for the light to change. This

UNR Times, October/November, 1984. Reprinted in the author's *Notes from the President's Chair: Reflections on Life in a University,* University of Nevada Press, 1988, pp. 103-05.

may lead to frustration, dyspepsia and a strong desire to kick your dog. (The loveable family canine, I hasten to add, has suffered no such indignity. For that matter, my stomach has been largely devoid of digestive rumblings. I would confess, however, to periodic bouts of frustration as my best-laid plans have gone awry.)

But one learns. There are reasons for these long waits. There is security, stability in those campus traffic signals. The university is an entity that emanates the need for change in the surrounding world, but it is also a conservative institution. It is anchored in ancient traditions, and there is an imperishable wisdom in those traditions. That wisdom can erect a barrier to changes that may seem at the moment imperative but, in the perspective of history, perhaps misguided. I have learned to respect this wisdom, admire the traditions that inspire it, even when it sends my plans to the discard heap.

The university is also a human—an intensely human—enterprise. It assembles, as well, the full range of human foibles and it displays often enough a very human resistance to change. Sometimes, tradition or no, it needs a push. Still, it can, when it needs to, make major adjustments in a hurry.

We have been in the process of making such adjustments lately. We are adjusting to a new demography, a new technology, a new set of demands for programs and services. We are caught up in the sweeping changes that have transported this country and its higher education system into a new era. We are not the institution we used to be.

Then again, we are. We begin this new academic year with a vision not unlike that which has inspired us for a century and more, with a purpose that has guided us through decades past. Our principal missions are unchanged. We are still a safe haven for questing intellects.

There is much to be done this year. There are additional adjustments to make, directions to forge, challenges to meet. There is a legislative session to prepare for and bacon to be brought home. There is a history to honor and a future to be won. We will need to stay in sync. We begin with confidence. We will know some sleepless nights.

On one of those nights, I may just arise from bed, put on my combat fatigues, camouflage my car, and launch a surprise attack on Ninth and Sierra.

≈

Home Sweet Home

NEARLY 24 YEARS AGO I CAME TO THE UNIVERSITY, just out of graduate school, as an instructor in political science. I had a six-month contract. I did not then think of the institution as much more than a stop along the road to some other destination. I expected to have a transient acquaintanceship with Nevada, and then move on.

Well, I was wrong. My transient status was soon abandoned. I began to think of this university as home. Not home as in where you hang your hat, but home as the place where roots are set down and nurtured, where much of life's drama is played out, where one builds a repository of lasting memories.

Home is also a place you miss when you're away from it, a place you long to be at certain seasons. Autumn is my favorite season on the campus. It's the back to school season. Excitement is in the air, along with a refreshing hint of the frost to come. The leaves are turning. The Quad is lovely. Homecoming is upon us, and that means our alums are ... coming home!

I am away from home this season, holed up at Oxford, getting some reading done, and writing, and thinking on such matters as why a university can get such a grip on people who work there, or go to school there, or went to school there in bygone days. There are reasons, I know, but that grip is not altogether a rational matter. It is in part, maybe in very large part, an affair of the heart.

I can say unabashedly that I love this university. It has given me the good fortune, as a faculty member, to take part in a marvelous mission, to help prepare over the years thousands of students to meet their futures. I have had the singular and immensely rewarding opportunity to serve for almost a dozen years now as its leader, to help it move—indeed, virtually to see it moving—to meet its future. I have had the privilege of sending my four children to the university, three now themselves alumni, the fourth still attending, all of them much better for the experience. I know it in so many ways by this time. It is such a great comfort to me, so inextricably a part of my identity. I know that in the quiet of an English night, if I listen carefully, I can hear it tugging on my heartstrings.

It is not just me, of course. It's all of those who are and have been a part of the institution. The point was made most poignantly for me

UNR Times, Fall, 1989.

last spring, at a reception in San Francisco for friends and alumni of the university. A couple of very special people were in attendance. One was Dorothy Bird Nyswander, Class of 1915. Dorothy has had a long and distinguished career as an educator, having received a Ph. D. from the University of California, Berkeley, taught at that university for many years as a professor of public health, traveled the world as an emissary of health education. In 1985 she was honored with a Centennial Recognition Award by our alumni association. Dr. Nyswander is 95 now. Every time I see her, she tells me that her elevator still runs to the top. It's been running there, inside a skyscraper mind, for nearly a century.

Mr. William Fife was also at the reception. A member of the Class of 1917, Mr. Fife had gone on to a great career, all over the world, as a mining engineer. He had been unable to attend his Commencement ceremony because he had gone off to help fight World War I. Seventy years later, at the 1987 Commencement, he came back to campus and walked across the stage to finally receive his diploma. When I saw him in San Francisco, he had just returned from a trip to Antarctica, at 93 apparently the oldest person ever to have set foot on that hard and far-off continent.

As it happened, Dorothy Nyswander and William Fife had been good friends during their days on campus, two of the 450 students then enrolled. However, they had not seen each other for 74 years. There, at the San Francisco reception, before a 100 people who could not help but be touched by the tableau, they renewed their friendship. They were, in that way that only a common identification with alma mater can provide, home again, together, after three-quarters of a century. Dorothy and William share this affair of the heart with 40,000 other alumni. I am not a Nevada alumnus, but I share it, too. I wish I could be there this fall when the alums come home. I'll be thinking of them, wistful but secure in the knowledge that a few months hence I'll be coming back myself, back to the campus that has given so much meaning to my life, back to a place I love, refreshed and enthusiastic to be absorbed once more in its great adventure. Back home.

≈

Patience Pays

THE LAST TIME I WROTE IN THESE PAGES, I was sitting at a desk in Oxford, enjoying a sabbatical leave, soaking up the glories and traditions of that wonderful place, but missing home as well. I went to Oxford to get some distance from, and do some thinking on, another university: this one, the one that has given me life and livelihood for almost a quarter-century. I went also to explore the marvelous resources of the Bodleian Library on a subject close to my heart and mind, and sometimes close enough to my stomach to interfere a bit with its normal operations.

The subject was the American university presidency. I wanted to read everything I could find (and there was much to be found) on this unique office. I wanted to learn more about its origins and evolution; about how it had survived and, on occasion, prospered; about its changing role in the institution it was designed to serve.

The literature on the presidency is full of testimony on what it takes to make a president successful: Timing, skill, energy, judgement, courage, prudence, tolerance, a generous thickness of skin, and luck (especially luck) all seem to contribute. According to the literature, all these attributes may not be enough. In certain situations, maybe most situations, an additional virtue is needed. If you are a university president and you don't have it, the experts say you better learn it. That virtue is patience.

This was not in the category of new knowledge for me. After 11-plus years in the job, I knew what a conservative, slow-moving institution a university usually is, what happens when you put inertia and a fresh idea together in the same room and tell them they can't come out until the issue is resolved. I knew also that patience is required not only of the president. It is needed by the whole institution, and perhaps even more by the community that loves and supports it and sometimes wonders whether it is getting where it ought to go as quickly as it should.

We have our share of inertia here, and often enough it plants its weighty peresence squarely in the path of progress. Fortunately, we also have a lot of ideas. When a good idea confronts an inert presence, however weighty the latter might be, the idea is likely eventually to win. It may drop a little of its luster, shed some of its poundage, but there is no presence, no boundary, no line of defense, no immovable object that can fend off forever the irresistible force of a good idea. If we are patient.

Well, we have been patient at the university. We have had this idea for a long time of turning a good institution into a great one. We understood there was much to do to make this possible. We knew our idea required major and sustained growth in state funding. In 1985, after a good deal of planning and preparation, we turned the corner on such funding. Since that year, the state has increased its assistance to the university by 64 percent. It's not enough yet, not by a considerable margin, but it is a significant beginning after a long wait.

We knew that public universities achieve greatness only when private dollars provide the extra help that excellence requires. So the university established a foundation in 1981 for the purpose of raising those dollars, saw donations gradually increase to $3.6 million a year by 1984 and, at $7.4 million, to more than double that figure by 1989.

We knew that great universities get that way through the recruitment and retention of outstanding faculty members, and that a widely recognized test of faculty strength is competitiveness in sponsored research. Such research has more than doubled in dollar value here in the past five years. Research and training grants have grown from $10.5 million in 1984-85 to $22.9 million in 1988-89. Further, it is clear from the quality of applicants for faculty positions, and from our ability to compete in choosing the best of them, that the university has come to be regarded as an institution with a very bright future.

We knew we had to build programs—at graduate and undergraduate levels, and internationally, as well. And that we had to build buildings—new or expanded structures for business, engineering, the fine arts, mines, medicine, journalism, judicial education. And that we had to equip them with the finest instructional and research equipment. And fill them, through strong recruitment efforts and an expanded scholarship program, with the brightest students. And that we needed to expend significant sums remodeling existing residence halls and building new ones to house a growing student population. We have done, are doing, all these things.

I went away for four months in part to get some perspective on all this, to evaluate from the tranquil precincts of Oxford how far we have come, how long it has taken us, what price we have paid, how close we are to the realization of that good idea, to the achievement of our goal of greatness.

We have come a long way, and it has taken awhile. We have paid a price in effort, dedication and disappointment. We have known travail. We have known triumph, as well. The "we" involved here is not the royal, presidential or editorial type, but a collective we that comprehends the committed, enthusiastic and persistent labor of legions. Greatness requires that kind of labor.

We have been patient. We are close. I am back from Oxford, happy to be home and inspired to be among the laborers again, and caught up in the excitement of an idea whose time has come.

~

A Matter of Definition

IT IS APPROPRIATE TO BEGIN HERE WITH SOME DEFINITIONS, with some thoughts on what we are and have been, and on the distinguishing characteristics of the institution we share.

We have just begun our 117th academic year, our 106th here in Reno. That long history defines us. For most of that history, we were the only institution of higher education in Nevada. Everything that now comprises the growing, complex and ambitious University and Community College System of Nevada had its beginnings here.

To put it another way, we are, have been, and will always be the senior institution of higher education in this state. Obligations go with that standing. We are required to be equal to a distinguished history, to safeguard the noble traditions that our long history has established, and to provide leadership, particularly in times of critical need. We live, I believe, in just such a time. We intend to meet our obligations.

We are defined as well by the land-grant charter that is responsible for our birth. The terms of that charter are the time-honored missions of the university: teaching, research and service. We are bound to bring to the people of this state a wide range of educational programs and services. We are bound to bring to the citizenry the fruits of our research, the practical applications in the field of what has been learned in the laboratory.

Silver and Blue, Winter, 1991.

The land-grant mandate was originally focused on agriculture and engineering, but it now encompasses far more than that, reaching into a network of research and service centers in most of our colleges and schools. The land-grant tradition is a tradition of problem-solving. It is a tradition of partnerships, in which the university provides assistance in numerous forms to agriculture, business, industry, and state and local government. It is a proud tradition that explains much of our history and points the way to our future.

A third point of definition, relating also to past and future, and tied irrevocably to our land-grant orientation, is the statewide scope of the university. From the very beginning, we have been able to say—as the great Wisconsin educator, Charles Van Hise, said of his institution—that "the walls of the university are the boundaries of the state." That is the reason we built a network of cooperative extension offices and agricultural experiment stations reaching into every county and corner of Nevada.

That is the reason we established the School of Medicine, which is extensively involved in training physicians and resolving health-care problems in Clark County as well as Washoe County, and in delivering medical care and services across the vast distances of rural Nevada.

That is the reason we developed the array of programs, facilities and services that now comprise the Mackay School of Mines, the College of Human and Community Sciences, the Area Health Education Centers, the Nevada Small Business Development Center and a host of other organizations that serve social, economic and educational needs across our state.

Our statewide profile is reflected also in our student population, 25 percent of which comes from areas of Nevada outside Washoe County. Eight percent of our students comes from Clark County, and every county in Nevada is represented by our student body. We have always been an institution with statewide obligations. They help define what we have been about for more than a century, and what we will be even more emphatically about in the century to come.

A fourth defining characteristic of this university is its long-standing position of leadership in graduate education and research. Graduate enrollments continue to grow substantially, and there has been an even more impressive growth in sponsored research funding.

We are properly embarked on a path to becoming a major graduate and research university. That is an attainable goal. It is also, in and of itself, a major challenge. State assistance will be required and, again, we will have to help ourselves if we are to attain this goal—as I am sure we will. As we continue our momentum in that direction—and this is clearly a part of our challenge—we must take care to keep our teaching mission in the forefront of our minds. We do not set out to become a major research institution by sacrificing our standing as a major teaching institution. Such sacrifice is neither necessary, nor anticipated, nor tolerable. Teaching and scholarship are not mutually exclusive. We must work hard to assure that the natural relationship between the two is the relationship that thrives at this university.

A fifth defining attribute of the university is its leadership in international education. We have developed for our students a variety of opportunities to study abroad. We pioneered the establishment of a consortium of universities offering programs at San Sebastian, Spain, Pau, France, and the University of Turin, in Italy. Many of our students have profited from our London Study Program. We are looking now at additional possibilities in eastern Europe, Asia and South America.

Similarly, we have worked hard to make of this campus the kind of global village that greatly enriches the lives of the entire university community. More than 60 nations are represented here now, including Japan, where we have established an international division and where—in Tokyo—students from this campus will soon be able to spend a semester or more.

Finally, we define ourselves by our determination to retain our identity as a residential campus. We trace our lineage, in residential terms, to 1896, when Manzanita and Lincoln halls opened their doors as men's and women's dormitories. Ninety-four years later, those halls still stand, one dedicated now as a home for honors students and our Honors Program.

In the past few years, we have spent $3.5 million to modernize our dormitories—Manzanita and Lincoln halls included—to make them more secure and comfortable. In the next few years, we will spend $5 million to $6 million to build residence hall space for another 250 students. That expenditure is a statement of our identity as a residential campus.

We are a much, much larger institution now than we were when Manzanita and Lincoln first housed our students in the late 19th century. And our student population has a vastly different demographic profile. But there remains a special flavor here, the flavor of belonging to a residential campus. That flavor defines us, as it always has. We intend to retain it, to rally around it, indeed to expand it, even in the face of growth and change.

We started the 1980s surrounded by forecasts—in the nation and in Nevada—of a gloomy future. The portents were unpleasant. Progress was not to be expected. It would be next to impossible just to hold our own.

Well, we held our own through the early years of the decade just past and went on from there to make the last half of the '80s a time of advancement and excitement for the university. Through it all, the good years and the bad, this university held fast to one overriding commitment. That was, and remains, our commitment to quality.

We enter the new decade with the comfort born of a job well done, the hunger born of the knowledge that there is a big job yet to do, and the enthusiasm inherent in the understanding that there is a great future out there to achieve.

I'm grateful, humble, proud and excited to be part of this university and associated with all of you in the adventure that awaits as we begin confidently to make our way now, in the 1990s, toward the next millennium.

~

An Arduous Voyage

THE YEAR WAS 1981. After a long period of planning, proposing, discussion and debate, the Board of Regents approved the establishment of the University of Nevada, Reno Foundation. It was a good decision, but we weren't out celebrating in the streets.

The foundation was formed to give the university a leg up in private fund-raising. The institution had long enjoyed the benefactions of certain generous citizens — the Mackay family, for example, and the Fleischmann Foundation. But we had a long distance to travel before we could say we were satisfied with the dollars coming from the private sector. The new foundation was to be the vehicle to take us down that road.

Silver and Blue, January/February, 1996.

It was a shaky creation back there in the early 1980s. The university community— a significant part of it, anyway—was not sure it wanted to join the trip. The community at large wondered why a public institution, already the beneficiary of taxpayer contributions, should be out asking for more. "Didn't we already, in effect, give at the office?" that community asked.

It was a good question, and it took us a long time to answer it properly; to convince our friends and supporters that the old, sharp distinction between public and private universities had dulled considerably over the years. Public dollars had come to be spent, and sometimes lavished, on private institutions. State universities, thinking that fair is fair, had concluded that that famous (and elusive) margin of excellence could be achieved only through philanthropy.

So, we gathered up our rubber bands and glue, our wings and prayers, and launched our new foundation on its hopeful voyage. By 1984, we were raising more than $3 million a year, and we had completed successfully—surmounting in the process a conventional wisdom that said it could not be done — our first substantial campaign. It was initiated to raise $2.8 million to match $6 million from the state for a major expansion of the Church Fine Arts complex.

We were feeling pretty cocky. We thought the time had come, by the mid 1980s, to begin the university's first "capital campaign." That meant big-time, multiyear, multipurpose fund-raising. We discovered we were wrong. We were not ready; not within the campus, not out in the community. It was an idea whose time, for us, had not come; not yet.

However, we *were* ready by the time we turned the corner into the 1990s. We were bringing in more than $7 million annually, through the efforts of the foundation. We had the infrastructure in place. We had willing and eager volunteers. We wanted to raise $105 million in half-a-decade. That was a big number, big enough to startle quite a few people when they heard it; big enough to stretch us to the outer boundaries of our stretchability; big enough to give our bold venture a name: *The Century Campaign.*

It's over now, just ended. We got beyond $105 million— to nearly 125 million. Our annual giving level, the firm, predictable funding year in and year out, is up to almost $17 million. Thousands of donors contributed in sums large and small. It was a heck of an adventure. Now, nearly 15 years after the foundation got underway, it is not a shaky creation anymore. It is solid. It has won a great victory. It has arrived in port intact after a long and arduous voyage. The time has arrived to celebrate. And to say thanks.

~

The Write Stuff

I ATTENDED A SPACE-AGE MOVIE A FEW YEARS AGO that depicted a great war in the heavens over an exotic but vital mineral resource. The resource was called "melange." I was reminded thus of my career as a journalist.

At the acme of that career, I covered high school sports for the *Fresno Bee*. One afternoon, following a baseball game filled with dramatic strikeouts and long home runs, a treacherous muse arrived, took up residence on my shoulder, and forced me to write a lead for my story that described the game as "a melange of missed and mangled baseballs."

This kind of writing might be acceptable, or at least forgivable, by modern standards of sports journalism. But a generation ago, if you covered high school sports, it was cause for either gentle advice or a dressing down from one's editor.

My editor was not from the gentle advice school. He told me, in effect, and in rather more colorful language than can be recorded in a family publication, that my job was to communicate with the reader. The reader, in this case, was interested in baseball, not fancy words and—forgive me—leads loaded with alliteration. He observed that I might leave the latter to the poets, and suggested a place where I could put my melanges.

I have written often about communication. It is an inexhaustible subject, in part perhaps because humans are so creative at obfuscation, so adept at finding ways to assure noncommunication. From time to time, our leaders wax wroth about the problem. Now is such a time, and with good cause. Our society has fallen well short of raising up our young to write well. Grammar has gone aglimmering. Punctuation is hiding under a rock somewhere. Spelling seems a lost art. So goes the refrain.

Silver and Blue, Fall, 1988.

I suspect that it is not just the young who suffer. None of us is in a position to cast the first stone. We've become a nation of lazy writers. I confess that I cannot parse a sentence as well as once I could. And I don't worry a lot about that. Semicolons mystify me. I let it pass. Even though I took home a flower pot as the winner of the third-grade spelling bee, on one occasion—again in my journalistic salad days—I managed to write a photo caption that misspelled "misspell." These days, machines have taken over spelling, correcting automatically the errors of mere mortals.

So, we need to learn to write better. Education is in the process of quickening to the task. It is a serious matter, a most serious matter, to be sure. The problems are manifold and complex. The solutions are not altogether clear. Nevertheless, we are not just talking about the situation anymore. We are getting past the hand-wringing and impre-cation-muttering stage. We are beginning—at all levels of the educa-tional system—to act.

At the university, we have been engaged for several years in a very productive effort called the Writing Project. The Writing Project is a joint venture with the Washoe County School District and is housed in our College of Education. Although the work is complicated, the concept underlying it is a simple one. The concept is to teach teachers to teach teachers to teach writing to their students.

By this time, hundreds of teachers and thousands of students at the elementary and secondary levels have been reached through this project. The results have been very encouraging. The Nevada Legislature has begun to fund the project. We expect it to continue, and to expand.

In 1987-88, university faculty put in substantial time and effort to-ward planning a core curriculum. The objective here is to assure that all of our undergraduates, when they complete their studies, will have a common set of courses in the humanities, arts and sciences and will develop as part of all these courses a set of skills. Computation is one of those skills. Writing is another. We already provide writing assis-tance to students in need; and we will shortly establish, as part of the core curriculum effort, a writing center for all students to use.

This university, like others across the country, is moving purpose-fully to help people get their messages across. We believe we have made progress. We know there is much yet to be done. Despite our best ef-forts, we understand that the occasional melange may slip into a baseball story and a vagrant "s" may sometimes turn up missing in "misspell." Machines or no machines, we remain mere mortals. We will probably never solve the mystery of the semicolon.

But we are determined to do our part to help our people get the right words in the right places at the right times. And we know that, ultimately, the path to better writing is the same as the path to winning baseball games: practice, practice, practice. The preaching is behind us. The practice is under way.

$\sim$

The Most Beautiful
Campus in the World

NOT LONG AGO, a gentleman came to my office to bring greetings from a mutual friend and, as it turned out, to express a breathless sentiment. He had just taken a stroll around the Quad, hallowed ground here at the university. This historic place, where the campus heart has been beating for more than a century, is modeled on Thomas Jefferson's inspired plan for the University of Virginia. My visitor that day was a graduate of that university, but had not been back for many years. What rendered him breathless was a kind of homecoming experience. He told me he felt as though he had returned to Charlottesville and walked again in Jefferson's footsteps.

Our own graduates have a similar feeling when they come home to campus after years away. Their pulse beats a little quicker when they once again see Morrill Hall, that sturdy sentinel that has anchored the Quad since 1886. At the northern border of this celebrated terrain, just beyond Gutzon Borglum's statue of John Mackay, Mackay Mines still stands, 90 years after it opened, stronger now with a $9 million infusion of substructure, museum space and a beautiful new library.

To the east is the junior partner, Mackay Science Hall, built in 1930, and to the west is the Jones Visitors Center, once the university library, then the home of English and then of journalism. This small but charming structure was erected in 1913. From its doorstep, one can take in Clark (1926), Frandsen (1917), and Thompson (1920), and catch a

Silver and Blue, November/December, 1997.

glimpse of Manzanita Hall just across the lake and, to the northwest, the roof of Lincoln. These residence halls house women (Manzanita) and men (Lincoln) as they have since 1896.

So the Quad, with its neighbors, is a special place: green, tree-lined, beckoning, contemplative. The stories it could tell, tens of thousands of them, if it could but speak! Even in its silence, it communicates across the generations. It is mostly where the university lived, for most of the university's life. No wonder alums get misty when they walk there. No wonder my Virginia visitor was impressed.

But there are other quads now, down below where the life sciences are housed and, north from there, where engineering buildings cluster. And there is the Hilliard Plaza, bounded by physics, chemistry, social science, business administration and journalism, and a lovely spot in its own right. These areas offer testimony to the university's growth, to its determination to forge an exciting future on the foundation of its storied past.

A good place to find the future this fall is the new $18 million, 122,600-square-foot education building. It's mainly a classroom building, serving the entire campus, and it is equipped with the best and latest technology. Nevada's teachers of tomorrow will study in this building. Some of them will be able to take advantage of a five-story, 1,000-space parking structure nearby, funded by the 1997 Legislature and scheduled to be open for business in 2000.

I once wrote that if there were a fifth horsemen of the Apocalypse, Parking would be its name. I also suggested that a modern university needs two presidents: one for parking and the other for the rest of the institution's business. Nothing has happened to change my mind on either count, but those 1,000 spaces will help. It will help, too, that right next door—part of the same construction project —will be a new student services center. It will provide convenient access to services— from application to admission to matriculation to graduation— to the students of the future.

Another handsome addition to the campus, dedicated this fall, is our new Honor Court. This court is adjacent to Morrill Hall. Etched on its striking granite pillars are the names of donors to the university, of outstanding faculty members and classified staff and community recipients of university awards, and, most importantly, the student Gold Medal winners stretching back to 1910. The court is a place to celebrate both the university's history and its sense of community.

Returning alums can bear pleasant witness to all this growth. Past, present, and future will be there for them to behold. They can observe an alma mater secure in those traditions so stirringly manifest on the Quad, vibrant in putting new facilities to work to serve both ancient and modern purposes, and eager to take on the challenges of the 21st century.

Those alums can also see on university vehicles bumper stickers that read: "Welcome to the Most Beautiful Campus in the World." A bit of a hyperbole, perhaps, but — on the Quad, on those other quads, at our Honor Court, and elsewhere — we are working hard to uphold that claim.

$\sim$

Who Should Come to College?

OELWEIN IS A NAME YOU PRONOUNCE AT YOUR OWN RISK. It is also a name that, if you heard it pronounced but did not see it in print, you probably could not spell, either. Neither its pronunciation nor its spelling is important anyway, except to those who have at some time called it home. What is of some modest moment here is that Oelwein is a small town in Iowa where, some 30 years ago, a young man found himself at a crossroads.

He had completed, barely, his freshman year at the University of Iowa, after finishing high school with a record that did not whet the appetites of Harvard recruiters. He had spent the summer working at construction and had a few dollars in the bank. He was not sure he wanted to return to the university.

He had few alternatives. The construction job was over. He could not go back to previous employment as a car hop at the local root beer stand. That would have been both beneath his remaining dignity and, at 30 cents an hour, beneath his personal poverty level as well. He could not return to detasseling corn, either, because at that season there was no corn to detassel. Besides, in a previous summer, he and his entire crew had been fired by the Dekalb Hybrid Seed Company for dawdling in the cornfield.

There were then no jobs available in Oelwein. He was not quite

UNR Times, October, 1983. Reprinted in *Notes from the President's Chair...*, pp. 69-71.

ready for a conscript's life in the Army. His bank account could not sustain him for more than a few months. There was work awaiting him in Iowa City, as a busboy at a bar and grill adjacent to the campus. So, after contemplating the bleak alternatives, he went back to school.

Possibly, this was not the right decision. Nine months later, the young man left Iowa City, a step ahead of the university registrar. That worthy gentleman was prepared to serve him with an eviction notice, the young man having managed to fail every course during spring semester except, mysteriously, Air Force ROTC.

He received a D in the latter, which suggested to him that perhaps he was more fit for the Air Force than for anything else. To that branch of military service, in short order, he accordingly repaired.

The above, you may have guessed, is a chapter from my partially misspent youth. I include it here not as autobiography but as prologue to discussion of a major question facing modern public higher education. There are many complicated ways of asking it. Put simply, the question is, "Who should come to college?"

I do not presume to have the answer. The times suggest, however, that Nevada and other states, and the nation in general, will be required to provide one. The question, of course, has been asked and answered before. The democratizing forces that propelled higher education through the 1960s and 1970s answered it most recently, and emphatically: Public colleges and universities should be open, at one level or another, to all comers. That has long been the case in Nevada. Now, with education looming as a major national issue, with educational resources being substantially reduced across the country, with vastly greater numbers of students attending colleges and universities than attended a generation ago, and with those institutions devoting increasing time and energy to remedial instruction, the principle of open access is under scrutiny.

In Nevada, during the next year, the university system will take a hard look at admissions standards. It is possible, even probable, that at the state's two universities the standards will be elevated. Raising standards, however, can create other problems. These will need to be addressed before any final action is taken. The financial implications will have to be examined. Very likely, a new system for financing higher education will need to accompany any changes in standards. The impact of higher standards on the state's community colleges—increased enrollment pressures, for example, and a possible diversion of resources from occupational programs—will require careful consideration. Changed standards can affect high school curricula. Relationships between school districts and university system institutions will have to be strengthened.

The problems are numerous and complex and the task will be difficult. It is necessary, even so, that we undertake it. We will be called upon—the citizens of Nevada will be called upon—to determine whether public higher education is still to be governed by the principle of access to all who are interested.

There was a place for me when I returned to the University of Iowa in 1958. Had high and rigid readmission standards then prevailed, I could have been shown the door. Given an academic career that only with surpassing generosity could have been called checkered, perhaps I should have been. Instead, I was back in school: unpredictable, unpromising, on probation, and grateful for the opportunity.

As we set out now to decide whether the question of who should come to college needs a different answer for a different era, I hope we don't become too much a prisoner of numbers.

I hope we will remember that there are people out there—bright people whose intelligence may not be reflected in high school grade point averages or standardized test scores; possibly even some contemporary equivalents of that unemployed and uncertain carhop/hod carrier/cornfield refugee of the 1950s - for whom higher education may want to save a place in Nevada.

~

The Eight-Year Degree

W E ARE WELL UNDERWAY BY THIS TIME with the academic year that will lead us to the next millennium. There is something about a new school year that always seems to open the memory bank. By now, mine is full of deposits. I thought I might share a few here, and, that way, I can at least make room for more to come.

Way back there in the bygone days I went off to college from a little town in Iowa (82 from my high school graduating class) to a big uni-

Silver and Blue, November/December, 1999.

versity with a lot more students than that town had people. No one told me what to expect, and so, once I arrived, there were many, many things I did not know.

It would have been good to understand, for example, that, with other freshmen, I would be required to pass a physical-education test. Among the requirements of that test were carrying someone of equal weight on my back for 50 yards (I passed) and swimming a lap at the university pool (never having learned how to swim—there being in those days no place to do so in that small town of mine except a little spot known affectionately as Becker's Bare Behind Beach - I failed).

I wish someone had warned me that I would be taking classes in large auditoriums with several hundred fellow students. And that attendance was not taken in many of those classes, and no one seemed to care whether I showed up or not. And that sometimes I had to walk a mile (in Iowa, in wintertime, a very cold mile) from one class to another when those classes were scheduled just 10 minutes apart. And that, if I spent too soon the money my parents had provided, and didn't have a job, I would have to learn how to make do with several helpings of peanut butter and crackers every day. And that the job I would eventually take in order to diversify my diet and have a little loose change in my pocket would be scrubbing greasy pots and pans in a local eatery, and after that the grubby floors.

I wish I had known about the communication skills examination, when I had to give an actual speech before actual people (carrying somebody 50 yards on my back was easier). I also had to write an essay like this one, a big job for someone who did not know exactly what an essay was. (I failed the speech and passed, barely, the writing.)

I wish there had been some assistance available to help a kid just turned 18 deal with all these challenges. But there wasn't much; the notion of comprehensive admission-to-graduation student services hadn't been invented yet. This is probably why it took me eight years to get my degree.

That was a long time ago. Nowadays, students arrive on the Nevada campus from towns as small as the one in which I grew up, still needing more information than they have acquired. They don't have to carry other students around on their backs, however, or swim a lap, or give a speech, and they have available to them a wide array of caring services. There is probably something better now than peanut butter to sustain the underfinanced and underfed. These days, what you want to know is how—as they say—to "navigate the campus." You want to know what levers to push, how to access those abundant services. And there are lots of talented people around to assist you in these tasks.

You still need to prove you can write, though. The university is ready to help, encourage, educate. You have to write in a bunch of courses that did not previously require that you do so. But we have a writing center open to everybody. And we have the core writing program to go with it, so 40 years from now students will not be called upon to pen a little piece about how they wish they had learned, prior to their college days, the art of making a paragraph march across a page of paper, or to tell a split infinitive from, say, a dangling participle, or where and why and whether to deploy a semicolon, or how to write a sentence that, unlike this one, contains less (or is it fewer?) than 10 clauses, 13 commas, 11 ors and ands, and 104 words.

When I entered the college life in the 1950s, I didn't really know how much I didn't know. About everything. I learned then that that's why we have universities: to make us more knowledgeable. And so, despite all the personal problems—the overused back and the underused backstroke, the course discourse and the penchant for lengthy sentences, the big lecture halls and the small meals, the eight-year journey to a bachelor's degree—I decided to make the college life my own. And except for a detour here and there, it's a life I've never left nor wanted to. It's a life that always leaves me wishing to know more than I do, and understanding that the university is just the place where I can make that wish come true.

~

Reinventing the Wheel

W HOEVER INVENTED THE WHEEL WAY BACK WHEN, I suspect, did not know what he or she had wrought. Nor could that Bronze Age inventor have understood that what had been wrought then would be wrought again ... and again ... and again.

There are very good reasons to reinvent the wheel, of course. Circumstances arise from time to time that resemble those of an earlier period, and a similar response thus may seem in order. Or else we

Silver and Blue, April, 1993.

forget the lessons of the past and have to relearn them. Or the generations change and the new one has to learn for itself what the old one
came to understand through its own experience. In all these cases and
more, the wheel finds itself back in demand. And that's not a bad
thing, necessarily, because a better wheel is often the result.

This is the way it has been with American higher education. Every
once in a while, we have had to reinvent it. We have had to respond to
circumstances not unlike those of some previous era. We have had to
relearn, and reteach, the higher education lessons of the past. We have
had to facilitate understanding among new generations of students
and faculty, of the general public, and of key decision-makers. We
have discovered that we can, if we do the job right, make the new
wheel a significant improvement upon its ancestors.

Eliphalet Nott had an interesting idea back there at the dawn of the
19th century. He thought that his institution—a struggling little place
called Union College—could become a place where the sons of the
middle classes might come in some numbers to get a practical, as well
as a classical, education. They might take a curriculum in science, or
agriculture, or engineering: courses not then in favor in the prestigious colleges. And they might become the agents of social and economic advancement for a changing America.

Eliphalet Nott served as president of Union College in Schenectady,
N.Y., for 62 years, from 1804-1866, dying in office at 93. He lived to see
Union grow and prosper. For a while, it was the second-largest institution of higher learning in the country. Other influential college presidents were educated there. Francis Wayland, a Union graduate, made
heroic efforts at Brown University to democratize both the admissions
process and curricula of that institution. And Henry Tappan, who in
the 1850s showed the citizenry of a wilderness state—in the form of a
rawboned institution called the University of Michigan—what a public higher education could give them. Tappan, too, studied under Nott
at Union.

Andrew Dickson White took lessons learned from Tappan at Michigan, where he taught awhile, and convinced a wealthy New Yorker
named Ezra Cornell of their value. Cornell gave his name to a university that combined White's ideas (he was the founding president) with
U.S. Sen. Justin Morrill's land-grant educational concept. The doors of
Cornell were opened shortly after the Civil War. Its students believed
the eponymous benefactor's message and motto, which is still embla-

zoned on the university seal: "I would found an institution where any person can find instruction in any study."

It was a message like that, a vision like White's, a nod in the direction of Nott and Tappan and Wayland, a celebration of Sen. Morrill's grand idea, that gave birth to the University of Nevada. Periodically, here and across the nation, we have misplaced that message, lost sight of the founding idea. We have had, at such times, to reinvent it. We did it nationwide in the years after World War II, when tens of thousands of veterans found their way to college campuses courtesy of the GI Bill, and then, following graduation, went back into society to make a very large mark on the country.

We did it again in the 1960s when state and national governments made huge investments in programs and student financial aid, and changed dramatically the landscape of higher education. Millions of additional students have received college educations as a result.

We did it in Nevada once more in the 1980s. We got back to our roots. We summoned the young people of Nevada, sons and daughters now, and returning students, and senior citizens, and others, to participate in the great adventure of higher education. We asked them to become agents of change. We built strong support among the citizenry, and those who make the key decisions, for the notion that the future of our state was tied to the quality of its institutions of higher education and to the accessibility of those institutions to the people of the state.

It seems all too soon, but it is time now to invent the wheel again. State financial support is declining. Student enrollment growth is increasing, faster in Nevada than anywhere else in the nation. Student fees and tuitions are increasing, too, in our state and every other. The quality of programs and services is being tested. And student access, which has oiled the machinery of American higher education since the days of President Nott, is under severe challenge.

The fact is that college-educated men and women have long been major agents of change in America. Collectively, they have been the engine of change: irreplaceable contributors to the advancement of the nation. They, and the colleges and universities from which they graduated, have done much to make this country the envy of the world. Without visionaries such as Nott and Wayland, Tappan and White, Justin Morrill and those others who founded and opened wide the doors of great institutions of higher education across the country, many of those men and women would never have been in position to make their contributions. We would have been, without them, without a doubt, a poorer country in every way.

Open doors are the most important historical metaphor for American higher education. Access has been the key, the wheel we need now and then to reinvent, the lesson we need to relearn.

It is time now, with educational costs going up and resources going down, that the nation learns that lesson again. It is time, certainly, that we relearn it in Nevada.

~

By the Numbers

IF YOU WANT THE STORY OF AMERICAN HIGHER EDUCATION in a numerical nutshell, here it is: When the Civil War decade, the first decade for land-grant colleges and universities, turned the corner into 1870, there were 63,000 students attending classes on the nation's campuses. When, a few years from now, the 20th century turns the corner into the 21st, nearly 15 million students will be in class on those campuses, and the campuses themselves will have grown greatly in number.

Between the 1860s and the 1990s, a revolution occurred in higher education. This university has been part of that revolution. Land-grant institutions, charged with bringing educational programs and services to the people of America, have been in the vanguard of the growth and change that have opened college doors to the millions. The American success story, the story of progress, freedom and opportunity, is embedded in those numbers. So is our own experience. As the university has developed from the three young men who made up, in 1891, its first graduating class, to the 1,800 men and women of diverse age and ethnic backgrounds who graduated during 1993-94, it has contributed many chapters to that story.

Viewed in terms of what an educated citizenry means to a democracy, those chapters deserve telling and retelling. Viewed simply in terms of the economic options made available to college graduates—who can expect average lifetime earnings of $1,421,000 compared to $821,000

Silver and Blue, November/December, 1994.

for those who do not attend college—the practical value of higher learning is clear. Viewed in larger compass, in terms, say, of the impact the university has on the state's economy, the difference our institution makes is abundantly evident.

More numbers: During 1992-93, the last year for which complete data are available, this university's economic impact on Nevada was nearly a half-billion dollars. The university produced, directly and indirectly, thousands of jobs for Nevadans. Incorporating into the calculation all the institutions in the University and Community College System of Nevada, the economic impact was in excess of $1 billion.

The conclusion seems inescapable: Here is an institution, here is a higher education system, worthy of major investment; here is an enterprise that holds like no other the key to Nevada's future. The message becomes even clearer when one considers that Nevada is likely to lead the nation in the decade ahead, as it did during the 1980s, in higher education enrollment growth. Between 1985 and 2000, the UCCSN will have grown from 22,000 to 58,000 students—a 160 percent increase. From 1992-93 to 2001-02, the number of Nevada high school graduates is projected to increase by 70 percent. That figure leads the nation, too. One-third of those graduates can be expected to move on to a college education. Once again, there is a story to be told in those numbers.

For the past three years, higher education in Nevada has done its part to help the state through a difficult economic period. We returned nearly $16 million to the state's coffers, left hundreds of positions unfilled, reorganized, redirected scarce resources, developed energy-conservation programs, realized a variety of greater efficiencies of operation, and still created new programs to meet student and community demands. We saw our share of the state's general fund decline from 20 percent to 17.6 percent.

Now—as we observe major enrollment growth headed our way, as we reflect on the contributions we make as an institution and system to the economic, social and political well-being of the state of Nevada, as we envision the tremendous potential we have for enhancing those contributions— we understand how important it is that a once-again economically strong state restore to its higher education system the resources it has lost. We appreciate better what reinvestment in higher education can mean to Nevada's future.

They become our watchwords for the years ahead, indeed, for the legislative session just around the corner: *Restore. Reinvest.* We know that there are thousands out there, alumni and friends, organizations that depend on the continuation of our success story, who will be watching with us.

~

Homecoming!

I KNOW. I promised: No more narratives on how I spent my summer vacation. This was a solemn promise, one to which readers responded with overwhelming gratitude. I intend to keep that promise.

More or less.

Come early July, in need of some rest from the labors of a legislative session, I journeyed with Joy to Rhode Island. We had there a wonderful week at Weekapaug, a place hard by the sea where rest was available in large amounts. Another thing available there in large amounts was food. We dined extravagantly on the likes of lobster, scrod, clams, tuna, bluefish, steaks, salads in staggering variety, desserts that ran a range from really rich to even richer, and such Weekapaugian delicacies as cheese grits with crawfish, corned beef and sweet potato hash, macadamia nut mashed potatoes, and — according to local experts — the world's finest granola. No bite, nor flake, nor yet grain of granola having ever passed my lips, unless perhaps in disguise, this was a claim I could not evaluate. I was prepared to accept it anyway, since this granola included a generous infusion of chocolate chips. How could it be other than scrumptious?

The inn that furnished these treats had other desirable features: no locks on the room doors (and no worry about stolen articles); one phone booth serving everyone in the place (no phones in the rooms); and but one television set on the entire premises. Alas!, there was also (isn't there always?) a fax machine. On the other hand, I did not see in our seven days there a single cellular telephone in use. In an era when that pestiferous instrument has intruded so rudely on traditional patterns of civilized behavior, its absence in this serene setting was cause for jubilation.

The environment at Weekapaug was thus ripe for exercising the con-

Silver and Blue, September/October, 1997.

templative faculties. Contemplation was further encouraged by the daily brisk walks taken in an effort to ward off the growth of girth occasioned by consumption of the aforementioned cookery.

Therefore, I did a lot of thinking. What I thought a lot about was home — not so much in the physical sense, but conceptually: home as something with which one maintains a strong, almost ineffable, emotional bond. That got me right to Homecoming, which makes its annual visit to the campus very soon and which — yes, I have arrived there at last!—is the real subject of my musings here. Readers can appreciate that the road to this subject must perforce have run through Weekapaug. Elsewise, no musings. So I have kept my promise. More or less.

Homecoming! What a great tradition! What a time to celebrate! What a recognition of that strong emotional bond! And now, increasingly, what a challenge!

For this university, Homecoming is an idea, and a practice, that goes back to 1920. Earlier in the century, according to the *Artemisia* of 1908, alums would gather every year at Commencement, to visit their alma mater and attend a banquet. There were not yet enough graduates available to make for a very large banquet. The 1905 *Artemisia* lists the names of all alumni of the university to that time—all 236 of them. They were spread around the country, and, indeed, the world. Approximately a third were mining engineers, and 1905 found that group in far-flung places: the Transvaal, Mexico, Costa Rica, El Salvador, Manila, Liverpool, Butte and Boston; also in Gem, Idaho, Grand Encampment, Wyo., and Harrison Gulch, Calif. From most such places, in those days, it would have been difficult to get back to campus for a weekend of rejoicing and remembrance.

Fifteen years later—after 30 years worth of Commencements—there were enough graduates of the university to make the first annual Homecoming a reality. The yearbook for 1920-21 makes no reference to this event, but the following year, *Artemisia* took note of the second annual celebration. The Wolf Pack beat Utah on this occasion, 28-7. The fabled running back, James "Rabbit" Bradshaw, made his last home appearance. A highlight of Homecoming week was a "successful yell practice." The alums were pleased with it all. The event was accounted a glorious accomplishment.

This year, in mid October, nearly eight decades after the original, we'll do it again. No doubt, alums will be pleased and the affair will be glorious once more (though yell practice may attract a smaller crowd).

So, where, exactly, is the challenge? Well, it lies in the circumstance that—like the old gray mare — we are just not what we used to be. When homecoming began here, and for most of the time since, we were a small institution with a familiar profile. Students who came here at 18 and graduated at 22 were central to that profile. The yearbooks could run photographs of nearly all these students and, for the seniors, carry the highlights of their undergraduate careers. The campus was an intimate place, where getting to know people was relatively easy and where the changing academic seasons were marked by games, festivities, ceremonies, rites of passage and assorted oats-sowing activities in which nearly everyone participated. Homecoming, for the many generations of students who have passed through our portals, has always been a time to share memories of those days, those seasons and observances, to relive for a day or two those wondrous years of youth, and to pay homage to the institution that made it all possible.

We've changed, of course. That 18- to 22-year-old group is still central to our mission, still a significant part of the campus population. But we're bigger now, and continuing to grow. It's harder than it once was to get to know people and to get involved in campus life. Not everyone's photograph is in *Artemisia* now, and the highlights for seniors don't get printed anymore. These days, every fourth student is a graduate student, and every fifth is from someplace other than Nevada. Students from 60 or more foreign countries and from the other 49 states come to school here. Numerous others attend the university by way of technology, sitting in classrooms far from that hallowed ground around Ninth and Virginia streets. Older students — women with growing or grown children, people looking for a mid-career change, senior citizens taking a class or two or finishing a degree they started on decades ago —are very much a part of the campus landscape. The rites of passage are very different for these students; the games and festivities don't mean as much; oats-sowing is not on their agenda. Down the line, one wonders, what will Homecoming mean to them?

It's a much larger question than that, of course, and a much greater challenge, as well. For all of the changes we have seen at the university, we still have an obligation to care for our students, to nurture them, to make their experience here personal rather than impersonal, to integrate them in some meaningful way into the life of the institution, and to forge thereby the tie that binds. That is an obligation that runs the gamut of demographic categories. It's what we need to do while the students are here if we want them to have that feeling of belonging when they're gone.

It's that feeling of belonging that is at the heart of Homecoming. It's a warm feeling. It will be amply on display here a few weeks hence, when hundreds of alums come home to join the celebration. Homecoming may not be quite the same 10 or 20 years from now. But, whatever shape it takes, I hope it will involve a cast of thousands, gathered in one place or in many, in a commemorating mood, honoring a fond and common allegiance to this university.

~

Hobson's Choice

THOMAS HOBSON KEPT HORSES IN CAMBRIDGE 400 YEARS AGO. He was an equal- opportunity stablekeeper. No matter the class of the client or the pedigree of the horse, every user of his services got the same treatment—the mount that happened to be closest to the stable door. For Hobson there was, as it were, no horsing around. You paid your money and *he* made your choice. He gave a name to an ancient human predicament: Hobson's Choice.

I didn't see any horses in Hawaii when Joy and I were there on a brief holiday in February. I did encounter, however, one of the several variant forms of Mr. Hobson's selection process. After several lazy days of reading, eating, walking and—there being but little sun—a bit of basking here and there, it occurred to me that I had some important appointments on my first day back on the job. And I needed a haircut.

That always comes as surprising news to people who, having observed the state of my unadorned pate, conclude that a haircut for me is an oxymoron. They may offer sympathetic comments of the grass-not-growing-on-a-busy-street variety. They may put forward suggestions regarding a cure, ranging eclectically from modern scientific breakthroughs to advice from Radford's *Encyclopedia of Superstitions* ("Anoint bald patches with goose dung and hair will grow again"). But a haircut! Are you kidding?

Nevertheless, there on the Isle of Kauai, in the waning hours of a week's vacation, I knew I needed one. Careful inquiry revealed that the nearest barbershop was 13 miles up the road, in Lihue. Or, I could go to the hotel a block away from our condominium where, instead of a barber, I would find a stylist. For someone like me, raised on 50-cent haircuts, the prospect of going to a stylist, to a salon full of fancy oils and fragrances rather than a shop with a striped pole out front and a pile of former forelocks on the floor, was daunting. Still, I was living now in the age of convenience. I called the hotel. I described to the stylist the long history of decreasing follicular activity atop my head, noting the likelihood that a complete styling job on that location would take her less time than the two minutes required for me to walk from my condo to her salon. And I asked her, given this description, the price of such a job. "Thirty five dollars," she replied.

I called the shop in Lihue. A haircut there would be nine bucks, the barber told me. But no appointments. You just drop in and take your turn. Hobson's Choice: an easy walk to an expensive stylist or a 13-mile drive in busy traffic, and maybe a long wait, to do business with an honest-to-God, low-cost barber?

I apologize. I have taken a circuitous route to get to the point (nothing unusual for me). We're talking about choices here and, as it happens, the university has arrived at one of those critical stages when important choices are in the offing; the kind that have to do with repositioning a large and complex institution.

It's not as though we haven't been there before. In my time alone, we have faced a myriad of hard choices on budget allocations, program priorities, organizational arrangements and community relationships. We elected, for example, to invest significantly in a new core curriculum, a revitalized honors program, and expensive Presidential scholarships. We decided, against the odds, to move forward jointly with a strengthened undergraduate program and a major growth emphasis on graduate education and research. We chose to combine a number of unhappy departments into a new college (Human and Community Sciences), and to give a long-standing and strong department status as an autonomous school (the Reynolds School of Journalism). We formed a private foundation after an uphill fight and, later, facing an even steeper incline, asked that organization to take on a capital campaign of truly challenging dimensions. In the current decade, we opted for a strategy of partnerships with assorted community entities and enterprises.

All of these choices were controversial to the point where it was often hard to see where advantage lay with one alternative or another. Hobson's ghost was summoned up by some, but it was clear to those many who bore the burden of decision that the choices, painful as they were, were theirs. We were not riding off on the horse that was closest to the stable door.

Now, we are on the threshold of a new era for the university. It's not simply that the millennium is upon us, though its arrival does seem to focus thinking on various paths leading to the future. These days, we have choices to make about enrollment management, recruitment and retention, technology, distance education, diversity, campus expansion, the best uses of our multiple existing properties, along with a host of academic program and organizational relationship issues. Underlying all these choices is the question of how to finance the university of the future. In that respect, we are bound to look different in the 21st century than we have looked in the 20th —less reliant on the state, creatively seeking new sources of income, establishing more partnerships. None of this will be easy, but, again, the decisions will be ours. Mr. Hobson can keep his stable door locked. And when the choice is between the nice-appearing $35 model and one that works just as well for a quarter of the price, the latter is the likely option.

By the way, I drove to the shop in Lihue on that fateful, tressfull day. There was no wait. The barber smiled when he saw me—one of those easy, nine-dollar smiles. I was in and out of his chair quicker than you can say "hispidulous."

I admit to a desire to frequent one of those fragrant salons someday. When I do, though, I want to give the stylist something to, um, style. You can never tell about these scientific breakthroughs, or, for that matter, about superstitions. I would have more to say on this subject, but if you'll excuse me now, I hear some geese out on the lawn. I've got work to do.

∾

The Class of 2015

THERE IS A FRAMED PHOTOGRAPH on the counter behind my desk at the university. It features a young man wearing a cap with the letter N on it. In fact, in this picture, he is a very young man. He is only one hour old. His name is Benjamin Peter Joseph Crowley. His father, Neil, is a graduate of the university. Dedicated alumnus that he is, he placed that cap with the Nevada N on his son as very nearly his first act of fatherhood.

So there, I've done it. Neil being my son, I have declared in print that I am now a grandfather, joyous news I'm sure to legions of readers. This wonderful event—Ben's birth—occurred last May. It was followed in July by the arrival of Colleen Rose Corkery, daughter of our daughter Theresa (also a graduate of the university). Then comes Margaret Crowley-Magera, another daughter and yet another alum, who will provide us with a third grandchild in February.

Since it is all but a foregone conclusion that these infants will one day matriculate at the institution that serves as the parental alma mater and grandparental employer of long-standing, it is clear that the Crowley family is doing its part to swell the ranks of, say, the Class of 2015 or 2016. We are making our own future contribution to that notorious product of higher education's budgetary calculus, the Full-Time Equivalent student enrollment. Benjamin, Colleen, and Margaret's first-born (Ryan) will, alas!, one day be FTEs.

Well, not quite. FTEs, as I have suggested before, are not real. Rather, they are figments of computation. But they are important figments because they drive the legislative appropriations that fund our academic programs and services. And they are going to grow. They are going to grow a whole lot.

The demographers tell us that no state in the country comes close to matching the increase in the college-age population that Nevada is now beginning to experience. Our state's higher education institutions, this one included, have grown steadily and sometimes dramatically, over the past decade. The next decade, however, will be something else again. By 2009, the number of Nevada high school graduates will increase over current totals by 198 percent! In comparison, California, at 81 percent, has the next-highest rate of growth.

Silver and Blue, January/February, 1994.

There is a story in these statistics. We get to tell it. We get to put the narration together. We can see in the future numbers a great opportunity to realize the educational promise—a promise of greatness—the foundation for which, by dint of much effort by many people for many years, is now in place. Or we can forget the foundation, forgo this promise, fail to prepare ourselves, and create that way a future that will serve well neither our students nor our state.

We do not have an easy task ahead of us. It will be costly, in dollars, effort, and dedication. But the cost pales beside the rewards. The task begins now. It will take particularly concrete form next year as we prepare our budget request, and it will get harder as we pursue that request with the governor and the Legislature. We will send, in the measure of success we have here, a clear signal to the next century.

The students are coming in that century. That's the lesson. We will need to learn it, and serve them, well. Benjamin, Colleen and Ryan, and their thousands of classmates, will appreciate it.

I have baby pictures, by the way. Stop by and take a look at the student body of the future.

∼

Chapter Three

≈

Technology

NED LUDD WAS AN 18th CENTURY BRITISH WORKINGMAN WHO, upset about the arrival of newfangled knitting machines, took it upon himself to destroy these machines in the interest of preserving his job. His was one of the earliest revolts against that momentous development called the industrial revolution. What happened here was a technological sea change. Other such changes followed. (We are in the middle of one just now.) Those who, in successive eras, rose up to fight these changes came to be known as Luddites.

Some have suggested that the Luddite label is a good fit for me. This is because of my propensity, periodically, to revolt against this or that 20th (and now 21st) century technological innovation. I have not destroyed any machines, though truth to tell I have been tempted. My revolt has come by way of the written word. Some of the words I have written on the subject are on display in this chapter. An interesting challenge presented to me not long ago, in the form of a 19th century technological breakthrough, opens the chapter ("Down to the Wire"). The pieces that follow make clear that technology is a bugbear for me. But there is a bit of badinage here, too, and a recognition that technological change has a positive side. We are afforded these days teaching and learning tools we could scarcely have imagined a few generations ago. The growth and accessibility of information have fundamentally (and helpfully) altered the educational enterprise. We owe these advances to technology.

But, lest we forget, there are those new appliances that can drive us to distraction. Toasters belong to that category, as is observed in the article entitled, "Chopsticks," and they can impart larger lessons, useful to universities, on the need for making adjustments. Television, in its manifold current guises, demonstrates the need, which higher education helps to meet, to differentiate what is important from what is not. The value of knowing what has worth, as distinct from that which is mere elixir, is the subject of "Follicle Follies." "Sweet Talk" focuses on technology and communication, recalling along the way how once the two-way wrist radio seemed an impossible dream.

The sheer din of modern life, and the role of a university campus as a safe haven from incessant noise, provide the subject matter of "Sound Barrier." The public nature of contemporary privacy is explored in "Invasion *by* Privacy." Technology's influence in making the world a smaller place, and in driving its peoples apart, is taken up in this chapter, along with the salience of the university as an integrative force ("The Tie That Binds").

The author comes clean about his own dependence on technology in "True Confession," and reveals a part of his delinquent youth, and how it connects to the modern, information-accessing university library, in "Browsing." The chapter concludes ("A Voyage of Discovery") with a critique of the claim proffered by certain techno-soothsayers that the college campus will soon be consigned to oblivion. Instead, I argue, American higher education—campuses and all—will continue in the 21st century the challenging expedition it launched in the 17th. There will doubtless be some exciting new ports of call along the way.

≈

Down to the Wire

I WONDER: If Ned Ludd had been an American cowboy in the late 19th century instead of a British laborer in the 18th, how would he have reacted to the invention of barbed wire? That invention, which produced cheaper and more serviceable fencing materials, helped speed the end of the open range in the western states. And it led to bloody struggles between the pro-fence forces and those who opposed this new technology. One imagines that Mr. Ludd would have taken the latter side, and—who knows?—perhaps led a run on wire-cutter sales. I might well have joined him, given what happened to me 130 years later, in Ludd's own country.

Joy and I were on vacation in Dorset, in the south of England, one recent summer, staying in a village near the town of Beaminster (Eminster to readers of the Thomas Hardy novels). The weather had been problematic. After several days of intermittent rain, the sun came out one afternoon and I got the itch to take a walk. The fields and footpaths would be muddy, I knew, but I thought a stroll into Beaminster would be relatively free from muck and mire. The way was well-marked— so I had been told—and it was only a four-mile round-trip. So I donned my Nevada Wolf Pack cap and ventured out. The walk went well for the first mile. Then I came upon a part of the path where the forest branches overhead had kept out the sun and the mud appeared to be knee deep. There was nothing else for it but to forge ahead, finding the dry spot here and there to place a foot and keeping to the side, where the grass was high and the mud not puddled, whenever possible. The deeper in I went, the muddier the path and the sparser the high grass became. The prospect to my front seemed worse. I decided, in defiance of all my hiking instincts and experience ("stay on the trail, stay on the trail!"), to find another way.

A fence ran alongside the path and, soon enough, I came to a stile affording entrance to the field on my left. Off in the distance, at the other end of the field, I thought I could see another stile. That one would get me back on the way to town. Over the stile and into the field, accordingly, I went. The grass was wet and the terrain bumpy here, and numbers of cattle had obviously been recent tenants. Squishing along then, and dodging the large and fresh reminders the cattle had left to commemorate their tenancy, I made my way to the end of the field. No stile here, however; just a higher fence and, like all the fencing hereabouts, this one was adorned at the top by two layers of barbed wire. Muck and mire seemed a wiser choice, so I retraced my steps until I came to a point where I thought the fence looked surmountable. I couldn't get over it, but I thought, thin fellow such as I am, that I could squeeze between those top two layers.

Mistake! Grasping the top layer with my right hand and pushing up, and the bottom layer with my left hand and pushing down, I wedged myself halfway through. The outside foot came to rest on a narrow ledge above a puddle on the path. The inside foot, as I now discovered, was lodged approximately one inch from a very large—and very fresh—testament to bovine digestive regularity. Precisely at the moment of discovery, my cap took leave of my head and plummeted down in the direction of this execrable testament.

I had a decision to make. This was a Wolf Pack cap, after all, and it had served me well. It did not deserve to be besmirched by the fate now awaiting it. But I had only two hands. One was protecting my bent-over back from the invasion of a barb or two. The other guarded from the lower barbs an anatomical locale known to be highly valued by the male of the species. I chose to free up the hand that held the upper wire (surprise, surprise). I saved the cap. (Of course, it helped that the hand I sent after it happened to be on the same side of the fence as the cow manure.) My back got barbed. Almost. The barb, I now determined, was imbedded in my shirt rather than my skin. I still had a predicament —how to get to the footpath side of the fence with barbed wire stuck in a shirt that was, in turn, stuck to my sweaty body. A good deal of deft and delicate maneuvering got me about three-quarters of the way through. But I could not shake the barb. I heard voices off in the distance. I did not want to be found—an ignorant colonial—in my current compromised position. I resolved to remove my shirt.

It is difficult to describe the contortions required to achieve this resolution. Picture a bent-over body, still concerned about barbs in both the higher and the nether regions, still worried about a descent into the mire on one side and a cow pie on the other, twisting and turning rather in the mode of Plastic Man imitating Houdini, to get that shirt off. The voices came nearer. The shirt climbed my body ... one arm out, no damage to either region; the other arm out, still no damage; over the neck and over the head, and I was free! I grabbed the shirt, torn as it now was from the rigors of a battle hard-fought but won. I put it on, redonned my cap (which bore the colors of the winning side, though it could well have borne another color) and walked off through the mud—humming the Wolf Pack marching song, bidding a cheerful good day to two hikers coming up the path from town.

~

Chopsticks

A FEW YEARS AGO, during one of my periodic mental revolts against the 20th century, I wrote a little piece about the frustrations of modern technology. There is much I dislike about that technology, ranging from amplified music, through premixed milkshakes and toothpaste tubes, to ZIP codes. This piece focused on toasters, which have caused me great grief down through the years. I wrote it in that state of high dudgeon peculiar to those who don't like their bread burned for breakfast and, as with the letters to the editor one composes in a similar state, I thought better of it later and let it go unpublished.

What brought me to the point of writing that piece was the current family toaster, latest in a long line of such machines to malfunction with remarkable regularity. I was a poor student when I got married 26 years ago. I offered my wife a modest dowry: one ancient toaster that, age notwithstanding, behaved itself rather well. This is not something that could be said about any of its successors. These latter routinely singed their contents, or refused to disgorge them, or catapulted them across the room. Or, I swear, simply ate them, caused them to vanish without a trace.

But the last one, ah, the last one. It was to be a marvel of sophistication: knobs and dials galore, computerized selection mechanisms to suit the most discriminating tastes in toasting. It had a price tag to match its technical excellence. However, it did not work. It gave me perfection on one side of the bread and ashes on the other. The width and length of its apertures were such that it was quite particular about which type of slice it would take in and which it would not. Despite all

UNR Times, September/October, 1987. Reprinted in *Notes from the President's Chair...,* pp. 115-17.

entreaties, for example, it refused to accept in good grace an English muffin. And there were times when it declined to let out that which it had let in. There was no catapulting with this machine. Pop-up technology seems to have compensated for previous shortcomings in this area. Perhaps it has overcompensated, given that its recent products often have no up to their pop at all. This one, anyway, did not appear to know up from down.

That is why I wrote the paper I did not publish.

One must be patient in these matters. Successful long-term relationships are built on a mutual willingness to adjust, to compromise. My toaster and I are getting along pretty well these days. I don't swear at it anymore, don't turn it upside-down and shake it violently anymore. For its part, the toaster brings its power to bear more even-handedly now. It is less given to singeing. It admits, even if reluctantly, almost all comers, even English muffins. And, as for its periodic pop-uplessness, well, we got that problem resolved amicably. The solution was Yankee ingenuity, or more accurately, Yangtze ingenuity. The solution was chopsticks.

The chopsticks container in our home is kept, for no special reason, on the shelf above the one on which the toaster resides. One morning, seized by angry inspiration when the machine was holding fast to a fat piece of homemade whole wheat, I grabbed a chopstick, inserted the narrow end inside the toaster, and effortlessly wedged out the toast. The practice is now routine. The toaster doesn't mind a bit. (I wedge gently.) And there is something wonderful about bringing together, to help produce my breakfast, contemporary kitchen electronics with one of the oldest culinary implements known to humankind.

We don't do much with toasters at the university. But we are familiar with the frustrations of modern technology. Our offices run on that technology as, more importantly, do our classrooms and laboratories. Often enough, despite the science, skill, and dedication that go into its production, it just does not work. Sometimes it does not work when one most needs it to work. When that happens, especially if it happens regularly, one is seized by the urge to turn the offending apparatus upside down and shake it violently. However, the apparatus is likely to cost a whole lot more than a toaster, so one resists the urge.

Instead, in the grand tradition of the university, we adjust. We find ways to make the technology work. We employ our ingenuity. We find, figuratively, a helpful chopstick.

Higher education has long survived—more than that, prospered—because it has learned how to mix the new with the old, in terms of both how to deliver knowledge and how to expand it. The humanities professor uses a computer for research. The scientist understands that the application of laboratory advances must be informed by enduring human values. The learning process itself proceeds from old lessons to new discoveries. That is how we got technology in the first place.

None of this is easy. It is merely necessary. Technology is here to stay; it will just keep getting newer. We can always find a way to make it function if we are willing to adjust. And to remember that, while things in general aren't what they used to be, some of what used to be is still available to help get us where we want to be.

That's how you get toast the way you like it in the morning.

~

Follicle Follies

WHEN HE WAS IN HIS EARLY 20S, my older brother discovered a disturbing process at work among the hair follicles atop his head. They were not functioning the way they once did. He was shedding hair by the handful. He was going bald.

Dismissing the fact that baldness ran like sap down the branches of the family tree, he invested a tidy sum of money in a cure: bottles of nice-smelling, multicolored liquids that, when applied regularly and vigorously, promised to restore his scalp to its former glory. The restoration project, needless to say, was a failure.

That was 40 years ago. These days, malfunctioning follicles are as common as they have always been. So are the balms that purport to repair them. So are the people who buy the balms. But there are differences, big differences. Television is one of them.

Hour-long programs are now given over to testimonials from happy people whose locks have grown long again thanks to some magic formula discovered in a secret scientific laboratory in, maybe, Liechtenstein. This is a substantial improvement from the old elixir salesmen, on display in a thousand Western movies, or the one who sold my brother that remedy for an irremediable condition. The principle is the same,

UNR Times, Spring, 1989.

to be sure. (Mr. P.T. Barnum put it into words for us a long time ago.) But the money to be made is greater by far than the potion peddlers of the old frontier ever imagined. Flimflam lives, and prospers! Television contributes (and there are plenty of other contributors) to this prosperity.

It's not just a matter of cures for baldness, of course, or wondrous diets that make your body look like something it did not look like when you first noticed it, or wizard slicers that cut everything every which way (including, perhaps, a stray finger), or ingenious schemes to make you rich in a day or two with no money down and not much in the bank.

No, television carries far more consequential challenges to the intellect. It sells (literally) salvation. It conditions preferences in culture and commerce. It controls political life in a measure that could scarcely be imagined in an earlier age. The recent election campaign, with its stupefying lack of substance, is evidence enough of such control, of the triumph of flimflam in politics.

To be sure, all this is but one side of the coin. Television has also educated millions, expanded greatly our cultural vocabulary, provided us knowledge and understanding of our world to a degree and with an intensity and propinquity unsurpassed by any other medium in any other era. But with all its power to enlighten and emancipate, it has a similar power to obscure, to dull the senses.

Higher education has always had a responsibility to develop in students a mental discipline, an ability to view the world and all its wonders with a critical eye, to tilt when necessary at conventional wisdom (and even on occasion at windmills), to separate intellectually the wheat from the chaff, to apply information and reason across a wide spectrum of choices. And to recognize flimflam in its sundry and sometimes sophisticated manifestations.

We have done this job reasonably well, I believe. With the power of television, the advances of technology, and the enormous increase in the amount and availability of information it becomes ever more difficult to distinguish what is genuine from what is just another elixir. For that reason and many others, we are thus challenged now to do the job better.

To that end, we have recently developed a new core curriculum for our undergraduates. Its requirements—among them an expanded emphasis on critical thinking and a much more comprehensive stress on writing and computational skills—will assure that our graduates are better prepared to make the distinctions and decisions forced upon them by the complexities of modern living and the often potent allure of modern panaceas.

We have developed, as well, a much more demanding honors program that will expect much from the students who undertake it and deliver much to them in return. Those who complete the program will not be daunted by complexities and they will not be taken in by false promises and premises.

We are answering the challenge, in these and other ways. We are attracting excellent students and excellent faculty. We are refining existing programs and offering new ones of high quality. As we look toward the arrival, one year hence, of the last decade of the 20th century, we are required to prepare our students to make the difficult but necessary choices that will help to shape the world—and diminish its reservoir of flimflam—at the dawning of the next millennium.

∽

Sweet Talk

I ONCE RAN AFOUL OF A COMMUNICATION SYSTEM that was used by the University of Nevada, Las Vegas during campus sessions of the Board of Regents. The system featured microphones that sat flat on the table. They were oblong in shape and dark- brown in color. In fact, they looked a lot like brownies.

The regents customarily provide nice things to munch on during their meetings, including a wide variety of sweetstuffs and, especially, chocolate sweetstuffs. I always help myself to the latter because, at the sight of chocolate, I tremble shamelessly. It is a continuing occasion of sin for me, a terrible temptation that the nuns at Sacred Heart School did not tell me how to avoid.

During one regents meeting at UNLV a few years ago, I found myself caught up in a raging discussion over some question of great and contentious import. I delivered, indeed, one of the finest speeches of my life. It was elegant, eloquent, poignant, persuasive, replete with the full range of rhetorical flourishes; oratory in fullest flower at its finest

UNR Times, Spring, 1988.

hour. Webster, Gladstone, Bryan, Churchill—they would have been pleased to be there. When I was done, exhausted but proud, and certain I had won the day, the board members seemed unmoved. They regarded me quizzically, uncomprehendingly. One of them asked if I would mind repeating my remarks.

It was then that I discovered I had not been speaking into a microphone. Having succumbed to temptation just before the discussion got underway, I had been speaking, instead, into a brownie.

When I was a lad back there at Sacred Heart School, one of my heroes was Dick Tracy, the great constable of the comics. Mr. Tracy brought notorious criminals to justice, in part through the use of his famous two-way wrist radio. The radio was an outlandish idea, of course. But that's what the comics are for, to carry us far beyond the bounds of reality. Readers understood that there was no possibility people could ever communicate with each other, like detective Tracy, by talking into a wristwatch to the guys back at headquarters.

This was in the days when television was considered a magical invention, when crowds would gather at night in front of the appliance store to watch for hours a TV set that showed nothing but snow. This was the pre-beeper age, a time when anyone caught speculating about something like cellular phones and electronic mail would have been shipped off forthwith to the home for the addlepated.

I have learned that communication, if one takes the word to mean that both parties or all sides to a discussion will carry away the same message, does not come easy. I have learned that it is a constant struggle for people to emerge from a conversation or a conference with a shared understanding of what went on there. I know that, though Dick Tracy was doubtless a man ahead of his time, even the best efforts of modern technology cannot stand in the way of one person swearing he heard what the other person did not say. And maybe I'm not the only one who sometimes speaks into brownies.

Recently, I got involved in the settlement of a dispute that was the stuff of which communications breakdowns are made. It was a negotiation over space and dollars, a task to test the mettle of the most talented negotiators. It's a long story, but, to boil it down to its awful and quintessential ingredients, it had discussions moving up and down and from and to staff, deans, vice presidents, two presidents and one chancellor. It called forth the full array of technological wizardry. Beepers beeped, speaker phones spoke, electronic mail heated up the cables.

Through it all, befuddlement grew geometrically. At length, when two people were instructed to sit down in a room and produce an agreement, we discovered that we really had no disagreement in the first place. We had simply not had the wit—until frustration and frazzled tempers forced a solution — to find the right way to communicate with each other.

In a few weeks time, the Class of 1988 will march in stately procession down the Quad toward Commencement. Inside the minds of the graduates, one expects, will be a goodly store of knowledge and pleasant memories, a sharpened ability to understand the world they will now inherit, and some thoughts about how to make it a better one for succeeding generations. This is a class that has grown up with beepers, for whom a two-way wrist radio would be considered as outlandish as the setting of the sun.

Our graduates will have learned about the technology that now helps people get their messages across more effectively. They will know about how and why people exchange messages without a word being spoken. They will understand the role of rhetoric and the importance of clarity. They may even have some inkling as to how, these days, folks are able to speak back across the centuries to themselves in earlier incarnations or how electronic preachers talk to God about church finances. They will probably figure out how to avoid talking to chocolate confections, and maybe how to avoid chocolate. They will leave us, in short, with a heightened appreciation of the fine art and frequent necessity of proper communication. And they'll need all that because they will ultimately share the responsibility of assuring that this planet of ours, around which now communication flows so plentifully, does not someday, because of miscommunication, get buried under mushrooms. We wish them luck. And skill.

By now, UNLV has installed a new communications system and I have pretty well forgotten the embarrassment caused me by the old one. It could have been worse, I tell myself. I could have eaten a microphone.

~

Sound Barrier

I READ SOMEWHERE RECENTLY that by the middle of the next century there will be no need for college campuses. Technology will make it so: One can simply sit at home at one's computer and punch up a course, a lecture, a library, or a little advice, perhaps, on career options. Maybe an examination administered by robot-monitors programmed to keep you from fudging.

How sad a development that would be, for many reasons. There is, for example, the ancient and honorable idea of the campus as a sanctuary, a place protected against at least some of the hustle and bustle of life outside its boundaries, an environment designed for contemplation. That idea would die with this particular triumph of 21st century educational technology. How sad, indeed.

It's travel, probably, that gives rise to such troubling thoughts. I have been doing a lot of it lately, hither and thither around the country, in and out of airports, on and off of airplanes. Often, I go through Dallas-Fort Worth (DFW in the argot of the airline trade). There, in case I miss my daily exercise, I can count on a long walk through narrow, noisy, teeming corridors to make my connection. I am certain to have an opportunity to play dodge-'em with one of those passenger transporters that zip through DFW at a rate just this side of the speed of light. ("Excuse the cart, please," the driver shouts. I excuse it with alacrity, giving the cart, as it were, carte blanche.)

If there was once romance in air travel, well, that's a rose that's lost its bloom. Loud and crowded airports give entry to loud and crowded airplanes. Even ear plugs cannot hold back the din of engines and cramped humanity and the captain explaining in laborious detail the history and topography of Shiprock, Ariz.

The planes do get you to cities, though. There (in, say, New York) you can find yourself headed the wrong direction at the wrong time up Broadway, against an oncoming throng aiming for the theaters or the variety of tawdry temptations available in the area. Or you can set yourself down among aggressive alms-seekers in downtown San Francisco. Or, if you go west from there, you can end up in the Far East, in the middle of Taipei, where the sounds of traffic can wake the dead and where, as well, there are devices that tell you, precisely and discouragingly, the prevailing decibel levels.

Silver and Blue, January/February, 1995.

And, of course, anywhere you go you can have a drink in a place where the music is cranked up to maximum volume. I recall one such establishment with no-smoking warnings everywhere, a menu based on the premise that nothing remotely bad for you would be served, and a big sign asserting that patrons ought not ask to have the music turned down because, harrumph, it is meant to be heard! Fortunately, the noise of conversation is not added to the mix in such places, inasmuch as it is impossible — save at grave risk to vocal cords — to have one. It is only fair to note that sonic boom music is also available these days at almost any intersection, where automobiles pass by with windows down and radios up (way up!), generously sharing exotic rhythms and (fortunately) impenetrable lyrics with people living within a one-mile radius.

Technology is doubtless in many ways a blessing, but when we consider that in the next 50 years it may put college campuses out of business, it would be wise to remember that it has also led to less beneficial consequences, including a fearsome ability to produce noise. Would it not be good, then, to keep those campuses around as bulwarks against what may be the even more fearsome noise of the future?

There are, as noted, a number of wonderful reasons that the campus as a physical presence should remain, to yield its manifold pleasures to our children and grandchildren, and theirs, as well. That presence is a noble tradition which, properly nurtured, affords an environment in which intellectual life prospers and fond memories take hold. Surely that is true of the tranquil, verdant precincts of our own campus, lovingly developed and universally admired over the past 110 years.

May those precincts, affronted only rarely by incursions of amplified sound, stand forever!

～

Invasion *by* Privacy

WE LIVE IN AN AGE OF GREAT CONCERN ABOUT THE MANIFOLD, media-abetted invasions of our privacy. There is, to be sure, ample
reason to be worried. Even so, as I read somewhere last year, it is worth
remembering that there is another side to this coin of concern. That
would be the increasing tendency of some people to share that which
should be private with the public. This, too, is worrisome. It is, in a
measure, also media-abetted. And it is, in many ways, a consequence
of our great, galloping, sometimes galumphing passage into the technological lifestyle. Nowadays when we ask ourselves that trite old question, "Will wonders never cease?" we are compelled to answer: "No!"
We can expect new ones nearly every day. All these wonders, however,
are not necessarily wonderful.

Take the cell phone, for example (please!). I know, I have mentioned
this *bete noire* of mine before, but consider it now in the context of the
aforementioned invasion. Why do I need to know the personal agenda
of the woman sitting in the adjacent seat on a taxiing airplane, or of
the guy at a nearby table in a restaurant? (I am now taking seriously a
cartoon I saw a few years ago, with the maître d' asking a couple arriving for dinner: "Cell phone or non-cell phone?") And, for heaven's
sake, why must I perforce overhear the gentleman standing next to me
in an airport restroom pursuing his occupational affairs over the phone
while otherwise occupied by the business that brought him to the
restroom in the first place? These folks are making their privacy public
and violating my privacy in the process.

And then there are all those nasty television shows where people
eagerly congregate to tell the world of their idiosyncrasies, indiscre-
tions and bizarre behaviors. (I know, just don't turn these programs
on; but how can a self-respecting channel surfer avoid them altogether?)
And some of the radio talk shows on which souls mired in the muck
are bared and—into the bargain—the language used does damage to a
civilized ear.

Speaking of ears, are they not assaulted as well by the personal musical preferences of those who drive around town with windows rolled
down and radio volume turned up to a level that can shake the very
air? What these people want to listen to is their own business, but
they ought not persist in sharing it with innocent others. That is an-

Silver and Blue, April, 1999.

other invasion by privacy.

We have found too many ways to communicate too much previously unutterable *stuff* to too many people in too many places. The valleys of public quiet are filling up with private noise.

Call me a reactionary (or maybe just guilty of selective recall), but I remember fondly the carbon paper era. Whatever was being typed in those days was going out to only five people, and it was not likely to burden them with the latest news about a person's peccadillos. Now, of course, one can run off a hundred or a thousand copies, or fax what should be a closely held message to the far corners of the planet. Or one can get an e-mail.

Truly, I enjoy e-mail. I have an address. I send off a lot of e-mail letters. I receive more than I send, since I find myself somehow plugged into networks—this is something like receiving those mountains of unrequested catalogs—I never asked to be part of. On the whole, though, e-mail is a welcome addition to the growing repertoire of communicative capabilities.

But take care! People may be inclined to believe that what they put into their e-mail letters is just between them, their addressee(s), and etherspace. It can be, however, public record. And there have been choice communications that, on certain occasions, have emerged from the ether for all (or at least some) to titillatingly see.

And here's the latest: You can be sent anonymous e-mail. I have had some come my way of late. People can convey it to you through a technological thingamabob called an "anonymizer," the purpose of which is to, well, anonymize you, so you can write whatever you want, launch verbal fusillades at your target, reveal your innermost quirks, and just basically travel incognito through the Internet.

In the end, I suppose, a person has to understand that there is a price to be paid for the tremendous growth in availability of information that technology makes possible and that education profits from so handsomely: We get, that is, a fair share of information we neither want nor need that in an earlier era would have seldom been transmitted. So, close your eyes and hold your nose when you surf through the Jerry Springer show and its odoriferous cousins. Carry earplugs for those times when the dashboard boom boxes in passing automobiles expose you to their clamorous rhythms. Get yourself anonymized and send an attack e-mail to one (or more) of those radio foulmouths.

Oh, and about cell phones? I have a confession to make. Keeping in mind the sounds of hypocrisy echoing around the corridors of power in the nation's capital these days, remembering those biblical injunctions about casting the first stone and judging not lest ye be judged, and considering the law of social physics that calls to our attention the coming around of what goes around ... I have to own up to an episode of awful shame. I beg pardon if this confession intrudes upon your private space. In an urgent moment recently, when I had to make a call and there was no public phone available, I borrowed one those devilish cell devices from a friend. Furthermore, I *used* it. And I was caught by a camera *in flagrante delicto!* There is photographic evidence! There is a negative!

I'm only human, after all. And this is just one of my many frailties. If I had more space here, I'd like to tell you about some of the others. In great detail. Maybe next time. Maybe not.

~

The Tie That Binds

I WRITE THESE LINES ON THE LEE SIDE of that great divide known as Y2K. It seems fitting that the shorthand reference for the arrival of the new millennium is borrowed from the technological vocabulary. One wonders at a time like this about Y1K (when few were fluent in that kind of vocabulary) and, for that matter, Y0K: What was the catalog of worries as 999 approached its last days? The end of the world was nigh, then, some folks believed, but the world itself—its multiple dimensions, features, geography and peoples—was known to no one. And as for the approach of the year 0, well, since its arrival was unheralded, there was no big changing of the calendar to cause concern.

If you are reading this piece on the other side of the Y2K divide, it is fair to assume that we have sailed boldly forth before the digitizing winds, navigated a passage through the cybernetic shoals and arrived safely on the farther shore. Now we can look backward for a bit, consider what has been wrought since 999, and conclude that it has been one hell of a millennium!

Silver and Blue, January/February, 2000.

The world no one really knew about 1,000 years ago is well-known now, though mysteries remain, and that's a good thing. Our world is tied together in sundry ways. Its far corners and exotic crannies are reachable by phone and fax and, if you have a little time, you can go expeditiously to explore a distant nook of your choice in person. Or, you can travel there and absorb its sights and sounds by using the Internet highway. One thousand years ago, vastly more of the world was out of reach than in. Today, we can reach wherever through that magic carpet we call a mouse pad. And talk with whomever, from almost anywhere, about almost anything via that ubiquitous device, the cellular phone.

The recent history of Mount Everest makes the point well. When Sir Edmund Hillary and Tenzing Norgay made it to the summit in 1953, it was just them and the mountain. Forty years later, the area around Everest had become a kind of tourist mecca, and climbers, armed with advanced technology, were simply part of the scenery. In spring 1996, some 14 separate expeditions, involving upwards of 150 people, gathered in that far-off place to assault the summit. That sad season will be remembered for the dozen climbers who died then on Everest's slopes. But perhaps the most poignant remembrance is of the leader of one of the expeditions, freezing and dying six miles up in the summit snow, speaking his last halting words, by telephone, to his wife in New Zealand. It is, indeed, a small world after all.

And yet, and yet ...

There is, as there always is, this interesting bit of irony to consider: If technology has made the world smaller, better understood, more interrelated, its peoples more—much more—accessible to each other, it has also provided the wherewithal to drive us apart, to diminish the ties that bind us into a community. These days, many of the tasks that have historically brought us out into society—shopping, banking, taking college courses, even job responsibilities—can be performed without leaving one's house. Anonymity has become for many a preferred way of life. It has become almost the norm to have an unlisted telephone number, or, if one is in the directory, to list only an initial or two in front of one's last name, while showing no address. If you want to call Roger Smith in Washoe County, and you don't know the number, you will have to choose between 24 R. Smiths in the phone book (five with addresses).

I recently lost a long-running battle with the folks who produce the university telephone directory. I fought hard, against mounting odds, to list my home number in that directory. It was once the case that practically all faculty and staff members had that listing. Over the years, those home numbers gradually disappeared. I was among the last to continue the practice. As a public servant, I thought I should be readily reachable, even though it meant taking some truly strange calls, often made in the middle of the night. You won't find my home phone in this year's university directory. I asked why, and was told that the computer cannot do this anymore. You show your campus number (and e-mail address) and that's all. However, if you are retired, you can show your home phone, but no office number. Is this a hint?

I don't understand this desire for anonymity, this business of un-listed numbers by the slew, and I worry some about the increasing temptation to just stay home and let technology take care of things for you. Still, there are ways yet available to forge the ties that bind. The university is one such way. A recent issue of our alumni magazine, for example, discusses our graduates at work in the Andes, in Kosovo, Borneo, and Japan; in Chicago playing baseball, near Gerlach grow-ing garlic, and near a Nevada Indian Reservation practicing medicine. What unites them is their common tie to this institution, one that gave them nurture and learning, and sent them proudly forth on their journeys 'round the planet. We are doing our part to keep it a small world.

The world can still find me listed in the Reno phone directory, with address. Call me if you have the urge, before midnight if possible. As for the number, well, you'll have to look it up

∾

True Confession

TIME FOR A CONFESSION.
Readers—the hardy few—who have followed my musings over the years may recall that on occasion I have tilted at the windmills of high technology. This caused me to take on, in curmudgeonly fashion, such diverse targets as the modern sneaker (formerly tennis shoe), egregiously

Silver and Blue, May/June, 1995.

amplified music, malfunctioning toasters of diverse ages and stages of sophistication, and the contemporary propensity to converse in computerese (shall we interface?, where's your throughput?). I have long thought of myself as something of a Luddite, someone who smiles when high tech goes goofy, a man who continues to do his writing on lined yellow tablet paper, an individual who might have been better set down in an earlier century.

But that's not the confession. This is: I now have a personal computer! Furthermore, I like it. I am very much on a learning curve with this machine, and I expect to be snaking my way along that curve for some time to come. I'm starting late and I'm far behind. I am both dazzled and frustrated by the complexity of my little laptop. But I see a future for myself now in a century different from the one (say, maybe, the 19th) in which I have often thought I belonged.

This other century, of course, would be the 21st. It's my job to help the university prepare itself for the promise, the possibilities, the perils of that new century. How that job must be done has become increasingly clear to me in recent years. I have seen our campus cable network expand; seen, as well, how much we have to do in that respect. I have seen what can be accomplished, the great advancement of the teaching art, through our "smart" classrooms. And I know that there are many more that we must build. I have noted the delivery of interactive television courses to locations such as Elko through our distance education program. And I have come to understand the urgent need for public higher education to spend millions of dollars to realize the potential of this program. I have observed our students filling to capacity (and then some) our computer laboratories, and I know those labs need to be expanded, to provide up-to-date equipment, longer hours, increased staffing.

The University and Community College System of Nevada has before the Legislature a request for $40 million in equipment funding for the 1995-97 biennium. That seems a large figure, but it should be understood in a context of the next-to-no equipment funding we have received during the past four years. The governor has recommended $20 million. That would certainly help. We hope to improve on this recommendation in the coming weeks. We are at the threshold of a new century, a technologically challenging and rewarding century. We will not cross that threshold in terms of those challenges and rewards unless the state of Nevada faces up to the investment required. Forty million dollars is not too much to ask — indeed, it is a modest request — given the task ahead.

So I have my computer to help me warm to that task. And, lo and behold!, I am using e-mail, as well. I'm on the Internet. And a student has offered to get me a strand of sorts on the World Wide Web. (I accepted.) My wife has a fax machine. I use it myself without fear. It is a cordial type, user-friendly, as they say; what you might call a reasonable facsimile (sorry). Thus, I am now, I admit, a bit of a technological voyager, and I am enjoying the trip.

Still, there are places I won't be visiting on this voyage. You won't see me, for example, strolling around with one of those cellular phones applied to my ear. I like telephones, but I like them stationary, the way Alexander Bell intended them. I see people these days talking on their cellulars in sundry places — on airplanes, in automobiles, walking, jogging, at basketball games (during the action!), while dining in restaurants, at concerts, in elevators, in airport restrooms, at meetings of all kinds.

I think the sun will still rise, and civilization will still advance, if we wait to make or receive those calls, just like we used to. I think our health might be improved. I'm sure our manners would be. I'm not taking the cellular trip.

But I'm enjoying the scenery on my PC ride. The other day, my daughter, who has a similar machine, punched up her encyclopedia and showed me on her screen the motion of an eagle diving for its prey. She showed me, too, a full-color picture of a quetzal, a South American bird, and had me listen as the computer gave out the quetzal's call. It's a very pleasant sound. Better, infinitely better, than the sound of a cellular phone ringing in places where phones were not meant to be heard. Better, for that matter, than the squeak of a high-tech sneaker hitting the pavement (sounds very much, by the way, like a low-tech tennis shoe) and the blast of full volume music shattering glasses and eardrums around the neighborhood.

As you can see, I have not given up windmill-tilting entirely.

≈

Browsing

RECENTLY, I HAD A TOUR OF THE GETCHELL LIBRARY HERE ON CAMPUS. I spent a lot of time there in the old days, but my job had kept me mostly away from its comforting environs for 21 years. I marveled at the changes: the Patricia L. Chase Study Area, a gift from a loyal alumna and her husband; the technology that now governs so much of the library's work; the access to information that has made the place as much a gateway to the world's knowledge as a repository for some of it.

And I walked leisurely through the stacks again, surprised that, as I entered a row, an electronic eye espied me and turned on an overhead light. Stacks lose some of their allure when the lights go on. But I still felt that old urge to stop and browse, to spend a few delicious hours just hanging out there in the aisles.

That's how an ancient memory caught up with me, and for a moment I was frozen again by the fearsome stare of Sister Angelica. And warmed by what came later.

The Sisters of Mercy were the keepers of Sacred Heart School in my home town. They were teachers such as Sister P. (who gave me all A's because she loved spelling and I was the third-grade spelling champ); Sister M. (a no-nonsense nun who taught me altar boy Latin, and the effective discipline of ruler-rapped knuckles); Sister J. (who, in her distracted way, presided—or tried to—over 11 o'clock study hall my first year of high school).

And, of course, Sister Angelica. In the history of naming nuns, there had never been a greater misnomer. She was not angelic. She was a Sister of Mercy, yes, but the order did not fit the person. She was not merciful. She was grim. She was frightening. Her smile muscle, apparently, had been severed at birth. Sister A. was the principal!

Sister J.'s study hall was a place made for mischief. Tommy the Great was a senior, and mischief was his middle name. He was our leader. It was Tommy who initiated the notes telling all the study hall boys the exact time when we would place hairpins under the desk slats and twang them loudly. Or when we would bend our heads back and examine the ceiling. Or when we would launch our arsenal of spitballs. Or, if the demons truly possessed him, Tommy would have us at these

Silver and Blue, September/October, 1999.

things in sequence, while doing other deeds that must remain unmentioned.

Sister J. was not pleased with these displays of anarchic behavior. If she caught you in the act, she moved you to a front seat for awhile. I got caught, eventually, and was transported frontwards. This restricted considerably my participation in Tommy's hijinks. I could occasionally stare at the ceiling, however, and was doing just that one day with 20 or 30 fellow-students when my peripheral vision discerned a presence in the doorway. I turned my head in that direction, and locked on to the paralyzing eyes of Sister Angelica. In a trice, I was reduced to a stupefactive state. Those eyes held portents of doom.

Sister A. spoke: "All those who were looking at the ceiling, raise your hands!" Mine went up, and I expected a sea of hands to do likewise behind me. Wrong. No on else volunteered. Not Tommy the Great. Not anybody. Just me.

Steering by my ear, Sister A. marched me down the hall to her office. There, she gave me the kind of lecture a warden might give to an unruly prisoner. Then she put me in solitary confinement. In a closet, with the door closed, the light on, and a bible to read while I contemplated the difference between good and evil. I heard her make a phone call. To my mother. To come and get her delinquent son.

After 30 minutes or so, Sister A. retrieved me from the closet, told me it would be several hours before my parents would arrive at the scene of the crime, and sentenced me to spend those hours in the school library. I was to talk to no one. I was restricted to a single activity: browsing.

I was a veteran reader by then. My parents started me early with newspapers and comic books, and our house was well-stocked with children's literature—adventure novels, Louisa May Alcott, the complete works of Horatio Alger. If you've read one Alger, you've read them all, but I read them all, anyway. Though I had often visited the local library, I had never had the luxury of spending three hours, without interruption, browsing in the stacks. I had that opportunity now. I wasn't quite sure about evil yet, but I knew that this was *good*.

My folks took me home late that afternoon, and kept me there for a week or so. Sister A. had suspended me (to be truthful, I had had a few prior offenses). This made Mrs. Swenson happy. She lived down the street, and had predicted when I was 5 years old that I was destined for reform school. Grandpa Cornelius Crowley, who lived with us when

I was a tyke, had doted on me a bit—"catered to your every whim," was how my mother put it; "spoiled you rotten," was my sister's version. "Brat," was the word of choice from Mrs. Swenson.

Mom found lots of work for me to do around the house and yard during the days of my suspension, and when all that work was done, she invented some more. But there was time to read, as well, to summon up a vision of Sister A's fierce visage as she stood in the classroom doorway, and to offer a silent thanks for those hours of pleasurable solitude amongst the books in the Sacred Heart High School library.

That's what I thought about on that recent tour through Getchell. And about what has happened to libraries since that memorable day at Sacred Heart a half-century ago. About the information age we live in and the technological advances that produced it. About the passing of card catalogs and the Dewey Decimal System. About the computerized processes that now rule the Getchell roost. About the access we now enjoy to hundreds of scholarly journals (full-text articles, all of them, from the beginning of all those journals' existence to the latest volume), not on-site but on-line: Punch a button and on your screen is whatever you want from, say, the *International Journal of Pediatric Otorhinolaryngology*, or the *Journal De Chimie Physique Et De Physico-chimie Biologique*. It's all right there, and it's doing wonders for the pursuit and dissemination of knowledge.

And I thought about the electronic eye that lights up the stacks. And about the stacks themselves (may God help us to always keep them open!). I had a sudden pleasant feeling toward Sister Angelica— the first one ever!—and thought that, if she were standing there with me in the well-illuminated aisles of Getchell Library, I would reach over and give her a big, big hug.

∾

A Voyage of Discovery

THE SKY IS FALLING IN AGAIN. That's what the pundits are saying. It's falling in on higher education, as we have come to know and love it. Sometime in the not-too-distant future, most of the college campuses in this country will be gone, or at least out of business. They

Silver and Blue, March/April, 1998.

could survive as museum pieces, artifacts of a glorious yore, tourist sites such as the Roman Colosseum or the Pyramids of the Nile. But they won't be doing education anymore, since they will be unable to adapt to the demands and developments of the 21st century.

Oh, the prestigious universities may still be operating, just because, since we are human, we will always value prestige. And the so-called convenience institutions, places just down the street that you can get to with little effort. And the colleges and universities that don't need a campus, that deliver their programs through distance education. You only have to commute, in this case, to your computer, maybe to your television set. These types of higher education entities, and perhaps a few others, can survive, possibly even prosper. But lots of campuses that don't answer to such descriptions will have to close down because they can't keep up.

That's what the pundits are telling us.

I think they're wrong.

They forget—these soothsayers do—what a marvelously adaptable enterprise American higher education has been. It is an enterprise that has met and mastered huge challenges in its three-and-a-half centuries of life. It moved a formidable distance (and not without pain) from its former long-term mission to train ministers and nurture Christian values in young gentlemen. It moved away, often in battle formation, from the old hard-and-fast fixed curriculum to incorporate the radical notion of elective courses. In the 19th century, it took on new disciplines, programs it had never contemplated before: agriculture, business, journalism, science (yes, science!), modern languages. In the 20th century, it welcomed the challenge of access, of opening its doors by century's end to 15 million students. Those doors had let in only a few hundred-thousand at century's beginning. It dealt successfully with threatening ideas such as public (instead of only private) education, graduate education, coeducation, lifelong education.

It even made headway with parking.

In the face of these daunting historical adaptations, the soothsayers tell us that many colleges and universities will be unable to cope with the challenges currently posed—by high technology, by a growing desire for more practical degree programs, by the sense in some quarters that the degree should be brought to you rather than you to the degree. We should know by now that, if you listen to the soothsayers, what you are going to get, in the end, is a lot of ... sooth.

It's time for another dog story.

I have written before in this space about the family pooches. There was Andy, a prolific and sometimes embarrassing designator of territory. There was Oscar, who was not of the gender that she once seemed to be. Now, there is Molly.

Molly is an *omnium gatherum* of breeds, in and of herself a veritable smorgasbord of canine multiculturalism. She is in large part Belgian barge dog. (Schipperke is the fancy name.) She is in smaller parts— quite a few of them, actually—Springer Spaniel, Labrador, Border Collie, and of assorted other ancestry. She is, in truth, a beautiful dog. But she has her peculiarities.

She will eat anything, and I mean *anything:* avocados, pomegranates, asparagus spears, olives, oysters, anchovies, exotic entrees from around the world, and, of course, Brussels sprouts (natural sustenance for Molly).

She has a quaint little habit of lying on her side and raising her rear leg high in the air when someone walks by. The first time you see her in this pose you wonder—could she somehow be preparing to ...? But no. It's a position she can maintain for an hour. She can even sleep in this position. It's a greeting of sorts, and an invitation to lean over and pat her sprout-filled belly.

Molly is a dog who periodically gets into a mood we call "the rips." She is swifter than a greyhound at these times, as she tears around the house, in and out of rooms, up and down the stairs, with utterly reckless abandon. This is, I think, a kind of therapy.

What really sets our pooch apart, however, is her devotion to walking. There is nothing, not even eating, that she enjoys more. When she is on a walk with me, she seems to own the great outdoors. She strains at the leash, to go faster, to see more. She sizes up strangers, greets canine colleagues along the way, emits empathy whimpers for other dogs barking alarms behind the fences. Mostly, though, she sniffs.

A walk for Molly is snifferama. There are the hydrants and trees, of course, and other jutting objects that are bound to attract attention. But there is much else. For Molly, wherever the wind and whatever the weather, the very air is always redolent, the pavement packed with pungent attractions. Every walk is an aromatic adventure, a true voyage of discovery.

And—to get back to the argument at hand—that is very like what American higher education has been doing for 350 years. It has lived a life of constant adventure. It has been on, will always be on if it is true to its heritage, a voyage of discovery.

For those of us privileged to be aboard for part of this voyage, challenge is never in short supply. The wind changes. The weather changes. The sea itself can be expected, on occasion, to change. We adapt, as did the voyagers who went before us, as also will those who sail the vast expanse of the 21st century. The campus will still be here, doing what it was ordained to do, when that long journey is done. Technology will have changed it, but not destroyed it. This has happened before, and will very likely happen again.

This can be a hard life. Once in a while, frustration can lead us to engage in therapeutic exercises, to undertake our own version of "the rips." Once in awhile, we need a pat on the back if not on the belly.

Molly seems to understand these things. She would make a fine sailor. Her nose, I know, would love the salt air. And if the sky falls in, no matter. For her, it would just be something new to sniff.

∾

Chapter Four

~

People

THIS CHAPTER DEALS WITH THAT ONE INDISPENSABLE ingredient of life at a university, the thread that joins job to institution to technology and to a whole lot more, the material from which past, present and future are wrought. That would be people, of course. You just can't say enough about them.

I have said quite a bit, actually, written my share about people—the people of the university, a wondrous lot—over the past 23 years. I have discussed them from the perspective of history, with stories gleaned from the campus yearbook ("Artemisia Archives"). I have harvested more history from visits with alumni in assorted locations, examples of which can be found here in a piece on our alumni reunion travels to the other side of the country ("Eastern Hospitality").

There is a tale to be told also in the discovery of individuals of very different backgrounds and interests bound together at a certain time by their successes and their common and considerable associations with the university. That tale is related in "A Four-Star Foursome." In a somewhat different way, it is related again in an essay ("On Call") about Nevada (the state and the university) as a place where the impersonal is impermissible, where you can reach out and touch someone and it may be the governor. And then there is yet another tale—"A Woman's Place(s)"—that celebrates the triumphs of trailblazing Nevada females over the course of a century and more of institutional growth and development.

Some people I have written about at length, including two memorable members of the Board of Regents whose contributions are noted in "Nancy and Bob" and "A Letter to Louie." Others, unfortunately, one comments on too late, citizens of the university who have passed on; individuals who left something consequential behind for the campus to recognize. In that regard, I include here some thoughts ("Keeping Up with the Joneses") on Clarence Jones, who left us after 65 years of service and remarkable generosity; Harry Chase, almost the first campus person I met, a legendary teacher, and one of my closest friends ("A Farewell to Harry"), and a trio of graduates from different eras who did not know each other but whose deaths came close together, and who each gave us a heritage to remember ("Three Who Mattered").

One thing about a university: It is a constantly renewing institution; people striving, others dying, still others just arriving. We send out new alumni every year in May, and three months later we start the process of creating new alums all over again. Sometimes, we invent labels for these new arrivals, call them a generation of something or other, overgeneralize their values and practices. But we are very glad to see them, these freshman students who will later move on into life carrying alma mater with them wherever they go. They are important people, given pleasurable attention in the chapter's final essay ("Fountain of Youth").

∼

Artemisia Archives

I AM A REGULAR READER OF THE *ARTEMISIAS* OF OLD. They give me a feel for the campus of times past, for the students and faculties of earlier days. They join those days to the present. They chart the development of the university and give context and particulars that cannot be found elsewhere.

Not long ago, I took a look at the yearbooks of 1925 and 1939. I was interested in the volume from 1925 because a member of that year's graduating class would be attending our mid-winter Commencement ceremony. At age 93, 70 years after she crossed the graduation stage herself, Eleanore Mollart Lemaire would be on hand to watch her grandson do the same.

Mrs. Lemaire's fellow graduates, I learned, included Albert Lowry of Winnemucca, later to have that community's high school named in his honor; Alice Norcross, from the same family as Frank, who was one of the three members of the first graduating class, in 1891; and Everett Harris, later an engineering faculty member, whose son, Richard, would serve as a student body officer here.

On the faculty that year were the likes of James Church, Peter Frandsen, Stanley Palmer and Reuben Thompson. The football team lost more games than it won, but the debate team defeated almost everybody, including Oxford. The freshman class, as was the custom at the time, went up Peavine Peak in the fall to paint the N.

As for 1939, well, I went to that volume to look for a swan. Someone admiring the seven swans who now call Manzanita Lake home had mentioned to me that swans had been on the lake at least since the late 1930s. Sure enough, on Page 12 of the 1939 *Artemisia*, there is a picture of just such a beautiful bird, described in the caption as the lake's "most distinguished occupant."

Professors Church, Frandsen, Palmer and Thompson were still around that year. David Goldwater was ASUN president. The football team had another losing season, and the debate team continued to be a winner. The campus players that year presented "The Torchbearers," and something called "Washington Jitters," a familiar condition nowadays.

So there is history between those covers, and there is visible on those pages a great potential for accomplishment. The yearbooks convey a

Silver and Blue, March/April, 1996.

convincing message about the power of the university to make a difference, as that potential comes to be realized. And, again, *Artemisia*
ties us together, those of us, past and present, who have shared the
institution. We see that in the Lemaires, in the Harrises, in the line
that runs from the Frank Norcross of 1891 to the Alice Norcross of
1925 to members of that family from later generations who came to
school here. We see it in ways as diverse as the always successful debate
team, the swans that still grace Manzanita Lake, and the Peavine N,
still painted in the fall as it has been for 84 years.

And then there are those faculty members who fostered so many
memories, people such as Church and Frandsen, Palmer and Thompson, all of them with us still in the form of buildings named in their
honor.

If you think of the university as an institution with a seamless history, whose writ runs across the generations, then *Artemisia* speaks to
you with a kind of eloquence. You see the institution compellingly in
the faces of its faculty; better yet in the faces of its graduates: Eleanore
Mollart in 1925; David Goldwater in 1939; and, in the 1901 yearbook,
a young man named Pat McCarran.

Pat was a member in his senior year of Nevada's first-ever debate
team. The debaters did not fare so well that year. The football team,
for once, had a better season. Pat, however, did all right for himself
later on. And many graduates to follow, whose photographs graced
the pages of *Artemisias* down through the decades, enjoyed Sen.
McCarran's patronage in Washington on their way to fame and fortune.

~

Eastern Hospitality

IN NOVEMBER, for the second straight year, we took the Century Campaign back East. We had some news to spread—$57 million pledged
or collected in the campaign so far—and people to greet. We saw some
familiar faces, and some we had not seen before (but expect to see
again).

There was Scott Hill, for example. He turned up in New York City

with his wife. Scott is the son of professor A.E. Hill, who built a distinguished English department faculty at Nevada in an earlier era. Scott,
now 91, graduated in 1923.

Then there was Katherine Mergen, who graduated in 1936 (though
she would have finished in 1932 had it not been for the Depression).
She attended our reception in Washington, D.C., with her son, Bernard Mergen. Bernard was a member of the Class of 1959, and is now
a professor of history at George Washington University. His mother
was once a professor herself, in the English department at the University of Nevada. She was hired to that position by A.E. Hill.

Mrs. Mergen attended last year's event in Washington, also. There
she encountered a former student who hadn't seen her in 40-plus years.
His name is Jim Wilson. He came west from New Jersey after World War
II to play football for the Wolf Pack. He came by train. He still comes
from his home state by train, several times each year, to visit his alma
mater.

The enthusiastic Dr. Michael Patmas flies when he returns to campus. He is from New Jersey, too. He came to the university as an undergraduate in the 1970s and stayed on to graduate from our medical
school. He's now 3,000 miles from the university he loves, but he never
misses one of our events in his part of the country. He attended our
New York reception.

So did Jane Creel, Class of 1946. Jane's father was Cecil Creel, former
director of Cooperative Extension (1921-52) and dean of the College
of Agriculture (1945-52) at Nevada. She did not know Mike Marley
prior to our reception. Mike arrived at the university from Boston a bit
before Dr. Patmas was a student here. He came to study journalism
rather than medicine. He wrote sprightly prose for the *Sagebrush*. Like
Bernard Mergen 15 years before him, Mike also boxed here under Jimmy
Olivas. Later, he was a producer for Howard Cosell in New York. Now
he manages professional fighters.

I knew Mike Marley in his student days at the university. I was teaching American politics then, an experience that I have occasion to remember often on my forays to meet alumni around the country. For
instance, in Washington I ran into Monty Pierce, a contemporary of
Marley's, a student of mine, and a campus activist in the days of yore.
And I encountered Jon Todd.

I was Jon's adviser during my first year at Nevada. It was his first
year, as well. He told me when we chatted at our evening in Washing-

ton that I seemed a little mystified by the university during that year. I told him I still am. Jon had a career as an Army officer after graduating in 1970. Next year, his son will be a freshman at the same institution where his father started school 26 years ago. Doubtless, he will get better advice than his father got from me.

Budget reductions may daunt us here at home. The success of the Century Campaign helps to temper the impact of these reductions. It's a pleasure to talk about the $7 million Sanford gift to support a center for studies on aging, and the many other donations that have kept our enthusiasm high during hard times. And there's nothing quite so heartening as the loyalty and support of far-flung alumni; of people such as Scott Hill and Katherine Mergen, of Bernard and Michael and Jane, of Mike and Monty and Jon; of dozens of others who came out on stormy evenings during our trek to the East to remember days of yore and raise a glass to Nevada.

~

A Four-Star Foursome

AH! THE UNIVERSITY. It is such a pluralistic place, a play of endless acts and scenes. It presents to the world so many different faces.

Dave Hettich's is one. Dave is well-known for a lot of reasons. For many years, concluding with his retirement last summer, he pronounced the names of our graduates as they crossed the stage at Commencement. About 20,000 of them in all, he reckons. One year I wrote of Dave's Commencement duties that he would "warm up with a Ho, a To, a Hug, a Vig, a Yau, and a Yup, sail through five Browns, four Grays, three Greens, two Joneses, and 10 Smiths, and wend his way with consonantal command and dipthongic diplomacy among an Abdollaholiaee, an Ashoftehfard, a Kolahiaghdam, a Mohd Talb Sabre, a Papameletiou and a Szecsody."

In later years, the names got even harder.

What does one say about Dave? Thirty-two years a member of the English faculty, beloved of his students, outstanding teacher, wonderful adviser, actor, director, presenter of readings, and ... Wolf Pack football fan! Dave is at every home game, sitting in the same seat he has

Silver and Blue, September/October, 1993.

always had. I did not encounter him that Saturday at halftime in November 1986. I was standing near the press box, waiting to go down to the track for an award ceremony. We were being beaten soundly by Georgia Southern in a play-off game. I was surrounded by people who, like Dave Hettich, were pronouncers of names. In this case, they were bad names, names brought unkindly down around the head of our football coach, Chris Ault.

To that point, in that year, the Wolf Pack had won 13 games—more than any college football team had ever won in a single season—and lost none. We were concluding our 11th successive winning year under Ault. He had compiled the greatest overall record in the university's football history. But it was not good enough for those pronouncers of bad names. They wanted Coach Ault's hide.

Fortunately, Chris survived that assault and the others that always come the way of coaches, guided the Wolf Pack to five more winning seasons, became an outstanding director of athletics here, and—somewhere along the way—awarded Dave Hettich's loyalty by giving him one of the Pack's old football helmets.

Chris Ault, another of the faces the university presents to the world.

Marion Motley's is yet another. Like Chris Ault's, his is a football player's face. Marion's face is black, and when he tore up the gridiron here in the early 1940s he was one of the few black men in America to be playing football at a predominately white university. He went on to play eight years with the Cleveland Browns, to be elected to the pro football hall of fame, to be recognized as one of the greatest to play the game. His legend lives on, here and around the nation, 50 years after his college-playing days. He has returned occasionally, to watch Chris Ault's teams play, to remember, perhaps, when the public address announcer pronounced his name at Mackay Stadium, a celebrated name, over and over, touchdown after touchdown.

I suspect that Joanne de Longchamps never made it to the stadium, but her name went out across the campus more times than she could remember. And across the state. And the nation. She took every art class the university had to offer. She was an artist herself (collage) and a renowned poet, a composer, a teacher of creative writing. She moved in famous company: Craig Sheppard, Charlton Laird, Walter Van Tilburg Clark. She published poetry with the likes of Conrad Aiken and Theodore Roethke. She was yet another of the fabulous faces the university has shown to the world.

Joanne de Longchamps, shortly before she died 10 years ago, decided to give her house on Center Street, just below the main campus entrance, to the university. We use it to house visiting artists, speakers and scholars. More faces.

If you like—and you should—you can learn a lot more about these four storied individuals whose names, for a variety of reasons, are just now in the limelight. These are four very different people, upstanding citizens of this institution, accomplished characters in a century-old drama still unfolding.

~

On Call

A WEEK OR TWO AFTER I ARRIVED AT THE UNIVERSITY IN JANUARY 1966, I was invited by Father Leo McFadden to attend an evening meeting at the Newman Center. The governor would be there, Father McFadden said. It would be a good chance for a student of politics to see Nevada's version up close.

I arrived early, anticipating the large crowd that governors typically drew in other states where I had lived. Well, Nevada is not like those other states. When the governor and his aide arrived, 14 people were on hand to greet them. We arranged our chairs in a circle and spent two enjoyable hours having a conversation—that's the word for it—with Grant Sawyer.

I got to know Governor Sawyer well later on, as I have every one of his successors. That's just the way politics works in Nevada. We are a small state, even if there are a lot more people here than there were three decades ago, and our politics is a measure of that smallness. If you want to get to know the governor, you just go out and do it. If you have a problem, you pick up the phone and call him.

The university runs the same way. It's a lot bigger than it used to be, but it is still a small place. If you have a problem, you pick up a phone and call the president. People do that regularly—students, faculty, staff, alumni, folks from around town and around the state. That's the way life works here. We would not have it any other way.

When we talk about becoming the best small state university in

Based on articles in *Silver and Blue* issues, June 1993, November/December 1993, and March/April 1994.

America, we mean the kind of institution in which people can routinely call the president, or a dean, or any other administrator, or a professor. We mean the kind of institution that cares for its people and its friends, a place that values the personal touch.

One of those administrators who gets (and invites) a lot of calls is Patricia Miltenberger-Edgington. Pat was a student here when I sat down to converse with Gov. Sawyer. She knew that small feeling, that personal touch, in her student days. She has worked hard, as our first vice president for student services, to sustain and expand those institutional qualities. She is also, by the way, an avid seeker of adventure. In that capacity, she climbs high mountains, descends deep canyons, races bicycles, runs marathons and rappels down multi-story buildings. But her true calling is to the continuing task (and one not without adventure itself) of assuring that we place students front and center at this university. She is willing to devote time, energy and fierce determination to that calling and, in the process, she helps keep us small (in the best sense of the word) and personal.

You can say the same for Angela Taylor. Angie is one of our graduates, too (bachelor's and master's degrees), and, like Pat Miltenberger, she played basketball for the university during her undergraduate years. She went to work here soon after graduation, as a part-time member of the sports information staff. She rose to the position of senior associate director of athletics—the No. 2 person in the athletics department. Angie is the individual most responsible for the dramatic rise of women's sports at Nevada. She attended high school with two of my children, and now, in her new position as director of alumni relations, she works with a third (my daughter Margaret, a member of the alumni council). That's a small-world kind of story, I suppose, but it fits Angela Taylor. She has done her part to make athletics a personal place for student competitors, coaches and staff. She is one of those administrators you can call when you need to talk with someone who cares.

You can be sure about Pat's and Angie's commitments to their alma mater. You can be just as sure about Grant Sawyer, a student here in his younger days. And, for that matter, about Richard Bryan, another Nevada governor (and, later, U.S. senator). Dick served as student body president at the university in 1960-61, a position that led to subsequent service as a state assemblyman and senator and then attorney general before moving to the governor's chair. His student presidential campaign was ably assisted by a fraternity brother named Frank

Fahrenkopf, destined one day for appointment as chairman of the Republican National Committee. Dick (a Democrat) and Frank went their separate ways in politics, but share some wonderful memories of that institution they called their undergraduate home.

In keeping with the state's tradition (and the university's, also), you can pick up the phone and get connected to these two national figures, just like you can with Pat Miltenberger and Angela Taylor. And while you can't reach the late Grant Sawyer anymore, you can call our Sawyer Center for Justice Studies, named in his honor, and get your questions answered.

The university is a reflection of the state that gave (and gives) it life. Like the state, it's a unique institution, still small, still welcoming. It's a place that still provides lots of opportunities, like the one offered me those long years ago, to have a good conversation with the powers that be.

∽

A Woman's Place(s)

A UNIVERSITY OUGHT TO BE A PLACE where conventional wisdom is challenged daily, if not hourly; where people are hard at work at the formidable task of shaping new directions. It ought to be an institution that welcomes people determined to go where few or none have ventured before, that provides an environment favorable to the blazing of trails. Let's chat a bit about some trailblazers.

American higher education has long offered both obstacles and opportunities to women. Its late-19th century Golden Age—when colleges grew into universities, great new institutions were founded, and students in much larger numbers began arriving on campuses across the country—offered ample testimony to this observation. Not many of these institutions opened the doors of their expanded curricula or their recently established professional schools to women. Women's colleges were founded during this era, to provide the opportunities denied elsewhere. Some universities, too, ran against the grain and gave women a chance to pioneer in a coeducational setting.

Based on articles in *Silver and Blue* issues, December 1992, May/June 1994, and March/April 1997.

Hannah Clapp was a pioneer at Nevada. In 1887, after a few years of uncertainty and tentative effort that followed the relocation of the university from Elko to Reno, she was the second person hired here. Only the president preceded her. She can be said, thus, to have been the first faculty member appointed in that new era. She was the institution's first professor of English and, soon thereafter, its first librarian. When Manzanita Hall opened in 1896, she was the first preceptress of that noble edifice. Other women joined the staff in these early years: Jeanne Elizabeth Wier, for example, a dominant force on the history faculty for four decades beginning in 1899; and Katherine Riegelhuth, a legendary professor of English and German from 1905 to 1943. Hannah Clapp blazed the trail that these two women—pioneers in their own right—were to follow.

Twenty years after Professor Riegelhuth retired, another woman took up duties in the Department of English, a woman who—though she would refuse to accept the description—would herself become the stuff of legend here. That would be Anne Howard, distinguished teacher and scholar, dedicated to her students, pioneer (there's that word again) of women's studies and women's welfare on campus, Chautauquan of note, and wise and candid critic of administrative misadventures. A few years earlier, Eleanore Bushnell had come on the campus scene as a member of the Department of History and Political Science. When that unit divided into its component parts, she became chair of political science. In that era, there could have been no more than a handful of women (if that many) in such a position. I had been a student of political science at three universities when I arrived here in 1966, and had encountered not one female among the departmental faculties. She was, by any accounting, another pioneer. It was Eleanore who came to the University of Washington, where I was in graduate school, to offer me a job at the University of Nevada.

The doors are open much wider now, certainly, thanks to the pioneering work of Hannah and Katherine, Anne and Eleanore, and others in between. The university welcomes women—now more than half the undergraduate population—to all fields. We are producing accomplished graduates in disciplines that once were inaccessible to aspiring females: engineering, medicine, the physical and life sciences, management, military science, and others. Consider the arts as one example (among many) of talent we have sent out into the world. Put Joan

Arrizabalaga, Class of 1962, on the list. She came out of East Ely. She paints. And sculpts. And carves. And welds. She has displayed her work in galleries from one end of the country to the other.

Or would you be interested in sopranos? We have provided more than our share since Ted Puffer joined our music faculty in the mid-1960s, and thereafter established the Nevada Opera Company. Dolora Zajick has performed in the world's greatest opera houses, including La Scala in Milan (with Pavarotti). Evelyn de la Rosa, a Zajick classmate, sang recently in Jakarta as part of a Far East tour. Other tours have taken her across the country, around the world, and back again to the campus, where she comes often to do some teaching, (and, once, to receive an honorary doctorate). Janet Iacovetti went to Fresno to sing in "Madame Butterfly" and stayed on to establish an opera company, as professor Puffer had done in Reno 20 years earlier.

While we are in the arts neighborhood, we should remember with pleasure the many talented actresses who got their stage education courtesy of our Nevada Repertory Company. Rebecca Judd can represent this group. She came to school rather later in life than our traditional undergraduate population, and discovered acting. Soon, she was playing leading lady roles. Then she was *the* leading lady. She had the part of Evita in the Nevada Rep production of that great play, one of my favorites. I saw that play in several venues, London and New York included, and Rebecca was hands-down the best in that challenging role. Now she is a professional, appearing on stage in key roles of major productions by prominent American theater companies. And, like Evelyn de la Rosa, like other eminent graduates, she comes back to campus from time to time to offer her services.

Thinking about Becky Judd, a non-traditional student in an era of transition, reminds me of another time, two or three decades ago. This was before we had much of a women's studies program here, before we had a Women's Resource Center. This was before women served as presidents of coeducational universities (or vice presidents, for that matter). It was before women became business executives, or newspaper publishers, or statewide office-holders; before they were members of engineering faculties, or medical school department chairs, or full-fledged college athletes, or collegiate athletic administrators.

This was a time when I encountered Beth-Ann (not quite her real name), who helped me see the future. She joined a dozen male graduate students in a seminar I taught here on American politics. It was the late 1960s, an era of ferment around the country. Beth-Ann brought some ferment of her own, feminist ferment, to that seminar. She became, now and again, our teacher, and we—the dozen male students and I—found the learning process uncomfortable. She challenged us, challenged our views on the role(s) of women in politics and elsewhere in American society. Often enough, we responded defensively.

I wanted to say, Wait a minute, Beth-Ann: You're talking to a guy who has changed maybe 5,000 diapers (OK, so my wife changed 20,000); who had often bathed the dirt from four children who had already taken baths of their own—prolonged mud baths— in preparation for the ordeal; who had read to those children almost every evening and answered their plaintive calls in the middle of many a night.

I wanted to say, Hold on here, you're dealing with someone whose mother— and I need to note she would have adamantly rejected the following description, and maybe me for suggesting it—was something of a feminist herself. There is not a household chore you could name that my mother thought of in gender-specific terms. She taught me, and my brothers and sister, to dust, sweep, mop, wax, vacuum, do the laundry, run the mangle, iron clothes, make beds, clean the windows, and manually wash and dry the dishes (and there had better be no weeping glasses in the cupboard!). She insisted I take typing in high school I hunkered down in that class with 25 or so amused members of the opposite sex. And, when I was about to go off to college, she taught me how to expertly fold my clothes and pack a suitcase.

I wanted to say to Beth-Ann, Why are you carrying on so about women in sports? Hadn't I grown up in Iowa, where, in a thousand small towns, girls' high school basketball ruled the roost? Spectators crammed the gyms to watch the games on Friday nights and, when the girls' state tournament came around, those towns went wiggy. (I did not stop to think that this was two-dribble basketball the girls played, that the guards could not cross center court, that these and other rules were designed to protect what was then considered to be the delicate feminine constitution.)

So, how about these for bona fides?, I wanted to ask Beth-Ann. But I didn't, and it would have made no difference, anyway. She cracked all our defenses and, grudgingly, at the dawn of the consciousness-raising era, we worked our way to an enhanced understanding. It was, as I observed, good preparation for the future.

A second portent of that future materialized for me in the mid 1970s, when I was serving as chair of the political science department. A single mother in her 30s—let's call her Hannah (another Hannah!)—found her way to my office. She wanted to go to college and was scared stiff. She wasn't sure she could do it. She wasn't sure she could find the time to attend classes, fulfill the assignments, do her job, and raise her daughter. She wasn't sure she had the confidence to match wits with bright 20 year- olds. But she was determined and, clearly, she was smart. I urged her to give it a go. She did.

Hannah was in the vanguard of a vast legion of women in their 30s and 40s— "returning women," we came to call them —who soon began to fill college classrooms across America. They changed the face of the campus population. They put smiles on the faces of professors, who found them generally to be superior students. Some of them eventually became professors themselves.

A few years down the road, I had moved on to become president of the university, and I had the pleasure of presenting Hannah her diploma. Later still, with Hannah on hand, I did the same for her daughter.

The future, whose harbingers hove into view back in the '60s and '70s, has now arrived. It's all about women who have succeeded in all sorts of circumstances, who surmounted those hurdles we discussed in that graduate seminar of yore, who found the university later in life, who broke through the academic and societal barriers. It's about business executives, educators, academic administrators, holders of high public office, engineers, physicians, miners, artists, journalists, philanthropists and more. It's about athletes who are no longer confined to two dribbles and few sports. It's about pioneers who set the precedents. It's about women who have in common their considerable accomplishments and their strong ties to this university. It's about women who would make Hannah Clapp and Katherine Riegelhuth proud.

In a way, this future is about my mother, too. She would want to know that I'm thankful for all the lessons (but grateful for the invention of automatic dishwashers). She would be pleased to learn that I'm still typing (and don't have to hunker anymore), and that I can still pack a suitcase with the best of them.

~

Bob and Nancy

I AM MUCH PRIVILEGED to give the American Lung Association of Nevada Tribute tonight to my good friends, Bob and Nancy Cashell. The university has enjoyed the privilege of a long and strong relationship with the Cashells and has honored them in its own way—Bob with a Distinguished Nevadan award and Nancy with an honorary doctorate.

As most people who know me know, I have a difficult time giving short speeches. Offering this tribute is doubly difficult because there is so much to be said about our honorees, and there is far too little time to say it. One has to choose one's words carefully to find the right way to communicate the kind of people Bob and Nancy are.

Where to begin?

Perhaps very near to the Cashell beginnings in Nevada. We learn something about our honorees at that point. We learn that Bob Cashell is the kind of man who would build a hotel-casino on the wrong side of the road. We learn that Nancy Cashell is the kind of woman who would remain married to a man who builds a hotel-casino on the wrong side of the road.

And we learn that between the two of them, wrong side of the road or not, that place was made to work. It prospered because it was friendly, because it was generous, because it had class. In a way, that's why the Cashells are being honored tonight—for their friendship, their generosity, their class, and because they have channelled those ingredients into a remarkable measure of involvement in the life of the community.

For Bob, that involvement has meant membership in—and often chairmanship of— organizations as diverse as the Commission on White House Fellowships, the Nevada State Youth Advisory Council, the Reno-Tahoe Olympic Organizing Committee, the YMCA Youth Soccer Program, the Sierra Arts Foundation, the Nevada Tourism Commission, the Nevada District Export Council and the National Petroleum Council.

It has meant service as a member of the University and Community College System of Nevada Board of Regents, as chairman of that board; as the Republican lieutenant governor of Nevada (and—before he changed partisan colors—as the Democratic lieutenant governor of

"A Tribute to the Cashells," American Lung Association Dinner, Nov. 6, 1991.

Nevada); as member and chairman of the University of Nevada, Reno Foundation Board of Trustees; as virtually permanent chairman of the university's Graduation Celebration.

And that just scratches the surface.

For Nancy, community involvement has run the spectrum from that same YMCA Youth Soccer Program, to the Sierra Nevada Museum of Art, to the Founding Board of Casa De Vita, to the Nevada Women's Fund, to the Manogue High School Advisory Board, to the advisory boards of the University of Nevada Press and the university's College of Education, to the virtually perpetual co-chairmanship of the Graduation Celebration Committee.

And that barely scratches the surface.

These are two relentlessly involved, unfailingly giving people. They have donated funds to more worthy causes than can be enumerated here.

When Bob left the regents some years back to serve as lieutenant governor, we issued a proclamation that said, in part, that Robert A. Cashell: defended the Board of Regents against all comers, including angry students, angry faculty, angry presidents, angry governors, angry legislators, angry editorial writers, and angry citizens; and ... as chairman, he expanded our parliamentary horizons by providing an entirely new interpretation of "Robert's Rules of Order"; and ... has enriched our vocabularies by his unique approach to words of more than three syllables and by liberally sharing with us a variety of poignant Texas expressions; and ... standing behind, beside and often well out in front of him has been his wonderful wife Nancy—holding his hand, twisting his arm, tweaking his nose, bringing him back to earth, keeping him from moving in four directions at once, guarding the only remaining family barbecue, and sharing with the rest of us her time, energy, wisdom and lots of funny stories about her husband, thereby helping him and us to maintain our sanity through four mad years.

They have gone on to other adventures since that proclamation was prepared, but much of the description still fits. Bob is still a defender of just causes, an unusual parliamentarian, a user of poignant Texas expressions; and Nancy is still full of energy, wisdom and lots of great stories, and still bringing Bob back to earth. They have never stopped being involved. They have helped. They have cared. They are two terrific people who represent citizenship in the highest and best sense of the word.

I can testify that they were thinking about healthy lungs long before I was. Years ago, I signed up to serve in the "Cashell Air Force" and flew many flights around the country on one or another of the Cashell airplanes. I was a smoker in those days and, 20,000 feet up on my first flight, I asked if I might light up. Bob said: "Sure, just follow the instructions over the cabin door." I walked up to the door and read the instructions. They were simple enough:

"If you wish to smoke, please step outside."

They are well and truly deserving of the award they receive tonight. I am privileged, the university is privileged, the community is privileged, to have them as friends. They are two people for whom the term "salt of the earth" was invented.

~

A Letter to Louie

I'M NOT SURE WHY PEOPLE talk so much about Louis Lombardi's 30 years of service as a regent. The way I calculate it, your relationship to the university goes back 55-plus years, to the day you arrived on campus in 1925 as a freshman member of the class of '29.

I do not know how much you recall about those early days on the Hill, or about your later associations with the university, but I thought it might be interesting to jog your memory a bit. The *Artemisia* yearbooks of the '20s record some memorable information. For example:

Procter Hug, Sr., was president of the Associated Students of the University of Nevada (ASUN) during your first year. Walter Clark was president of the university. Walter F. Pratt was chairman of the Board of Regents. Miss Sissa was the registrar and secretary of the faculty. Margaret Mack was dean of women and Raymond Leach was the master of Lincoln Hall. Buck Shaw coached the Wolf Pack football team to a record of 4 wins, 3 losses, 1 tie. Harry Frost scored the first touchdown of the season and Jim Bailey had a great year in sports.

As for Louie Lombardi, the record shows you to have been a starter on and captain of the freshman basketball team and a member of the Freshman Glee Committee. *Artemisia* describes your prowess in basket-

Written in commemoration of Dr. Lombardi's retirement from the Board of Regents in 1981, after 30 years of service. The letter appeared in *Silver and Blue*, Fall 1990, shortly after he died.

ball as "fast on offense," "a stone wall on defense" and "by far the best running guard on the squad." The yearbook offers no description of your performance on the glee committee. Maybe it's just as well.

Those were eventful years and there is more to tell about them than can be set down here. It would serve the purpose to move to 1928-29, your senior year, pausing in between only to remark on two events of note: As a sophomore member of the Wolf Pack tennis team, you were defeated by McBride of Sacramento J.C., 6-4, 6-1. As a junior member of that team, you lost to Mott of Modesto J.C., 6-2, 6-2. You did beat McBride in doubles. But not Mott.

As for 1928-29, it was a year when the university's enrollment increased to 1,037, the highest in history to that time. Mercifully in those days, the "Full Time Equivalent" student had not yet been invented. The library was the newest building on campus. Social organizations abounded, including the Whelps and the Buckgrabbers, Caucus and Clionia, Cap and Scroll, Mask and Dagger, Sabre and Chain, Trowel and Square, Square and Compass, the Cosmopolitan Club and the Sundowners of the Sagebrush. Count Ilya Tolstoy spoke at the University Lecture Series and, it is reported, he "deplored the state of civilization today and declared that it is in a dangerous condition." *Artemisia* referred to the university administration as "the shadowy and mysterious entity." Some things never change.

Plays produced by the students that year included "The Poor Nut," "The Old Soak," "He Who Gets Slapped," "Outward Bound" and "After Dark" (or "Neither Maid, Wife, nor Widow.").

A chap named Alan Bible was managing editor of the *Sagebrush*. Jake Lawlor was captain of the basketball team, which had a mediocre season whose high point was a 62-15 victory over Pacific Fruit Express of Carlin. The football team did not win a game. There was a new head coach the following year. You went off to St. Louis to become a doctor.

You next appear on the university scene, as a major personage, in 1951, the year you first took your seat on the Board of Regents. Silas Ross was chairman. Malcolm Love was president, Elaine Mobley dean of women, and Bob Griffin dean of men. Procter Hug, Jr., was an ASUN senator-at-large. Numerous luminaries-to-be were active in campus life. The football team, even with help from the likes of Ron Einstoss, Pat Brady, Scott Beasley, Stan Drakulich and Myron Leavitt, won one game and lost nine.

That was the first year. There were 29 more to come—big years, lean years, in-between years. The football team got better, no doubt with assistance from Dr. Lombardi, the team physician. The university grew, the university system was created and, ultimately, there were more students at its smallest institution than there had been in the entire university back at that high-water mark of 1929. Very likely, many of the 5,000 babies you delivered ended up on the campus you have so long called home, helping produce its continuing growth. The School of Medicine was established. Buildings blossomed, including the Louis L. Lombardi Recreation Building. Others disappeared. Some changed functions, such as the library—the newest thing around during your student days—which became Clark Administration. University budgets got into nine figures and funding formulas became part of the new math.

Well, much has happened in those 30 years, not all of it good, of course. But most of what was good got to be that way because you were around making it happen.   I have had the privilege of sharing many of those years. It has been my very good fortune to serve as president for some of them, working with the very rich heritage you have left us.

During your final year on the board, Proctor Hug III was a member of the graduating class. Maybe you can help deliver Proctor IV someday, and recruit him to the campus where three generations of the Hug family have known your leadership.

~

Keeping Up With the Jones

IT IS DIFFICULT TO DO JUSTICE IN A FEW MINUTES' TIME to a record that has run for two-thirds of a century. That is the period covered by Clarence Jones' relationship with this university. It was a relationship that took Clarence from his freshman matriculation here in 1927 to this room, this day, this service, nearly 68 years later. It was a relationship expressed in many ways.

It is reflected in those student days, for example, when Clarence majored in electrical engineering, an experience and a department he

"Eulogy for Clarence K. Jones," Nightingale Concert Hall, Jan. 21, 1995.

always gratefully remembered.

Clarence was part of the Class of 1931, about 150 strong, and so were Marv and Lucie Humphrey, Walter Van Tilburg Clark and Euphemia Clark Santini, Ellen Prince Hawkins, George Vargas, Howard Sheerin, Marjorie Ligon Rose, Jack Walther and Bill Woodburn. And Gretchen Cardinal Whitehead, Margaret Gottardi Hart, and a young woman with a lovely name and a long list of credits in the yearbook. That would have been Desert Rose Mahana, who was on the publications board, the Buy-a-Brick Committee, and the Student Union Building Committee; also the Soph Hop Committee, *Artemisia* and *Sagebrush*, Wolves Frolic and Spring Festival, and, in her junior year, became the 49er Whiskerino Beauty Queen.

I mention this because Clarence didn't see much of that kind of life, didn't have the time for a lot of on-campus activity, because he worked so long and hard *off* campus just to make ends meet. Even so, he participated in the Associated Engineers, ran varsity track for two years, and was chairman during his senior year of the "Get Together Dance." That chairmanship was good training for his later experiences, getting together, as he did, in a wide variety of ways, a wide variety of people in a wide variety of campus places to enthusiastically pursue the life of the university.

We know Clarence, of course (as we know his wife, Martha), as a remarkably generous person, whose approach to giving has encompassed a tremendous range of programs and projects and people over a long period of time. There is scarcely a corner of the campus, scarcely a nook or cranny of these 200 acres that does not bear his imprint (and hers).

I looked this week at a computer printout of Clarence's donor history (and Martha's, as well, since they have done everything together philanthropically). It covered only the past 12 years, although the record of Jones family giving goes back well beyond that. This printout contains several-hundred entries. These entries include gifts to virtually every college and school on the campus, and to an abundance of programs: to engineering and medicine, human and community sciences, education and arts and science, nursing and nutrition, journalism and juvenile justice, stress research and speech pathology, the Women's Resource Center, the Wolf Club, the Sun Dial Project, science and technology, scholarships and internships, the ski team and the cycling team, the library and the marching band, the Nevada Writers

Hall of Fame, the Morrill Hall Endowment, KUNR, oral history, the Oceanographic Globe Fund, and equipment in a whole host of locations—just to name a few!

It is appropriate in this regard that we gather today in this great concert hall next-door to the Jones Music Studio Center; and that many of you walked here by way of the Jones Visitors Center, which Martha and Clarence restored and reinvigorated for us; and that as you walked you probably passed a number of other places that bear the mark of the Jones family. Clarence and Martha have done so much for the university, have given so much to help so many that in letter after letter after letter I have had to write to them: "Dear Clarence and Martha, I have run out of ways to say thanks, and, furthermore, I have run out of ways to say I have run out of ways to say thanks."

Well, the list is so long and the coverage so comprehensive that there is this nearly irresistible temptation to remember Clarence especially through his donations. And we will remember them, of course. But there is more, much more. There have been so many other manifestations of his presence here:

• There is his attendance at university events of all kinds. One encountered him everywhere. At ball games, for instance. (He was at a basketball game last week   he seldom missed one — six days before he died. And I bet he was a joyful presence in spirit two nights ago when the Wolf Pack handed the UNLV Rebels a pretty sound thumping.) And at the thousand meetings he got to over the years, and the lunches, dinners, banquets, dedications and celebrations. We couldn't have had them without Clarence being there.

• And there was at all those events and occasions that memorable, friendly presence, those smiling, twinkling eyes so nicely magnified by the thick lenses of his glasses, that cherubic countenance that made everyone in the vicinity happy just to *be* in the vicinity.

• And his emotional involvement with this institution. It's always hard to describe something like that, to describe, I guess, what love is and how it works, but we are very secure in the knowledge that he loved this university, that he loved it well, and loved it all his life, and that that love will also be part of his legacy here.

There was that about Clarence, entirely separate from his financial commitments.

• And there was the modesty about what he and Martha and the family have done here. He never hungered for recognition of all that.

But he did like to hear about the impact his donations made. And when you told him about that (and he always wanted to know), those great, magnified, twinkling eyes would usually fill up with tears. They were tears of happiness, for sure.

It seems to me, in the end, that that was Clarence's greatest reward —to know positively, tangibly, that he had helped, to know *how* he had helped, to know *whom* he had helped, to know that he had touched people's lives, made those lives better, and through that, through those thousands and thousands of better lives, over the decades he had helped here, to know he had made this university a much better place, as well.

That, I think, is what moved Clarence Jones the most.

It's interesting, isn't it, how friends can speak to us after they have left us? Yesterday, when the flags on campus flew at half staff (as, indeed, they do today) in honor of Clarence, the Board of Trustees of the university foundation held one of its regular meetings. Clarence was a charter member of the board, a member for several years of its executive committee, an emeritus trustee also, active in the foundation for all the years of its existence.

In whatever capacity, he almost *never* missed a meeting. The day before yesterday, we got a card from Clarence saying he would be at this one.

I think he mailed it before he died, but you never know: He loved those trustees meetings. And he was there among us, anyway, getting us together again (like he had done at that Get Together Dance 65 years ago), in spirit this time, much on our minds and in our prayers.

The trustees observed a period of silence, again in honor of Clarence. Later, they voted to establish in his name (and Martha's) a $1 million foundation scholarship endowment. There will be 10 of these scholarships awarded for next year, and 10 more for each of the following three years, until we reach 40 of them, and then that year, and every year thereafter, in perpetuity, there will be 40 scholars on the campus as a result of this endowment.

Those scholars will be Clarence and Martha Jones scholars, every one of them, and in that way, as in many others, we are assured that his name, the name of Clarence Jones, a great and remarkable man and a wonderful friend of all of us and of his alma mater, will live on, on this campus, forever.

∾

A Farewell to Harry

DURING MY FIRST WEEK ON CAMPUS, in January 1966, I met the political science professor whose office was next to mine in the building that then housed home economics. His name was Harry M. Chase, Jr. We became the best of friends.

Thirty-plus years later, at the end of June 1996, I stood with my arm around Harry on the front porch of his home in San Francisco. We were saying our good-byes. Harry was dying of pancreatic cancer. In seven weeks, in the middle of the night of Aug. 12 and after a hard but hopeless fight, he would be gone. He was 72.

I have written often about the people of the university—students, faculty members, alumni, friends. They make the institution go. They protect its traditions and advance its purposes. They are a diverse, dedicated, challenging, chance-taking, entertaining, edifying and sometimes eccentric lot. They make my life interesting. They are worth writing about.

Harry was one of those people, of course, and he answered to many of those descriptions. He was a member of the active faculty here for a quarter-of-a-century, joining what was then the Department of History and Political Science during the 1956-57 academic year. That was a time when the university, like higher education across the land, was beginning a period of significant growth and change. Young faculty members, a postwar generation, were arriving in large numbers. Harry's colleagues among the recent arrivals included Wilbur Shepperson, Russ Elliott, Eleanore Bushnell, Don Driggs and Jim Roberts—individuals who would build to strength not one department, but two. Harry was at home, as a youthful builder himself, in this illustrious company.

Political science was on the move in more ways than one by the mid 1960s. The newly separate department had left its previous quarters for temporary lodging in Fleischmann Home Economics while its new home was rising from the glorious ashes of the old Mackay Stadium. That lodging ended in fall 1966. We moved then to Stewart Hall, soon to become ashes itself, and deservedly so. Most of that grand old structure had fallen victim to an earthquake and all that was left was the basement. Harry's office was near mine in those damp depths, as well. His problem was a leaky roof, a condition that plagued most of the building and one that was handled in the time-honored fashion, with

Silver and Blue, November/December, 1996.

buckets. My office was leak-free and bucketless, but it had a dreadful smell. Harry said it was dead mice, redolent rodents rotting away in the walls. He was right, as we later discovered, except that there were live mice in there, too.

In fall 1967, political science gladly, dryly, and with a sense of an improved olfactory future took up permanent quarters in the just-opened Mack Social Science building. There, until he retired in 1981, Harry Chase continued to grow his reputation as the department's premier teacher. He was a commanding figure in the classroom — tough, disciplined, charismatic, fair, caring. He asked for— he demanded—the best from his students, and they gave it to him. He was, in short, a legend.

Harry left high school in Indiana at 16 to join the Canadian army. He and his regiment, the Essex Scottish, took a major part in the Dieppe raid in August 1942. Five thousand Canadian infantrymen fought in that desperate battle. Just over 2,000 returned to England. The rest were killed, wounded or taken prisoner. Most of Harry's company did not come back. Harry did, and forthwith joined the U.S. Army Air Corps, as a B-25 radioman/gunner. He flew 52 combat missions from 1943 to 1945. He also served during the Korean War, was a longtime member of the active Air Force reserve and retired from that standing with the rank of colonel.

In some ways, Harry never stopped being a military man. He enjoyed martial music and military history. For years, one of his avocations was to create dioramas of famous battles, painting in precise detail the uniforms of the miniature soldiers. His years of service, he once wrote, had led him to appreciate "the value of human sacrifice for an ideal; the hopes of men afraid and yet able to carry on; and, above all, the need for prevention of future conflicts." One of the principal reasons for choosing a teaching career, he said, grew out of his wartime experiences: "We who are left owe something to those who are no longer with us." Honor, obligation and loyalty were central values to him.

Yet he was an academic through and through. He loved the life. He loved to teach. He read widely and voraciously. Though he did not publish a lot, he was a scholar. His students never forgot him, and he made his mark on thousands of them. For years at alumni gatherings around the country, no professor has been more asked-after than Harry Chase.

When I last saw him, Harry gave me his copy of the *Rubaiyat of Omar Khayyam*. He admired poetry, and had a habit of committing to memory the poems he admired most. He knew by heart every verse of the *Rubaiyat* and, even so, he read these verses often. In the copy he gave me, he wrote an inscription, asking me to think of him in the light of the final stanza:

And when Thyself with shining Foot shall pass
Among the Guests Star-scatter'd on the Grass
And in thy joyous Errand reach the Spot
Where I made one—turn down an empty Glass!

Consider it done, my friend; by me and by those many you knew and touched here and around the world, who join me now to toast your life.

∾

Three Who Mattered

IT COMES IN THREES, SOME PEOPLE SAY. Death does. Three people whose lives, taken together, comprised a significant part of the life of the university signed off recently. I knew them well, personally and in terms of their diverse university connections: three vital, interesting, memorable individuals, all of them Nevada graduates.

Death is seldom timely, and Bill Neeley died too young. He was 52. The Department of Political Science put in place a Ph.D. program here in the 1960s, when graduate education was booming across the United States. The university was just then joining the boom, establishing its bona fides as a graduate institution. Political science was (and is) my department, and I had been there but a few years when along came Bill Neeley as one of the new program's first doctoral students. He was *the* first to complete the Ph.D., and he moved on from here to teach at California State University, Stanislaus. He was a fixture there for more than 20 years, widely respected by his colleagues, and the leader of a graduate program in public administration that—before he was done —brought hundreds of students to him (and him to them) from pub-

Silver and Blue, January/February, 1997.

lic service positions in the area. Bill was a noble man in a noble profession; and he made a big difference for a lot of people.

Bill Neeley is buried not far from Stockton, Calif., which is where I got to know Kara Lucas Pratt 33 years ago. Her son-in-law and I were then graduate students together, and good friends. Mimi, as we all came to call her, was one of those larger-than-life individuals who left a big wake behind her wherever she went. She was a graduate of the University of Nevada, Class of 1929. She was from Fallon, a Pi Phi, a member of Clionia and the Women's Varsity Debate team, and she was senior class vice-president. Her brothers, Keith and Arthur, were in school here then, too, as was her future husband, Ken. Mimi graduated with people such as Jim Bailey and Louis Lombardi, Snowy Monroe and Jake Lawlor's older brother, Mike. Walter Clark concluded his 11th year as university president with this class.

The Pratts fondly remembered their days here on the Hill. Mimi was especially proud to come back 67 years later to watch her namesake granddaughter, Kara Votruba, graduate with the Class of 1996. The younger Kara had become part of a clan that by now included 72 children, grandchildren and great-grandchildren. During countless summers, Mimi led large packs of these progeny on strenuous hikes in the mountains around Greaegle, Calif. She was still climbing those mountains the year she died, and was laid to rest among them in November, in the Mohawk Valley Cemetery, at 88.

Then, of course, there was Clark Santini. Walter Clark Santini, actually; grandson of the university's president during Kara Lucas Pratt's years here, nephew of the great novelist, Walter Van Tilburg Clark, and brother of Jim, the former Nevada congressman. However, you didn't come to know Clark as someone's relative. You knew him because he was one-of-a-kind, a man of causes, a character out of Don Quixote, a modern day Sisyphus except that sometimes Clark got the boulder *over* the hill.

Clark was a graduate of the university, Class of 1964. He loved the place, I think, from the day he was born. He served on the alumni council for two decades, was president of the alumni association for two years, and he always referred to the institution as THE University of Nevada. Clark's causes covered a lot of territory, took a lot of time and consumed a lot of energy. But no cause for him engendered more passion and dedication than his university. He once described himself in a note to me as Nevada's "chief fanatical supporter." He was that, and more.

I knew Clark for 30 years. We had our differences, God knows. He could try Job's patience, and may be doing so right now. He thought in the later years of our acquaintanceship that I was taking the institution he loved in the wrong direction. No matter. We made our peace at the end.

Social scientists have wondered through the years what it is in an institution — a university, a church, a country — that can evoke such fierce love, such strong emotional ties from those who are part of it. I don't know the answer, and, when it comes to things that tug at our heartstrings, empirical analysis probably always falls short of the mark. But if you want an imposing piece of evidence of those ties at work, I give you Walter Clark Santini, fierce lover of his alma mater. Clark Santini, dead too soon, at 54.

So we have Bill Neeley, who showed to a large public officialdom the value of doctoral education at Nevada; Kara Pratt, who knew so well the small and intimate undergraduate institution of celebrated memory; and Clark Santini, whose family writ ran from 1918, when his grandfather assumed the presidency of the University of Nevada, through a span of 80 years and four generations of strong and varied attachments to the place. Bless you Clark, and Mimi, and Bill for what you meant to us, for the sense of the university's history you impart to us in death, and for the abundant pride of grand accomplishment you gave to us in life.

~

The Fountain of Youth

FIFTEEN YEARS AGO I WROTE A PIECE ABOUT CAMPUS LIFE in the 1950s and how it had changed by the 1980s. The '50s interested me because that decade was my decade on campus. Indeed, it had taken me most of that decade to complete my amply checkered undergraduate career. Eight years, to be precise; a period that covered early and emphatic failure, 45 maturing months of military service (and 19 success-

Silver and Blue, January/February, 1999.

ful credits from the University of Maryland Overseas Program), readmission to the University of Iowa (squeezing through by the width of a midge's whisker), and, finally, graduation in 1959.

We have a proclivity in this country to label people, especially young people, in accord with what certain pundits see as the major themes and principal changes manifest as the young come into adulthood. The 1920s, thus, was the era of the Lost Generation, a time between the world wars perhaps best symbolized by the rootless expatriates who peopled Ernest Hemingway's Paris. At the other end of the century, we find Generation X. Gen Xers, it is presumed, lay claim to their own special brand of rootlessness, having no identity to call their own, reliant on the fashions, the fads, the music of earlier periods. In between these generational bookends, we find the likes of the Beat Generation, the Me Generation, the Silent Generation (my peers, the group that came of age in the 1950s), and assorted others.

The labels seem full of meaning, but, when you get down to cases, the meaning is hard to find. Millions of young Americans did not go the Paris in the '20s. Millions did not arrive in San Francisco with Jack Kerouac and beatnik friends as the '50s ebbed away. Millions did not subscribe to the inward-turning, instant gratification behaviors that were the me-ness themes of the '70s and '80s. I can't think of a young person I know who perceives himself or herself as Gen X to the bone. And as for that Silent Generation— the group, it was said, that wanted mainly a career, two cars, two kids (maybe four), a split-level house in the suburbs and a life free of adversity, adventure and acquaintance with social problems—well, I didn't know a lot of card-carrying members, and I carried no card myself.

What is a generation, anyway? Not much more than a convenient category, a soft concept prone to collapse when you get to inquiring about its particulars. Yet we use it regularly, not just for the Lost, and the Beat, and the Silent, but to try to get a handle on what differentiates the young from the older and the older from the oldest, to try to define the boundaries of that peculiar social divide known as the generation gap. And we employ it especially in distinguishing the group arriving now on our campuses from the one that arrived a few years or a decade ago. We understand, of course, that the college campus is a very different place than it was in the '50s and '60s, or '70s. It's bigger, more complex, more diverse in terms of age, ethnicity, nationality. There are more graduate students, more married students, many more students we identify as non-traditional, and, percentage-wise, fewer who belong to that traditional cadre of 18- to 22-year-olds.

Still, we remain interested in that traditional cadre, in what they are thinking and doing, in their values, concerns and expectations. We measure this, after a fashion, every year, and we tend in that way to think of almost every new class as something of a new generation. We are often surprised when we discover that our latest young arrivals on campus don't seem to fit the mold set by the pundits and other label merchants. The surprise is often a pleasant one, reminding us anew of how privileged we are to live a large part of our campus life among the young. They always have much to teach us about our time, and about the wellsprings of hope.

As the profiles of 1998's young arrivals make clear, this is not a group whose members are lost, or beat, or silent, or turned inward, or searching for their identity in earlier eras. It's not the group of drinking, gambling, partying, devil-take-the-hindmost students the media sometime suggest are the archetypes of modern college life. It's a group that looks a lot like many, many others we have seen over the years: balanced, reasonable, rooted, optimistic, purposeful. They are not without worries, certainly, and how could it be otherwise? They may have soured on institutions we once held dear. They still have a lot of growing up to do. Some may require as much time to get there as it took me in the 1950s. But those wellsprings of hope are still abundantly evident.

For that we are grateful. And we are renewed. Our job will be to keep those wellsprings flowing.

∼

Graduate school, University of Washington, 1964.
Joe, Joy, Theresa, and Neil.

Professor Crowley of the Political Science Department in the office of good friend and colleague,
Harry Chase, 1968.

Joy and Joe, 1989

The Crowley Family 1985. l-r - Neil, Theresa, Joe, "Oscar," Joy, Margaret, Tim.

Inauguration address, 1979.

1993 - a proud grandfather with grandson Ben—destined for the Class of 2015.

With Sammy Davis, Jr. at a 1990 Black Students Organization reception

With Leslie Stahl of *60 Minutes* when he was NCAA president in 1994

Tennis anyone? l-r, Paul Page, Joe, John Marschall, Dave Seibert

Longtime donors
Clarence and
Martha Jones

Unveiling of the new (top, 1987) and newest (bottom, 2000)
university flags.

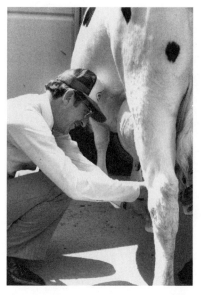

Ah, the duties of a university president

With super-alumnus Clark Santini, alumni breakfast, 1989

With journalist and longtime university supporter Rollan Melton.

President Gerald Ford, 1981

President Ronald Reagan, 1982

President George Bush and Judge Ernst Watts, National Judicial College

l-r, Senate Majority Leader Bill Raggio and Governor Kenny Guinn, 1999
Foundation dinner

General Colin Powell

With, l-r, former Governor Grant Sawyer and Dean Louis McHardy of the
National Council of Juvenile and Family Court Judges, 1987

Dorothy Gallagher, a member of the Board of Regents for 20 years.
A good friend and strong supporter of higher education.

Sharing laughs with comedians Bob Newhart (1999) and Jay Leno (1989).

Bill Cosby presents a $90,000 check to university athletics. Athletic director Chris Ault is on the right.

Vice-President Al Gore, 1996

Joe and Joy with Carol Channing - Hello Dolly, 1979

Bob Cashell, Dan Klaich and Joe with Debbie Reynolds 1987

Clark Administration Building, Joe's office for 23 years

UNIVERSITY PRESIDENTS

LeROY D. BROWN	1887 - 1889
STEPHEN A. JONES	1890 - 1894
JOSEPH E. STUBBS	1894 - 1914
ARCHER W. HENDRICK	1914 - 1917
WALTER E. CLARK	1918 - 1938
LEON W. HARTMAN	1938 - 1943
JOHN O. MOSELEY	1944 - 1949
MALCOLM A. LOVE	1950 - 1952
MINARD W. STOUT	1952 - 1957
CHARLES J. ARMSTRONG	1958 - 1965
N. EDD MILLER	1965 - 1973
MAX MILAM	1974 - 1978
JOSEPH N. CROWLEY	1978 - 2000

In the University of Nevada Honor Court, 2000

Part Two

≈

LETTERS

Letters

ONE OF THE MOST SALIENT FEATURES OF THE MODERN ERA is that it has given us a myriad of ways to get the word out. I have written elsewhere in these pages about our numerous vehicles of communication—faxes, e-mails and copying machines included. We can be instantly in touch. We can do so frequently. We can send out our missives in large volume, all thanks to advances in the technology of communication. These are useful advances, on the whole, although it is fair to say they have also taken away something of the aesthetic pleasure of corresponding with another person. Faxes arrive looking like what, in fact, they are: poor substitutes for the originals. E-mail, so quick and easy, encourages sloppiness—in spelling, syntax and proof-reading. The copying machine is going to give you, sooner or later, that familiar smudged appearance, and it can make an attractive letterhead look dreary. And then there are the faxes of copies, and copies of faxes, that have also come to serve the purpose of getting a message from me to you in a hurry. What all this will do to the art and science of archive-keeping, I am at a loss to say. Neither would I care to venture a prediction as to the fate of those instructive books that present the collected, selected, lifetime letters of important personages. Chances are that many such personages are producing their correspondence in e-mail form now, and that the historians and biographers of tomorrow will have a difficult time tracking it down in the mysterious vaults and peculiar passageways of cyberspace. Then, too, there are those boxes of correspondence your mother kept, maybe your father, too, that you discover after they have taken leave of this mortal coil. Those discoveries may pass from sight, as well.

That's why I like letters, in the old-fashioned sense of that word. Especially the ones that come in stamped envelopes. They have a long and gallant history. They have solidity. They impart a feel for relationships, good and bad, and a sense of the event and the personality that modern messaging devices can miss. If one takes care in the writing of them, as I think one is more likely to do, they can dispense pleasures harder to derive from these devices. Probably, somebody somewhere offered much the same argument when the typewriter came along, when the fountain pen replaced the quill, or when the ballpoint version (or the one that writes underwater, or the one that is guaranteed to write forever) entered the realm of correspondence.

Maybe I like letters because I have written and received so many of them, especially during the years I have served as a president. There have been thousands, some of which (quite a few, actually) have found a place in the university archives. I have culled a small number—exchanges of correspondence for the most part—for presentation here. There are letters (or portions of letters) from and to faculty, students, interested observers of the higher education scene; other letters dealing with memorable issues; still others representing the occasional vacations I took from serious writing in order to indulge my humorous (low humor, often) propensities. Low humor is a genre with regard to which it could be said I have an excess of ability that I am inclined to use excessively. This has been good therapy for me, though it may bring pain to readers.

Taken together, the letters selected for this chapter represent something of a commentary on the presidential life. Much of that life revolves around criticism, a constant (indeed, essential) component of academic discourse and, often, after a fashion, a building block in the decision-making process. Some criticism, on the other hand, is merely ill-informed opinion, and plenty of that comes forward in communications to the president. Both types of criticism are manifest in the letters included here. Presidents deal daily with issues large and small and covering a wide expanse of territory. A sample, as noted, is on offer in this chapter. Often enough, people write simply to ask for something they believe the president has the power to provide. You can find that kind of letter also in the pages that follow.

There are other varieties of correspondence not represented here. That would include anonymous messages, letters from people who want to lay before you their solutions to life's problems, their scientific discoveries (which may be perpetual motion machines, refutations of the theory of relativity or the first law of thermodynamics, mathematical formulae of sundry, sophisticated stripe, or reflections on Foucalt's Pendulum), their conversations and adventures with inhabitants of other planets, and declarations of a personal genius as yet somehow unappreciated by the wider world. Or, you may get an inquiry you had never expected (such as one I received from a gentleman in southern California wondering whether I would be interested in selling the university for cash); or a threat from someone whose request you have denied (such as one sent me by an angry nurse who had tried to have her son excused from paying a certain fee and, when she did not prevail, expressed the malign hope that I would get sick enough to land in her ward at a local hospital).

Or, there are those really creative people who find novel ways of getting their message across. One that stands out in this category came from a former faculty member, terminated by the university (with proper notice) within a few years of his appointment. He went to court and lost, appealed and lost. The case dragged on for an extended period, and, when it was over, we asked the court for award of attorney fees and related costs. The court agreed. The former faculty member sent a check that included this note on the bottom line:

For corruption and incompetence at the university, in the UCCSN*
and in the Nevada Judicial system.

A collection of such letters could yield some insight into the human condition; or provide evidence that eccentrics, lovable and otherwise, still dwell among us; or testimony in support of that emergent principle of American jurisprudence, that everything that goes wrong in one's life must be someone else's fault. But that would be for another time, another book, perhaps another author.

With a few exceptions, the real names of my correspondents in the selections that follow are not provided. Brief descriptive comments, offering a sense of what moved the letter-writers to write, precede the correspondence in each category. To conserve space, I have edited both their letters and my responses, while attempting to preserve the essentials: focus, objectives, arguments, evidence.

* University and Community College System of Nevada.

Chapter Five

~

The Faculty Speak

THERE IS A SIZEABLE LITERATURE DEALING WITH THE QUESTION of where to properly place the limits of presidential authority, with, for example, how far its writ runs in relation to academic departments. The department, typically, is the basic organizational unit of a university and the home of many consequential decisions. Should a president (or a vice president) get involved in some of those decisions, and specifically in matters of hiring new faculty? That is the issue addressed below by professor George A. A different kind of personnel issue is taken on by a mid-level administrator, John B., who is concerned about what he perceives to be inadequate support by the administration for a dean in trouble. Another faculty member, Dr. Max C., writes from the painfully personal vantage point of someone who, following lengthy negotiations, has resigned his position. Yet another, Jake Highton (his real name), scornfully questions the university's movement toward a greater emphasis on research. Rounding out this section is an exchange with Wilbur Shepperson, an influential, longterm member of the faculty who writes insightfully and critically of my performance during a trying time for the university.

~

George A.

Professor A., as his letter points out, had been a strong supporter of mine during a search process for the president's position that became, on the campus and in the community, very contentious. He was as outspoken then as he is in the following letter, which takes exception to what he sees as inappropriate intervention by the university administration in personnel processes where the department faculty's right to decide has been violated. He is concerned enough to copy his letter to 11 others

———

April 28, 1982

Dear Joe:

A friend with vast experience in ... academic-administrative affairs has advised me not to get into this unless I am prepared to spend a lot of time on research ... I respect but have decided not to follow my friend's advice. I do not have time for the research. Perhaps the Faculty Senate does. Perhaps the Faculty Senate will look into the conduct generally of your administration in hiring and promotion, especially to check how you have operated in light of ... the Code. I remember when the Code was unofficial law; some smart educators worked hard to devise it, and the entire ... faculty voted to abide by it.

What follows is submitted, respectfully, to urge you to stop hiring and promoting faculty members as if the university were your personal fiefdom. The way you have been operating is not the way, I think, to build a great department ... or a great university.

Before it was fashionable to support you, I supported you publicly, [and] asked how a man like you could not be listed among the finalists in competition for presidency of the university. I ... declared that Joe Crowley would bring to the presidency "a fund of that hard-to-codify quality called decency." So you and I began with a relationship that could not have been unpleasant for you. The relationship has, of course, changed.

Was it about two years ago a faculty-community committee [was] appointed by your administration to weigh and make recommendations to you (and tenured department members) on several applications for a job ... in the department ...? The committee decided that [one of the candidates] ranked third, considering all qualifications, including actual teaching experience. Yet you and your janissaries hired [her] ... The work of the committee had turned out to be a farce. Please note that not at issue here is [the candidate]. I have come to admire and like her. What is at issue is your apparent disregard for established academic selection procedures ...

[Recently, another] entirely unpardonable irregularity pulled my cork and caused me to write this letter. [It was] announced that Sam G. had been made a full professor. I know that no member of the full-time ... faculty had a hint that this was coming ... The miracle must have required your personal endorsement.

I guess I can understand, if I work at it, the expedience of your wanting to recognize Sam's help, and potential for further help, in the drive for the money required [by] the department. While [you and he] are wheeling and dealing for ... funds, who is going to keep the store open, performing the drudgery of teaching? What is left to teachers, in these perilous times for education, after the full-professorships have gone to creatures ... with little experience in education?...

I urge you to stop this policy of expediency and to return to running the university as if it were a university, not a bucket shop.

Very truly yours,
George A.

May 4, 1982

Dear George:

Thank you for your recent letter outlining concerns about certain personnel matters. We have covered some of this ground before; the hiring of [the faculty member you mention], for example. Obviously, that decision was a controversial one. I do not believe, however, that it signified, as you put it, a "disregard for established academic selection procedures." Those procedures call for the committee to make recommendations and the administration to make a decision, which as far as I am aware is what happened in this matter. I do not believe that a disagreement between committee and administration, however strong the feelings may be on one side or the other, constitutes a violation of established procedures ...

Now, as to Sam G ... I have not presided over any miracle in this matter. No one has. There has been no miracle. Sam has a temporary, one-semester, part-time appointment at zero rank. His contract does list his position title as professor and that does confuse things a bit, I admit. Still, he does not hold that rank. His official contract status is as a lecturer ... The bottom line is simple, and understandable, confusion. No miracle. No conspiracy. No promotion. By the terms of his contract, Sam holds the rank of lecturer.

Perhaps you will permit me a modest excursion into the realm of the bête noire. Technological progress, for all the undoubted good it does, produces many items that lead my bête noire list. Consider the copying machine. One need not offer testimony to the sundry nice things these machines do for us. One of the not-so-nice things they lead us into, in my humble view, is the terrible temptation to transmit our personal letters to long lists of possibly interested people. In the days when "cc" meant "carbon copy," this did not happen. Perhaps I express a hopeless and anachronistic commitment to the simpler days of yore, but I hold firmly to a preference for sending a "cc" only to those who are substantially and directly involved. That is usually a very short list.

I cannot help but observe that your letter expresses a different kind of preference. I am grateful that you sent it to only one regent, instead of nine, to only one media representative instead of to the universe, and that not a single member of the Nevada congressional delegation and the state Senate and Assembly was sent a copy. The governor also was not on your list. Many of the letters I receive are not nearly so selective ...

I have much respect for you, George, and for your views. I am sorry to hear, therefore, that you find my administrative performance to be more suited to a bucket shop than to a university. I have learned, somewhat painfully, that the longer one stays in a position like mine—the lengthier the record of hard and controversial decisions and, alas!, of mistakes—the more susceptible one is to charges of bucketry, or what have you. I have learned also that one is often enough called to account for decisions and mistakes one did not make. One pushes on with an effort of will, though others may see it as will-o'-the-wisp.

～

John B.

Dr. B. comes to the defense of a dean he sees as being abandoned by the administration. Comments he has read in the local newspaper have upset him, and he believes them to represent the view of the academic vice president (and probably the president, as well). He is bothered considerably by what he perceives as the encouragement the administration gives to faculty members unhappy with their dean. He wonders about the absence of loyalty, and expresses concern about a high turnover rate among deans at the university, caused, seemingly, by the loyalty problem. He wants the president to provide unqualified and public support for the dean, who in Dr. B.'s judgment has performed most ably. Dr. B. is a person who has himself experienced public criticism, and he may well wonder (though he does not say so here) whether the administration gave him, during his own time of trial, the support he deserved.

————————

April 3, 1995

Dear Joe:

I was extremely saddened with the article on Dean [White] in the *Reno Gazette- Journal* last Friday. The lack of administrative support was one of the low points in my administrative career. I will assure you this was a common concern from the calls I received... from Reno business leaders, university administrators and faculty. It was obvious, to the individuals that called me, that a dean who builds a quality college is not appreciated by the vice president.

The University of Nevada, Reno is the first place I have ever worked where employees (faculty) are encouraged to protest against their administrator. I believe this is one of the main reasons for the high turnover of deans at UNR. As you know, I have always supported higher administration and I want you to know that I am having difficulty this time because I think Dean White deserves more respect.

I have seen [him] build a quality college with limited resources. The vice president told the press that some of the best professors opposed Dean White but failed to comment on support from his best department chairs, which I think is more important. I have visited with several faculty in the college ... that have indicated limited resources over time is a major concern. I have attended many ... meetings where [Dean White] made great presentations for more resources, only to see the vice president's office not have the courage to shift resources.

Joe, I am writing to show my support for Dean White because I think he has earned more respect than he has received. I know [he] has the courage to face the truth, however I do not believe he is the major administrative problem.

Sincerely,
John B.

———————

April 10, 1995

Dear John:

I write in response to your letter on the matter of Dean White. I often find myself reacting to newspaper articles as though they contain God's truth, and all of it at that. I know better, of course. I know that, at best, such articles only moderately convey the facts involved in complex situations, that they routinely quote sources incompletely or out of context. And yet, I am as capable as the next person of making judgments about people and situations based on what I read in the papers. Something like that seems to have occurred in terms of your reaction, and that of others, to [a newspaper] story... [quoting the vice president.] He had other things to say, about the dean and what has produced the faculty discontent, that did not find their way onto the printed page. In other stories ... he has defended the dean strongly, has said the deanship is his as long as he wants to stay in it.

Did he say that some of the best professors opposed the dean? Yes, he did. He said it, I suppose, because it is true. That is precisely what makes the current problem in the college a serious one. We could try to line up those in the college who are for the dean and those who are against him and let them have at each other, ensuring in the process that just about all the dirty laundry in the college would be hung out to public view; ensuring as well that the college would not recover from the conflict for a long, long time to come ...

I am not sure what you mean when you write that this is the first university you have known where faculty "are encouraged to protest against their administrator." In my 17-plus years in this job, I cannot recall a single instance of such encouragement. If, however, you have in mind that the central administration will listen when faculty in significant numbers criticize their dean (or when deans criticize their vice president), then I plead guilty. I plead guilty to having heard such protests against every dean who has done good work here, to having, in every case, stood firmly with the dean, but also to doing my best to help the dean resolve the problems (which has often meant some involvement with faculty members). I have refused to ignore the presence of such problems. If all that amounts to encouragement, then you are right, for sure. I have listened to faculty, stood with the dean, and tried to help work out the problems, for example, in [seven different colleges, a couple of them twice.] ... I did so because I am loyal to those I ask to assume difficult responsibilities, and who succeed, and because above all else it is my responsibility to look toward the longterm well-being of the college or unit involved (and thus the university).

This is precisely the course of action being followed in [the current] case. The dean has done a great job. He deserves my loyalty and support. He has it. He also has a very serious problem in his college. I need to recognize that problem and help get it solved, in the dean's interest and the interest of the college. In all of this, [the vice president] joins me ...

I'm not sure how to respond to your comment about "the high turnover of deans" here. I take it as a criticism and am willing to consider whether it may have substance. I'm not convinced it does, though. On the average, I suspect, we have a lower rate of turnover than most places. The conventional wisdom is that deans stay in position, on average, about five years. I calculate our own average to be in the neighborhood of seven years.

I appreciate your support for the dean. He needs that, and he has many friends who have written or called to express their support as well. He has that kind of support because he has done a brilliant job. If I do not do my job and help the dean and the college get to the other side of the current difficulties, all of [his] fine work (most of it, anyway) will be destroyed. I do not intend to let that happen.

∾

Max C.

Dr. C.'s unhappiness is born of a long dispute over a research issue, in a department suffering from a history of deep divisions—regarding both programs and personalities—among its faculty members. He is a full professor who eventually decides he wants to leave the institution, and so engages the administration in negotiations leading, after much controversy, to that end. He receives what those involved believe to be a reasonable settlement, and writes a different kind of resignation letter. My response evokes a protest from him, through his lawyer, and I write back, through the university lawyer, with an offer Professor C. does not take me up on.

Dec. 21, 1994

Dear President Crowley:

Please accept this letter of resignation from my position as full professor at the University of Nevada effective December 23, 1994. I resign with both regret and relief. I came to the University of Nevada expecting the opportunity to teach and conduct research in a professional setting. Instead, I have been subjected to a pattern of harassment which has prevented me from publishing and has wrongfully resulted in a denial of tenure. The atmosphere in the college ... and the university as a whole is not conducive to effective teaching or productive research, and no effort is being made to improve these working conditions. The caliber of staff and students at this university will never improve without a change in attitude. Unfortunately, I will not be here to see such a change.

Sincerely,
Max C., Ph.D.

January 3, 1995

Dear Dr. C.:

This will acknowledge receipt of your letter of resignation from your position at the university dated December 21, 1994, the resignation effective as of December 23, 1994.

Your resignation is hereby accepted, with pleasure.

TO: Don Klasic, General Counsel

February 21, 1995

Dear Don:

My letter to Dr. C., accepting his resignation "with pleasure," is in the file. It would have never occurred to me to express my pleasure in this way had not Dr. C. written a far more insulting letter of resignation ... to me ... It seems to me that when someone is as lavish in offering insults as C. is in his letter, he should be prepared for a bit of the same in response. If he would care to replace his letter with a more conventional one, without the insults, I would be pleased to drop the "with pleasure" language (even though it's an honest expression) from my response.

∾

Jake Highton

Professor Highton was probably—over the course of two decades— my most severe and constant critic. In that time, he wrote me only a few brief, uncritical notes. However, he was a columnist for a small-circulation newspaper in the area, and, often, he used his space to lambaste me. The number he wrote after I announced I would be leaving the position of president was typical. He observed that I had "milked [my] mediocrity to the maximum;" had "provided no academic leadership, no intellectual leadership; had "no character, no vision," and was "a submediocre academic" who "presided over the intellectual decay of the university." Also, I had "surrounded [myself] with mediocrities," and [my] "cronyism was blatant." I was "far too partial to athletics," was given to "financial hanky-panky," required that "subordinates bend to [my] will," featured policies that were "close-doored and close-minded," and "thwarted people who wanted to make a strong contribution to the university." After years of describing me, despite my many failings, as a nice guy, he concluded in this final piece that I had been "a savage infighter." It would have enhanced my standing considerably if he had written that earlier.

On one occasion, professor Highton had awarded me a "C" for my performance as president. I wrote him a thank you note (we remained friendly despite the harsh appraisals) expressing the opinion that this was a much higher grade than the evidence he adduced in support of it seemed to warrant, and suggesting that he was in danger of damaging his reputation as a tough grader. His evidence, in any case, seemed to be mostly drawn from rumor, half-truth, whole cloth, and an occasional stray fact, and he had never discussed my job with me. Nor, as far as I know, did he ever describe in his column the desirable ingredients of good academic (or intellectual) leadership. It was only clear, whatever he believed them to be, that I did not possess them.

Jake deserves a place in these pages. Since he wrote no letters, a column he published on a major initiative of mine would seem appropriate here. That column, and my response, are found below.

––––––––––

Sparks Tribune, March 28, 1991

No institution in America is more trendy than education ... So it was inevitable that the University of Nevada, Reno would designate itself a research institution. Never mind that it is absurd. UNR is a land-grant school. Its primary mission is to reach. To pretend otherwise is ostrichism.

Research obviously is important for professors. It is one of their prime missions. Scholars need to battle on the frontiers of knowledge. Their scholarship can be important throughout the world. What is trash research to some can be treasure to another.

UNR has some fine researchers and excellent scholars. They should be encouraged. But it makes no sense for UNR to be a research school.

Compulsory research is the reason for publication of so much nonsense ...

Ah, but the research game is the thing. Research assures professors tenure, promotion, grants, sabbaticals and consultantships.

To think that an obscure university like [this one] can compete in the research big leagues with Harvard, Chicago and Stanford is silly ...

As Page Smith writes in "Killing the Spirit," the argument that research enhances teaching has been "thoroughly discredited by experience and by research."

"The best teachers are almost invariably the most widely informed, those with the greatest range of interests and the most cultivated minds," Smith writes. "That is real research and that, and that alone, enhances teaching."

But to universities, research is everything, teaching unimportant except to pay it lip service. Good teaching is no way to build an academic career.

Journalism school research, for instance, is so odorous that no working journalist takes it seriously. It has none of the critical analysis that would be worthwhile ...

Research in journalism, worthless as most of it is, is deemed essential in the academy. It is key to academic careerism ...

Good teachers inspire, challenge. They make students think, set lofty standards, turn out better human beings. Their imprints last the lifetimes of their students.

Nothing is more sacred than the minds of young people. Research never reaches those minds. Teaching must remain the essence of universities.

James Garfield, an alumnus of Williams College who became U.S. president, extolled "the value of a true teacher" like Mark Hopkins in a 1871 speech he gave to Williams alumni. The kernel of his speech should be engraved in marble—in big letters, in a prominent place—in the office of every university president.

"Give me a log hut, with only a simple bench, Mark Hopkins on one end and I on the other, and you may have all the buildings, apparatus and libraries without him," Garfield said ...

And as Michael Shenefelt of New York University reminds us, Socrates never published a word.

Jake Highton

—————

April 8, 1991

Dear Jake:

Recently I encountered a column you had written on research. You haven't asked for a reaction, but I thought I would provide one anyway. It seemed to me that the column summoned up a considerable rhetorical force to knock over—at least at this university—a straw man. The impression one gets is that, in your view, there is that group of universities which is comprised of the research institutions and that group which is not. Either you are or you aren't, no in-betweens. This university is in group one and thus seeks to compete with Harvard, Chicago and Stanford (to borrow your examples). Teaching, presumably, is left in the dust. So is our land-grant heritage. So is the tradition of Mark Hopkins, perched out there on one end of the log, with the student on the other end.

Well, I would agree that the Hopkins' tradition is gone. When he left the Williams' presidency, a year after Garfield's speech and 36 years after he assumed that office, Williams had an enrollment of 119. The enrollment was 119 when he assumed the presidency in 1836. If we had 119 students, we could order up some logs and have at it. However, we have 12,000-plus, and we are even at that a small state university. Mark Hopkins, by all accounts, was a great teacher. He taught moral philosophy in an age when higher education was almost exclusively the preserve of the privileged classes, when the curriculum was fixed and narrow, when rote recitation was the required form of student participation, and when the purpose of colleges and universities was to turn out good Christian gentlemen. No Jake Hightons need apply: There was no journalism curriculum. Nor, for that matter, were there curricula in a host of other disciplines that today we take for granted. The sciences were very suspect and the notion of teaching modern languages was still a revolutionary idea. I'm not sure this situation, the established order in Hopkins' day, is what you would want us to return to.

As for the land-grant tradition, you note that our primary mission, as a land-grant institution, "is to reach." I suspect, given the context, that this is a typo and you actually wrote "teach." However, reach is really a better word. The land-grant tradition is based on not one, but three fundamental and interrelated reaching missions—teaching, research and public service. Agriculture, of course, was the original focus and has been the organizational model: the college for teaching; agricultural experiment stations for basic research; the cooperative extension service to bring teaching and applications of basic research into the service of production agriculture and related fields such as home economics.

I believe we remain faithful to the land-grant tradition (a tradition Mark Hopkins found abhorrent, by the way). We seek to expand it to apply well beyond agriculture. We do not seek, have never sought, to become a Harvard, Chicago, Stanford. That would be silly, to use your word. That's the straw man you knocked over, stone cold dead. But it isn't this university. A commitment to enhancing research is entirely appropriate for us, altogether in keeping with our land-grant origins. I don't believe that makes us trendy. But this commitment is one of degree, of growth in what has been a basic mission from the beginning. It is not a commitment to be Stanford. No one has suggested that it is ...

I understand your distaste for, not to mention intolerance of, a certain kind of research in journalism. Beyond that, it is not clear to me what you consider to be trash. Would you want to include in such a category Kent Sanders' work on intestinal diseases? Trixie Gardner's research on primate communication? Baldev Vig's on genetics? Leonard Weinberg's on terrorism? Bruce Douglas' on the seismicity of bridges? Tom Cargill's on international banking? Jim Richardson's on religious cults? Morris Brownell's on the poetry of Pope? Barbara Thornton's on medical ethics? Don Hardesty's on Donner Party archeology? Who decides what is trash? Who will be the censor?

I expect there are some things we might agree on with respect to the research issue. We certainly disagree on the direction we see the university to be headed. I think you have done the institution an injustice. If we were doing what you accuse us of (to offer an example close to home) the name of Jake Highton would not have been advanced this year for promotion to full professor. That name has been advanced and approved, and deservedly so, because this is not the kind of campus your column makes it out to be.

Ah well, Jake; it is probably safe to say that sometimes in research, and sometimes in column writing, nothing exceeds like excess.

≈

Wilbur Shepperson

It was always a good idea, when the late Dr. Shepperson spoke, to
lend an ear; and, when he wrote, to read with care. He was an accomplished scholar, longtime chair of the Department of History, a well-
connected man on campus and off, and he spoke and wrote with the
voice of wisdom and authority. He writes here during a stressful period
for higher education in Nevada. For me, this was a time of great personal challenge. The circumstances were daunting, made the moreso
by ill-advised decisions on my part. The Board of Regents had determined that the *Code*, the governing document for all institutions in
the university and community college system, needed major changes.
The board and faculty members around the system were locked in highly
visible, heated conflict over these changes, and institutional presidents
were caught in-between. In addition, the state's economy was in recession, educational funding was diminishing, and there was no money
for cost-of-living salary adjustments for faculty and staff. Somehow, I
chose this time to launch an initiative called Comprehensive Program
Review, the purpose of which was to analyze all degree programs, close
down some of them, and redistribute the saved resources. In addition,
an attitude shift had occurred, whereby the regents, the chancellor's
office and the campus administration had decided that the time was
at hand to take back some lost ground, to be understood as the people
in charge of higher education in Nevada. And I had come to think of
myself—not such a good idea in academic circles, and worse if you
announce it to the world—as a manager. All this is what prompts
Professor Shepperson to write his letter.

March 9, 1983

Dear President Crowley:
    Over the past several days I have been somewhat indisposed, and
while sitting at home I have had an opportunity to sort out and analyze some of my thoughts. This letter is not a plea for myself, the
department or friends, all of whom want nothing more than fair play,

true leadership and a good university. Personally I have been treated well by this administration as I have by the six previous administrations. Nor am I a critical letter writer; this is my first in thirty-two years at UNR. However, I sense something is wrong, and differing from some others, I do not believe it is the shortage of money, or the legislature, or even the regents that are the root of our discomfiture.

Certainly the pressures for temporary expedients are now overwhelming, but when historians write the history of the university some years from now they will reflect on our philosophy and how well we maintained our direction during difficult times and not on finances or the coming of a sports plaza. They will ask whether we reduced or depleted or diminished our educational role, whether we made people more appreciative and aware of life, whether we provided pleasure through understanding, whether we offered a means to overcoming ignorance and prejudice. A computerized administration, professionalized athletics, and high-technologies may be instruments or tools or passing fads, but the core of a university, the liberal arts, does not really change. Our future historian certainly will ask, where was the administration when the props supporting a fragile academic freedom were removed? Where was the administration when a Comprehensive Program Review suggested shifting away from liberal arts? Where was the administration when the need for a broader understanding of the world led to the converting of resources to the provincialism of Great Basin Studies? The liberal arts by their very nature must study and be related to all of mankind.

Perhaps more significant than the above was the death of faculty governance and the rebirth of the chain of command. For the chain of command to work the commanders must be at their posts with answers and clear unconfused directions. Many of us were ready for a thoughtful, dynamic and progressive administration and a reduction of pointless committees; instead we have found uncertainty and ambiguity. We are always suspended, waiting for the other shoe to fall. It seems that there is a confusion between working hard and working well. Self-congratulations and boosterism, always in poor taste, seem to be the order of the day. The troops really know the quality of leadership shown by the captain. Or was Marshall McLuhan correct? Is style and form and image everything? Despite great diversification, a university above all other institutions, must not be managed, it must be led ...

I believe that the faculty is in a state of manic-malaise when it should be moderately-mobilized. In a university true resources are never material, they are always human. Therefore, I am shocked to learn that the CPR once it started took on a life of its own and produced results not "anticipated." However, since we have it now "we must live with it." I refuse to believe that programs or policies are in the hands of fate. Obviously administrators must respond to pressures from above but just as obviously they should devote their energies to leading and responding to those below. Strength of character, dedication to purpose, intellectual superiority are the hallmarks for such leadership. George Orwell once observed that with athletics the legs are the first to go, but with a society clarity of language and acceptance of responsibility are the first to go. Has 1984 come?

I hope that when the history of the university is written, this era and this administration will be seen as standing for the basic values of culture and learning, however, I do not think we are headed that way today. We have a mission, indeed it is the very heart of education, to raise the community's experiences and the scholar's intellectual expectations. This cannot be done if we accept short term personal and political expedients which lead to the abandonment of the traditional principles of our profession.

Sincerely,
Wilbur S. Shepperson

April 4, 1983

Dear Shep:

I was sorry to learn that you were indisposed, but pleased that your indisposition provided an opportunity to set your views to paper. Many others have done so of late, but none as thoughtfully as you. That is a compliment, I suppose, and may sound strange coming from someone whose leadership your letter rather emphatically calls into question. Though it may seem otherwise, criticism is still welcome in these precincts. It is never pleasant to be taken to task, but criticism is communication and, despite the sundry shortcomings of my stewardship, I continue to believe that communication is imperative if one is to function in this job with even marginal effectiveness.

I could not help thinking as I read your comments that if I were now, as I was six years ago, a resident of Mack Social Science* (an idea, I acknowledge, whose time many insist has come again), I would be writing the president a letter like yours. I would be, I suspect, as distressed as you by what has happened. I would probably be helping to lead the charge.

Alas!, I reside now in Clark Administration. It is doubtless not enough to say that the world looks different from over here, but it is profoundly true. It is not that one grows wiser in this position. Indeed, deprived inevitably of time for study and contemplation, in a way one probably becomes less wise. It is simply that one's understanding of the academy, the forces that comprise and move and sometimes obstruct it, and of what one does to lead (or try to lead) it, is not the same.

So I find myself not writing a critical letter, but responding to one, and doing so in the certain knowledge that you will find the response in some measure unsatisfactory because at some juncture our frames of reference diverge.

A case, perhaps, in point: You distinguished between managing and leading. I cannot, anymore. You distinguish between human and material resources, the former being a true resource and the latter something else. I cannot effectively make that distinction, either. I do not know how to lead in these times without managing, and I do not know how to develop human resources in the absence of some significant attention to the material kind. The Comprehensive Program Review was initiated out of a firm conviction that the university could be advanced, its historic purposes protected and its current obligations satisfied only if we could manage better our meager material resources. It is fair to suggest that charting such a course in response to demands for accountability from legislators, regents and influential citizens is expediency. But it is difficult to be daily besieged by clearly justified requests for more dollars in the service of educational programs, and to understand that the dollars available are unlikely to increase, without concluding that we need to find a way to manage better.

When your historian of the future examines CPR, he will look at the process and the results. I hope he will decide that the two are related. As you suggest, I did say that the process took on a life of its

---

* The building housing both history and political science, and where I had made my faculty home before becoming president.

own and that it produced results that were not anticipated. I did not mean to imply that we had placed it thus in the hands of fate, that once the process was in motion we stood helpless before its deterministic impulses. I take full responsibility for initiating CPR and for the decisions it produced. I have said that several times in several forums, but perhaps have not spoken clearly to the point. Still, I hope it is not inaccurate to maintain that the CPR process, any process for that matter, moved in some measure on its own momentum, moved in directions not foreseen at the outset, and affected the judgments and behavior of those participating. I cannot think of a process about which the same could not be said.

I can understand why CPR and other developments have led some to conclude that the death knell has sounded for faculty participation in the governance of the university. Collegiality, I think, is not necessarily an either-or proposition, though of course it can be. Rather, it is a matter of degree. Further, I believe it possible for the degree to change, and the underlying principle still be upheld, as circumstances change. It is my impression that we had moved considerably during the late 1960s and early '70s toward a greater decision-making role for faculty and a lesser role for administration. I admit that the pendulum is swinging back now.   Again, from where I sit, the times and the situation in which the university now finds itself demand that those in positions of authority exercise more authority. But I do not believe collegiality has died, and there is no intention that the institution now be operated in accord with military principles.

That brings me, at last, to a bottom line; yours, I think, as well as mine. I take seriously your view that my administration has been characterized by uncertainty and ambiguity, and can only count myself at fault for not making matters clearer. Although I am not sure what it is about my tenure in this office that appears self-congratulatory and boosterish, that reflects a consuming emphasis on style, form and image and a preoccupation with personal expedients, I agree that the troops are appropriate judges of the quality of the captain's leadership. I respect your judgment that my administration has lacked strength of character, dedication to purpose and the requisite intellectual content. It would be presumptuous of me to quibble with that judgment. I perceive myself as standing for the basic values of culture and learning and as having as my paramount guide in the making of decisions the best interest of the university. But I cannot, without assistance, see myself as others see me. Your evaluation of my leadership, or lack thereof, is therefore helpful. I take it as a constructive evaluation and I shall try to learn from it.

~

Chapter Six

~

Selections From Other Critics

THERE MAY BE AN ASPECT OF UNIVERSITY LIFE that inspires more comment—one way or another—than athletics, but I don't know what it could be. Higher education is criticized, and long has been, for the emphasis it places on sports. That emphasis is a reflection, in part, of society's priorities, as expressed, for example, in daily newspapers and television newscasts. Typically, the newspaper has a sports section, the newscast a sports segment, and neither has a regular component on education. University presidents routinely complain about the amount of visibility given to athletics and, hence, about the amount of time they must allot to the subject. Problems in the athletic program lead to prominent stories in the media, which, in turn, move people to take up their pens and write letters to the editor, or to the president. This hard reality of the president's job is given attention in a later chapter as well as in this one. Here, the focus is on individual athletes who have made the headlines. In one instance, an angry Texan (Charles D.) takes me to task for a decision made by a National Collegiate Athletic Association committee of which I was a member. In the other, an angry Nevadan (Marvin E.) expresses his views on the university's handling of a case involving one of our basketball players.

A different kind of letter comes from Loretta F., who is unhappy about the university's general education requirements. Arthur G. is abundantly disgusted with my management of a complicated property matter (and I, it is fair to say, am disgusted with Mr. G.'s use of the language). Joe Bob's correspondence is not simply a letter. It's more like a saga of sorts, in which he—over a period of several years—dispay cerns a series of shortcomings in my performance. Some of his letters are recorded here, along with my increasingly terse responses.

∾

Charles D.

Mr. D.'s letter came with a packet of clippings from Texas newspapers. Both Mr. D. and the Texas sportswriters are upset because the NCAA, through a committee ruling, had overturned a previous decision and restored eligibility to a player (at a major Texas university) charged with violating amateurism rules. As noted, I sat on that committee. The letter is addressed to the NCAA, with copies to committee members (listing first names only). The clippings refer to the decisions as "outlandish," an "injustice," a "fiasco," and testimony to the NCAA's "hypocritic oath." The case, however, was a complicated one. The committee, after extended discussion, determined it was, in effect, not proved. There was evidence of a serious problem, but, in the committee's view (which I shared) it was just not enough. The player was a talented young man. It occurred to me that, if he had not been, I might not have heard from Mr. D., whose loyalties, perhaps, belong to another university. That was a cynical reaction on my part, but, even so, it was one that arose from experience.

———————

Dear NCAA Staff:

The Durham decision reflects poorly on a National Collegiate organization. This doesn't present a very good image of the so-called "citadels of learning." It's no wonder that the U.S. Congress is considering getting into the act. Somebody didn't do their homework.

Charles D.

Copies to: Chuck, Joe Fred, Bill and Doris!

———————

Feb. 26, 1992

Dear Mr. D.:

Thanks for sending me a copy of your letter to [the NCAA] and accompanying newspaper articles. I can appreciate your concern in the matter of Mr. Durham's reinstatement. The confidential nature of the proceedings prevents me from offering a specific response. I will say that the issues in this case were very complex, that they have to do solely with the question of professionalization, and that in this regard precedent and intent become key considerations. It is the kind of case, in my opinion, with regard to which reasonable people can disagree. As far as the newspapers are concerned, a part of their responsibility is to offer criticism. There are, on the other hand, those who have the responsibility to make decisions. It is my experience, in complex and controversial matters such at the Durham case, that the critics have a lot easier job than the decision-makers.

Thanks again for writing.

~

Marvin E.

Students, like other people, sometimes get in trouble with the law. College athletes, unlike the rest of the student body, can expect to find their misdeeds—even relatively minor ones—given conspicuous attention in the media. That is what happened with the basketball player identified below as Mr. I. His behavior was a violation of athletic department policy, leading to a brief suspension, and the subsequent filing of a gross misdemeanor charge led to a longer suspension. Under athletic department policy, such a charge results in automatic suspension until the case is decided or the charge withdrawn. The suspension raises the ire of Mr. E., who reads about it in a somewhat confusing newspaper story.

December 7, 1994

Dear Sir:

It seems that you have a student and member of the UNR basketball team who has been accused of a crime. If convicted, he should be punished by civil authorities of competent jurisdiction. However, this young man has not been convicted of anything. Indeed he has not been officially charged with anything. Yet, in a "headline grabbing" rush to judgment, you have institutionally engaged in numerous public comments which will only serve as impediments to justice in this matter. Furthermore, with arrogant disdain for the entire process, you have actually instituted punitive action against him.

While no one seriously believes that a self-respecting institution of higher education (a clear contradiction in terms) would be caught teaching our Constitution, I had labored under the illusion that a few of you "older heads" had actually read the damn thing. Wrong again!

Very truly yours,
Marvin E.

———————

Dec. 12, 1994

Dear Mr. E.:

My goodness! Talk about (to use your term) a "rush to judgment," you managed to indict, try, and convict the university without a hearing, without even a semblance of due process. One wants to say, "Physician, heal thyself!," but one refrains in the interest of civil discourse.

As for the case that prompted your letter, be advised that the university took no action against Mr. I. that could be regarded as punishment for the crime of which he has been accused. We share your view that that, along with the prior question of his guilt or innocence, is a matter for another jurisdiction to decide. The athletic department, notwithstanding, retains the authority to punish athletes who violate the department's standards of conduct. Mr. I. clearly committed such a violation, without regard to the charges of misdemeanor battery. He agrees. That is why he was suspended for two games. He understands that the suspension would have occurred had no misdemeanor charges been lodged ...

Given the media's propensity to dwell on the negative in these matters, and the difficult challenge faced by both the accused individual and the university in getting their positions clearly and fully before the public, it is not surprising that you jumped to the conclusion that we were punishing Mr. I. for the crime with which he has been charged. What happens here is not unlike the jumping to conclusions involved with others in the reading and viewing public who decided, based on what they had read and/or viewed, that Mr. I. is guilty, even though they had only a small part of a complicated story. We should all know better, but, alas!, jumping to conclusions is an ancient, if distasteful, human indulgence ...

The Department of Intercollegiate Athletics has a policy, which I approved, that student-athletes charged with gross misdemeanors or felonies will be suspended from the team until the civil authorities have ruled on the matter. The policy was born of several harsh experiences. In this instance, too, the purpose is not to punish the individual for that with which he or she is charged. Because these situations are always front-page material, often on a sustained basis, there are usually serious negative effects on the individual, program and, indeed, on the entire institution; effects, we think, which can be substantially mitigated through our policy. The student-athletes understand this policy from the beginning of their matriculation here. It has been criticized, and one understands why. However, it represents an effort (thus far a successful one, I believe) to find that elusive balance between individual rights and community welfare. Perhaps you would agree that that is a familiar refrain in the Constitution, a subject, by the way, on which I have taught courses for 32 years.

Thanks for your thoughts. Don't hesitate to share some more of them should this response move you in that direction.

~

Loretta F.

Ms. F. is returning to college after some years away, and she does not want to waste time taking classes—the general education curriculum— she regards as useless. She is indignant, as well, that she is required to pay for certain services which she believes should be free of charge. She senses a conspiracy at work in both the course and service fee require-ments, the money from them going (as she sees it) to pay the high salaries of administrators and the unjustified costs of athletics. Ms. F. copies her letter to the Board of Regents, the governor and a member of the Nevada congressional delegation.

Oct. 17, 1994

Dear President Crowley:

I would like to take this moment to air a few complaints I have with the so-called "University System" of Nevada. Currently I am attending WNCC in Carson City and have an Associates from a junior college in New Jersey. Since deciding to re-attend college, the curriculum, in my opinion, is ludicrous. My feelings are that the university is trying to get extra money, for whatever reasons, (probably to pay your salary along with the high paying salaries of your athletic staff and other staff members who probably do not rate for such a high salary) out of the poor, paying students so that your establishment can say that we received a well-rounded education. Taking physics, geography, chemis-try, and biology classes is not a well-rounded education, in my opin-ion, especially since I am an elementary education major. I will have to take science and social studies and reading and language arts classes for the elementary school. Further, if a student has taken English com-position 101 and 102, why take more? Oh, I forgot, the university system needs money, so charge the student once again for classes we will not learn anything more in. I also don't agree with having to take Western Tradition classes (UNR) aka European Civilization I & II. Sur-vey of American Constitution (WNCC) is understandable since the Department of Education requires such a class. I have taken the Ne-vada and American Constitution exams through the Department of Education and passed them both. But you are telling me that I must pay to take the classes because students are not allowed to test out. What's the difference, again, it's money! I do, however, agree with classes pertaining to elementary education (e.g., School Math I & II) so I can learn how to teach the young child today. Please do not tell me these are stepping stones for the upper classes. We both know that's not so. When I went to college, you took classes related to your degree, not these extra curricular classes that absolutely have no meaning at all in life unless you are an English major, or science major, etc.

Also, does my experience in life account for anything? I not only have two children of my own... but I have been working with children, either volunteer or salaried, for the last 9 years. I feel this should be applied somehow. What more general education can you get than actual hands-on experience?

As I mentioned earlier, I do have an Associates degree (64 semester credits), but unfortunately I cannot be placed into the Professional Program at UNR because I have not met the General Education requirements. Not only do I have to take classes that I don't feel are pertinent to my field, I also must submit to taking an examination that costs about $60-70. I will be paying for extra classes plus this exam. May I remind you that this exam will test my abilities in reading, writing, and math. Now tell me, does this sound ethical to you? Well it doesn't to me! Explain to me Capstone courses, what is the purpose for taking these (6-credits total)?

I recently read an article in the Reno Gazette-Journal. I was appalled to read that the University of Nevada's President, Joseph Crowley, has asked for more aid for students and scholarships. If you stopped paying the high salaries of the university staff, mainly athletic staff and professors who many times have an Instructional Aide teach the class for less money, you may have more money for student aid and scholarships. I also feel that there should be less emphasis on sports scholarships and more on academic scholarships. That's the problem with this country, everyone is more interested in sports than academics.

Speaking of making money, I was shocked when I phoned the admissions office to have a course catalog sent to me and they informed me that you now have to buy them from the University Bookstore for $5.00. I honestly could not believe my ears. I asked the person if this was another way to the university to make easy money. If I am a potential student who wants to attend your establishment, what a sure way to turn me off by charging me $5.00 for a course catalog ...

These are my complaints. While I know it may not change anything for me right now, I would at least hope that the Board of Regents, the Curriculum office, yourself, and any others who may be involved in the course curriculum could find it in their hearts to take into consideration all that I mentioned above and if it gets changed for the next person, well then I did my duty. Remember, I am not an 18 or 19 year old student. I happen to be in my thirties. I would appreciate a response from you, but please do not flatter me with "We want you to have a well-rounded education." Life is my well-rounded education.

Sincerely,
Loretta F.

———————

Nov. 14, 1994

Dear Ms. F.:

Thanks for your letter of Oct. 17 dealing with curricular and other requirements of the university and suggesting that the principal reason for such requirements is to pay for high salaries and sports programs. I'll try to answer all your questions, though you raise many and I may miss one or two. Feel free to make an appointment to further discuss these matters with me, if you wish.

I'm sorry that you find our general education requirements so onerous. What you criticize here is the very foundation of a university education, one that has been around, in one form or another, since the first European universities began to develop 800 years ago and, indeed, can be traced back to early Greek civilization. The notion of a general education was the overwhelming focus of American higher education from the early 17th to the late 19th centuries. At the latter time, professional education (including teacher training programs) began to be established in American colleges and universities. Obviously, these programs are vital components of modern higher education. However, the general education core—the Core Curriculum, as it is called here—is the basis for these professional programs, at this institution and at every university worthy of the name.

What you take issue with, in other words, is the most important thing we do. If I may say so, respectfully, the fact that you find the general education program so unnecessary, that you characterize its components as "extra-curricular classes," is the most compelling reason I can think of that you need to have that program.

Hands-on experience is not a substitute for general education. Life experience, as you put it, is not the same thing as academic experience. If it were, universities would clearly not be necessary. And, I might add, society would be impoverished by the absence of them. I cannot imagine sending teachers into the schools without the benefit of the academic foundation a general education curriculum provides. Even if we wished to, accreditation requirements, I can assure you, would prevent us from doing so.

To put the case succinctly, we are proud of our Core Curriculum, proud of its quality and rigor, and we insist that every undergraduate student experience it.

It is understandable that you would prefer not to pay for such things as testing requirements and catalogs. All of us would prefer that these things be free. It would be nice to have the state subsidize them, and to pay as well for all costs of public higher education. The state does not, of course, and is unlikely to start doing so. That means that services provided by the university, which require staff, time and other resources to produce, will have to be at least partially paid for by consumers. I don't believe this an unusual arrangement ...

As for the university's expenditures on athletics, most of them are from funds raised by the athletics department through game attendance, advertising, private fund-raising and other non-state sources. Approximately 60 percent of the department's budget, including most of its scholarship dollars, is from such sources. The athletics budget is modest in comparison with other Division I institutions and the same is true of salaries paid to coaches and athletics administrators. We do have to operate in the marketplace in this respect, as we do for professors and university administrators. Again, by easily demonstrable national compensation schedules, our salaries are nevertheless generally below average.

Thanks for your comments. Best wishes in your course work here.

∼

Arthur G.

In the late 1990s, the university was involved in lengthy and difficult negotiations with the city of Reno over a piece of property owned by the institution and desired by the city. At one point in the discussions—a low point, to be sure—I appeared before the city council to explain a decision I had made that was adverse to the city's interests. The decision caused consternation among a number of citizens attending the meeting. One of them (Mr. G.) wrote to me soon thereafter, expressing his reaction in no uncertain terms. He says that my decision is "appalling," and the reasoning behind it "ridiculous." The university, he observes "takes from the community at will, but often fails to give back ..." We demonstrate a "gosh, golly, gee whiz ... attitude," have "summarily trampled on the efforts of those community activists who worked in a good faith" and "failed in [our] due diligence efforts ..." There has been a "major mistake." Mr. G. concludes:

Who is going to be fired for this error? Don't tell me, I already know—nobody!! This is government and no matter how egregious the error, no one is ever responsible! Well guess what Mr. Crowley, there are citizens like me who happen to believe that there is responsibility in government. I can only conclude that your administration is so poorly constructed that all of us in the 'public' will be paying a large price for this and other follies for a long time to come.

So I write back, more or less in kind:

June 4, 1999

Dear Mr. G.:

Thanks for your recent communication. Criticism is always welcome here, even the kind that is born in heat instead of light, relies on vituperation rather than reasoned comment, substitutes attack for analysis and reduces complex situations down to simple bromides. Fustian may make one feel good, but I have yet to see it solve a problem.

Best wishes.

～

Joe Bob

Joe Bob is a man of strong views and, in his letters at least, rambling style. He is one of those people who is sure that the path to truth and virtue is known best (and maybe only) to engineers, but believes that the state of Nevada needs only one engineering college. The creation of an engineering school at UNLV, in the mid 1980s, and my support for that initiative, stick in his craw. He is angry because he is convinced I took action to prevent him from being hired to teach in the university's Mackay School of Mines. He despises politicians, and considers me to be one of their number. He wants me to resign, and never tires of encouraging me to do so. Eventually, I decide I have heard enough from him.

Sept. 4, 1991

Dear Joe,
    From one good Joe, to another— resign! UNR is headed by a Ph.D. in Government, not Education ... Mistake: Empire-building—Dr. T. gave me an opportunity to teach, by getting me gasoline money for commuting— when you reneged, on the promised instructor and professional slots! ...
    Joe, you began your fund-raising about several years later than UNLV President Maxson. Why?
    If this hullabaloo over President's stadium seats, and the enclosed elevation of UNR to "the university" aren't enough to make you seek retirement, wait a bit! Your mentors ... are weakening.
    Try retirement, Joe, I like it! (since 1982)

Joe Bob, P.E.

"Nemesis to the Machinations of all Politicians"

Sept. 18, 1991

Dear Joe Bob:

I thought maybe you had retired from letter writing as well, since it has been so long since I last heard from you. I enjoy your views, even though I usually disagree with them.

Thanks for your advice that I retire. Others share your perspective, I'm sure, but I respectfully decline. I'm still enjoying the job ...

As to my reneging on a promise to hire you here, I must say, Joe Bob, I haven't the faintest idea what you're talking about. I don't generally make hiring decisions for professors' positions. (They are made at the level of the department and the dean, with occasional participation by the academic vice president.)   I have never promised such a position to anybody ...

You observe that we began our "fund-raising several years later than President Maxson. Why?" Joe Bob, a good engineer like you should have his facts straight before he raises such a question. Here are the facts.

It is well understood that private fund-raising is most effectively accomplished by universities through foundations established for the purpose. When I became president in 1978, there were no foundations for any of the campuses in the university system. The effort to establish them was led by guess who? Me. It took three years. [Our] foundation was the first one in the system. We have been raising private dollars on a substantial basis, through the foundation, for 10 years. Virtually every year, we raise more money, in cash and cash equivalents, than UNLV.

What we launched last year is what is known in the trade as a "capital campaign." This is an extensive effort over a limited period of time (in our case, $105 million by the end of 1995). UNLV has not undertaken this kind of campaign and ... does not intend to do so. No institution in Nevada has undertaken a campaign of this magnitude, ever.

Those are the facts, Joe Bob.

Good to hear from you. Don't wait so long next time. I'll probably be here for a while.

Best regards.

Oct. 18, 1992

Dear Joe:

I haven't written you with one of my ironic/sarcastic critiques for some time.

Congratulations on your NCAA (possible) appointment. You had better resign as UN(R) President since the Legislature (through the media) is after you for the unreliable market research ... on the [Nuclear] Repository. Note: The state is having a large portion of any market research done at UNLV, now! Your people gave [the governor] what he wanted to hear!

Your School of Education doctorates have flunked out ... WNCC is starting a farm club for your Political Science degree, rather than beefing up Machine Technology. Need I go on?

I wonder whether you can make $250,000 or more (gross) as NCAA head, alone. The "perks" from your "special" funds are being uncovered by the media ...

Your past is catching up with you. If you don't recall, you and I met on the balcony of the Legislative building almost six years ago.

When my wife saw you and Dr. Maxson on TV after you got your raises to above $100,000/yr., her comment was: "He's president of UNR; no wonder it's barely in the top 100 universities and colleges in the U.S." We both recognize that the Vice Chancellor is responsible for counter-acting your high administrative costs (and favoritism), and kept the quality education on schedule with the slim budget you left him.

Remember also, I taught for ... the School of Mines and learned a few things you reneged on for teaching slots in that school, after promising it to the Legislature ...

Farewell Joe, you've got to go!

Joe Bob

Oct. 29, 1992

Dear Joe Bob:
  Thanks for your thoughts, such as they are.

Best wishes.

March 13, 1995

Dear Joe:
  ..... Don't you wish you had been chosen head man of NCAA?
  With a strong Chancellor of the consolidated university, some of
your past will catch up with you. Of course, it all depends on those
political Regents! Your advanced degree in government (machinations)
will help you there, no doubt!
  Yet, UNR is better planned for physical plant than [the university]
where I got my M.S. in Chemical Engineering. The Legislature [there]
made the same errors as ours! [Other state schools] were funded heavily
with engineering, yet [my university] remains the primary engineering
school in the state. Could it be because of we alumni? ... However,
please note: Things really got screwed up when the second law school
was built in [that state]. Nuff said. With the superfluity we have of
attorneys in this state, we need a law school like a hole in the head!
Let them commute to Sacramento.
  [One of your former regents] is my friend today since she helped us
engineers fight the UNLV Engineering School ...
  .... So, watch your P's and Q's Joe. It is later than you think.

Sincerely,
Joe Bob, P.E.
Citizen Lobbyist to the Nevada
Legislature in Education since 1988

————

March 20, 1995

Dear Joe Bob:
    Thanks for the usual letter.

≈

Chapter Seven

~

Some Student Views

STUDENTS ARE LETTER-WRITERS TOO, although their communications are more likely to reach others—a faculty member, department chair, dean or associate dean, staff in student services offices (especially those offices!)—rather than the president. The introduction of e-mail has changed that in some measure. My e-mail address is in the university directory and readily available on the Internet, so I seem to get more student messages these days. As with the letters, and letters to others copied to me, these messages tend to focus on matters of concern or interest to the individual student—a financial aid problem, difficulty in enrolling in this or that course, an argument over this or that fee, a complaint about a grade, and the like. This type of correspondence tends to get prompt attention, usually by requesting a response from someone in the institution with the responsibility to deal with the matter at hand.

There are students, of course —many of them —who go beyond the personal to take on larger questions and who are not shy in offering answers or expressing criticisms. One of the things I have missed most since becoming an administrator is the regular contact with students, particularly those willing to challenge ideas, practices or policies. Accordingly, when students write to me to lay down such challenges, the administrative routine can be enlivened and the critical faculties engaged. The three students whose views are set forth in this chapter are good examples: Matt Black (his real name), who comes to the end of his undergraduate career in a sour mood; Edward J., a student leader who believes his constituents have been wronged by a controversial decision; and Ernest K., a young man I came to know when I helped teach a course one semester. Ernest became, for awhile, a regular and single-minded correspondent.

∾

Matt Black

Matt was one of those students you want to have around, and have more of (but not too many more). He liked to stir things up, and he usually found innovative ways to do the stirring. He was smart, funny, personable, provocative and impatient. He wrote to me on occasion, was in my office to promote his ideas a time or two, and once in awhile expressed his opinions in the student newspaper. By the time his graduation arrives, he becomes disenchanted, with me and by what he sees as the foot-dragging pace of institutional change. He gives vent to his uncharacteristically somber mood in a newspaper column. I regard this as a kind of last letter to me, so I provide Matt a reply.

―――――――

May 2, 1995

At the end of the semester, illness can be debilitating, almost crippling.
Whether some sort of palsy grabs you by the coccyx or you just end up with a sinus infection, you can measure your success by your ability to weather it all. That is pretty much the way I feel as I plink out these last few thousand characters amidst worries of my impending graduation, nursing a cold.
I still can't believe the nightmare is finally over. For the last five years of being a ... student in the UCCSN, I have been plagued with proving to the faculty that I have a brain and that I can use it.
I guess that's what having a diploma is supposed to mean.
Or is it?
Judging by the class of this university and since, coincidentally, he is at the Hilton on May 20, we'll probably end up with [G. Gordon] Liddy as our keynote speaker at Commencement.
Also, knowing the keen eye for cash that our fossil of a president

has, we'll probably give Liddy, a convicted felon lest we forget, an honorary degree in communications or political science or something else in his bailiwick.

My point? I guess my point is that a degree doesn't really mean anything. It just means that you've poured ... your hard-earned cabbage into another diploma mill. It could be worse. We could get bilked ... like a lot of my friends back East did. Also, we could have a reputation like Grenadan medical schools have.

Hell, I don't know. I could call myself disillusioned, but that would mean that I had an illusion to start with. I guess I'm fed up. I should move on, out of this one horse town.

It's just time that the university and I broke up. It's been an uphill climb these five years we've been seeing each other. The things that thrilled me about my school when I met her just don't seem to thrill me anymore. I remember her teasing me with all the things about her that I liked.

I'd drink with her but when it came to telling the world about us, she left out the fact that she had a drinking problem so she could have other people around. Keeping up appearances you know. She said I could make something of myself with her but she kicked me back when I tried.

When I criticized her, she crushed me by threatening to throw me out. Who would have believed it? After all we'd been through.

I can't say it was love, since I constantly had my eye on other schools. The fact is she had broken me, financially and emotionally. Like the battered spouse that I was, I stayed with her until it was over and I was strong enough to tell her I was leaving.

As I packed up my things, I told her that she had hurt me all the times she didn't listen to the criticism I gave her ... I tried to change her as much as I could. Trying to push her when she did good. Trying to hold her back when she was obviously, shamelessly doing wrong. I did it all because I wanted the best for her. Even in the end. But it's over now. I can move on. But perhaps not without G. Gordon Liddy.

Matt Black

May 15, 1995

Dear Matt:

I read your May 2 column in the *Sagebrush*. It disappointed me. Not because you consider me a fossil—that's mild—and not because you think so poorly of the institution that will soon be your alma mater (rather bad writing there Matt, really). No, I was disappointed because you sell yourself so short. You have in fact made a difference here. You are irreverent, bright, creative, a gadfly; in short, a refreshing presence. I have enjoyed getting to know you, reading your material (some of it, anyway), seeing you push us along a bit. Institutions move ever so slowly, and universities lead the class in that respect. If you are going to be a gadfly (you could make a nice living at it), you will need to learn to take satisfaction in modest progress. The obstacles that have troubled you here can be found most everywhere. You ought not let them get you down.

So keep pushing. Don't go through life as a stick-in-the-mud. It's such an easy course to take, and you can do better. Lock that bothersome bitterness in a closet and hope for a burglary. End of lecture.

Good luck.

∽

Edward J.

A controversy arose during 1991-92 over the location of the Alumni Museum. It was a space issue. Space is one of those constants of academic life, answering to a mysterious iron law which holds that there is less of it available after more has been added than there was before the adding was done. In this case, more was needed to house the staff in Morrill Hall and, to meet that need, a decision was made to move the museum. It was small, had been housed on an upper floor in Morrill, and had attracted few visitors during its dozen years of existence. Nevertheless, it stood high in the hearts and minds of some active alumni, who launched a persistent and passionate campaign to keep it where it was. Notwithstanding, a decision was made, following extensive discussion, to distribute its contents to more accessible sites around campus.

Edward was a veteran of student government, a person who served as a tireless champion of student causes. He was an able leader, sometimes given, though, to leaping before looking. That is what he did in this instance. His letter to me has been lost to history. But in it, he recounts his disappointment that student views on the matter had not been sought, his indignation at the injustice of the decision, and his certainty that, once again, the people he represents had been treated as second-class citizens. One of Edward's many positive attributes is that he is always willing to engage in dialogue, always ready to be educated. That could necessitate, and does in this situation, a stern stance on the part of the respondent. I respond sternly, then, intending to turn his loss of temper into a lesson.

Feb. 12, 1991

Dear Edward:

I have your letter of Feb. 8. I have read it several times to try to understand the reasons for its angry, lecturing tone and content. I'm still puzzled.

I gather that, in your view, the Alumni Museum has become a place that students visit in significant numbers. Therefore, the Alumni Council and its Morrill Hall Committee should propose for action by [student government] any alterations they contemplate in regard to the museum. Since this did not happen, the university has admitted that students are second priority and, to quote your own language, "the university for the sake of the university will always be ahead of the university for the sake of the students."

Wow! It takes a real leap of faith and, I think, a commitment to a particular ideological stance to accept this kind of logic. Perhaps there is another way of looking at this matter. Let me give it a try.

The Alumni Museum is not a place that carries with it the grandeur of the ages. Neither the soul nor the history of the university reposes there, despite claims to the contrary. It has only been in existence for 12 years. It is badly located for a facility needing adequate access to function properly. It would come as news to the staff that students often visit the museum. Indeed, hardly anybody visits the museum ...

Morrill Hall, not this out-of-the-way museum, is the soul of the university, and a lot of history reposes there in a lot of ways. It nearly came down in the 1970s. The university, with the assistance of the Alumni Association, raised nearly a million dollars to save it. The Morrill Hall Committee was formed at that time, [and it] has played the critical role ever since. No decision about uses of Morrill Hall gets made without the committee's consideration. No entity is more committed to preserving the tradition and sanctity of Morrill Hall than this one.

Edward, you can't just claim ownership of the Alumni Museum because students visit there. All campus facilities belong to the university, but many of them are viewed by their principal occupants as belonging especially to them. Thus, the College of Business Administration has a special role in relation to the Business Building, the Department of Music in relation to the Nightingale Concert Hall, the Department of Intercollegiate Athletics in relation to the stadium. ASUN has that relationship with the student union. The Alumni Association is not asked to pass judgment on major physical alterations in the student union, though virtually all of its members have spent many memorable moments there. The association would not expect to be asked for its approval.

Well, Morrill Hall has *its* special relationship with the Alumni Association and the Morrill Hall Committee. Over the years, despite many changes ... ASUN has never suggested a right of approval, or a right of consultation, for such changes. Now, you appear to claim such a right. I'm sorry. I disagree.

As for the business about students as second priority and that baffling language of yours I quoted above . . . best to write it off, I think, as a case of emotion running ahead of reason. It's like letters one writes to the editor in a fit of pique. Except, if one is wise, one lets the letter sit for awhile and then either throws it away or rewrites it so that reason, not emotion, governs its language. Such wisdom comes through learning experiences. That's why the university is here.

∼

Ernest K.

In fall 1994, missing the classroom, I joined with professor Steve Tchudi (Department of English) in teaching a freshman seminar on society and its problems. This was a rubric that gave both instructors and students a lot of room to roam. Ernest took advantage of that flexibility, roamed far and wide, and ended up with an argument that the United States could be best understood as a cult. Ernest was a very bright student, who seemed to take pleasure from provoking his classmates, and me, as well. I admired that trait, and I liked his mind. I did not buy his argument, however. He left the university after that semester and, subsequently, he initiated a correspondence with me which continued for nearly a year. His letters were rambling, grammatically loose, and, most of them, very long. Still, I found them, Ernest's ideas, and his insistence on pushing them stimulating enough to sustain my end of the exchange. He is interested here in achieving two objectives: 1) convincing me that his argument, drawn from cognitive psychology and a concept called "biasedly accumulated schemas," explains everything; and 2) getting me to award him (no need to worry about curricula, examinations, term papers, grades) a university degree. For my part, I join the argument and decline to give him a degree.

Dec. 22, 1994

Dear Mr. Crowley:

You may not remember me but I am the one student who argued with you a little in Mr. Tchudi's and your class about America in actuality being nothing more than a cult. So if you remember that you must now be remembering with dread that I also asked you for a degree not that long ago.

The concepts in this letter and in my larger paper developed out of years of questioning and over that time noticing patterns. Over those years the one thing I never tried to do was make something work; my primary goal was to find what was there and not what I wanted to be there. What I came up with in the end was neither that hopeful or gratifying.

I began with the scientific perspective, that life itself is seen as nothing more than the consequence of chance reactions. From this perspective there would be no intrinsic meaning. The survival of the species could not even be justified, but only be the goal of the evolutionary process not serving a purpose of having any type of meaning attached to it. This perspective also coincides with that portrayed in history ...

The question is where did we get all of these ideals, meanings, beliefs? Just as these vary among different regions, they find similarity within regions, groups, cultures. To avoid a long, drawn out review of the process of acculturation or socialization I will simply refer you to the area of schemas in the literature. Cognitive psychologists have developed the concept of schemas to better explain this process of acculturation. Cognitive schemas are learned, internalized patterns of thought-feeling that mediate both the interpretation of on-going experiences and the reconstruction of those memories ... Everything you are is schemas; your ideas, your goals, your beliefs, and these will affect your perspective. Yet we know that you develop these schemas biasedly by the fact that people demonstrate more similarity within regions than to other different regions. You are exposed to different cultures, ideals, etc. It is the same with language; you learn the language exposed to you. So you are a biased creation ...

This process of creation is why the world is the way it is and why you and I are the way we are. Now I have not stretched or warped anything to get to this point. Everything here is very plain and almost unquestioned in the literature. The difficulty develops in the conclusion that we are nothing, that we are just a creation, that what we believe to be true has about as much validity as my speaking the English language and not Korean. Knowing that there is nothing does not change what we are; we have been created. We are the schemas we developed ... Like most or all cultures, there are avenues of change. Cultures have been around for a long time and are very good at dealing with the biased creation and differences in beliefs ... I see such cultural avenues perhaps being more detrimental to humanity than good, and what I see is this university continuing them.

Okay, I have explained that scientifically there is nothing, that we are nothing more than the product of chance reactions and the evolutionary process. I have explained how we as humans develop and are created ideals, beliefs, supposed intrinsic meaning in light of there being nothing ... The belief that there is a correct or true context is what I refer to as the "false pretense." ... We are and we live by the biasedly accumulated schemas we hold. We are our schemas but we need to understand that these schemas are nothing more than creations we have biasedly accumulated ... I do not partake in the "false pretense," as this university currently does. This nation and its government partake in the "false pretense.".... I do not believe in the "false pretense" where this university does and therefore I am leaving. Let me explain first that I understand the world's dependence upon the "false pretense" and in that context I respect you, what you have done, and are trying to do at the University of Nevada, Reno. Look at my own advancement. I do not want to make it sound like your university is doing irreversible harm; it is doing exactly what it is supposed to do in its contexts ... You and your institution are doing a good job in the current contexts, and like you said it is a place to expand ideas even though ours are diametrically apart. But there is a time when a student must leave his teacher and strike out on his own. All I am asking for is a degree ...

If you are not convinced that I deserve a degree or even an honorary degree I would be interested in hearing why. If there is anything that you do not understand or simply find fault with in my argument I would also be interested in hearing it.

Thank you for letting me take up so much of your time. And so, I should be expecting my degree in the mail any day now?

Sincerely,
Ernest K.

Jan. 4, 1995

Dear Ernest:

I do indeed remember you, your observations about America as a cult, and your request for a degree during a recent conversation over pizza. Your letter is certainly a thoughtful and provocative one, and I enjoyed reading it. It suggests that its author has a very able, nimble mind, the courage of his convictions, a trace of intellectual arrogance not unbecoming in one of youthful years (though offensive when found among individuals of older vintage), and a refreshing forthrightness. Those are all interesting and welcome qualities, but they are not enough to get you a degree just for the asking.

Your explanation of the human enterprise, with all its schemas, and of the university's role in it (with schemas of its own), is a challenging one, though rather too mechanistic and deterministic for my tastes and— or so it seems to me—not really a product (though you claim otherwise) of scientific method. When all is said and done, you imply, just about everyone and everything is imprisoned in these schemas except ... lo! ... Ernest K.

Well, Ernest, you are right: You *are* outside the schemas. But so are lots of other folks and institutions, the university most especially included. A university is the very place for you to develop your ideas, to present them, defend them, have them criticized, refine them, throw them out (which latter course of action I humbly recommend for the idea at the core of your letter). It operates by rules, of course, and must. And it can be a very conservative institution. But if one loves the life of the mind—and all the joys and frustrations, the dead ends and newly discovered intellectual highways that go with it—this is where that life is lived. There are no walls, no bars or boundaries, indeed no schemas, that can hold back a questing mind or repress a good idea.

A college degree may mean different things to different people, in a material sense. But symbolically it signifies intellectual success. It suggests that, despite obstacles, conventions, bureaucracies, whatever, the holder has won a victory, has become educated, is now a full-fledged learner.

You are a bright young man, Ernest, but you have a lot to learn. You have to earn a degree by learning, and you aren't there yet. When I was your age, I left college life and made my way in a hard world for nearly five years before heading back to campus. I learned from the experience, too, and among my lessons was that there was so much more learning for me to do. At one campus or another, I've been at it ever since. I think of myself as something more than a product, as you put it, of "biasedly accumulated schemas." I think of you that way also. There is more to life than contexts. There are people inside those contexts, people of independent mind and spirit, and you know what? They make their way out. They cause change. They've been doing that since the dawn of time. They are doing it still. There is no better place to do it, for all its faults, than a university. Perhaps, as I did nearly 40 years ago, you will one day reach that conclusion, as well.

In the meantime, I wish you well in whatever is next for you. In the absence of a degree by mail, as you requested, this letter will have to suffice.

———————

Ernest persisted for nearly a year. In a letter dated Jan. 12, 1995, he writes:

You were right in defending the degree. My request ... was a feeble attempt, ... a shot in the dark. The degree stands for something which I have not completed ... However, I still believe you wrong in your response to my core argument ... You stated that [it] was too deterministic for your tastes. It is for mine too, but that is no reason to discard it ... I could only show that we have a limited free will, based on history and change ... The issue of free will is not essential to prove or disprove my argument.

Before I go, I was just wondering if you could find it in your heart to give me a degree? ... See I am not outside schemas, I still have an irrational need for a degree ...

———————

Feb. 13, 1995

Dear Ernest:

It's good to know that you see yourself, as you see everyone else who is or ever was (or presumably ever will be) as just another prisoner of biasedly accumulated schemas. Sorry I was wrong about that. And you are correct as well in another self-appraisal: You do like to argue!

However, you haven't convinced me. The argument, in one form or another, has raged for ages. Free will and determinism, I mean. Sometimes, it has produced revolutions, as when Martin Luther posted his theses on the door or Karl Marx wrote *Das Kapital* and placed us all in the steely grip of dialectical materialism. I do not believe that the biasedly accumulated schema view of the world will lead to that kind of result. For one thing, it's simply dreadful terminology, incapable of inspiring a march on the barricades. For another, it is negative to the point of nihilism. The latter is good for those disaffected folks who get their jollies from throwing bombs, and for anarchist intellectuals who argue politics in seedy French cafes. But nihilism never built a cathedral, and never will. Neither will a view of the world that proceeds from a biasedly accumulated schema.

Anyway, I'm beyond convincing, Ernest. I enjoy reading your thoughts. You could help build a cathedral some day. Keep reading and using your brain and the time will come when you'll get these schemas in perspective as an intriguing idea but one hardly capable of encompassing the vast, wild, unpredictable, and sometimes elevating experience of humankind.

Sorry, no degree. Best wishes instead.

––––––––––

On June 7, Ernest writes again. He now addresses me as *"Dear Joe,"* and he asks:

––––––––––

Hey Joe what's up? It is me again, the America is a cult guy ... Perhaps you are right and the argument about schemas is too negative. Even before I received your letter I was slowly coming to the same conclusion ... Yet I feel bad, should I discard it just because it is too negative? No one has seemed to have yet proved it wrong. As I would leave it right now, it would still stand true ... I have always been one to try and help people understand themselves and the world, but as I am learning they do not want to know. So ... I packed it away on a back shelf.

So since I came to this grand conclusion, can you give me a degree? Come on, I have searched, learned, and become totally bewildered by what I found and had to give it up. That is least worth something ... I hope I have not been too much of a nuisance...

––––––––––

June 26, 1995

Dear Ernest:

I'm glad to see you are sticking to your unshakable certainty regarding schemas, and even gladder to learn you're abandoning the notion anyway. It's good to have something to hang onto that helps make sense of the world, and it's good to recognize that the time has come to stop insisting that others hang onto it too. While you insist you are leaving it because others find it too negative, you might consider that others resist it because it does not make sense of the world to them, or perhaps because in some ultimate way the world makes no sense or doesn't need to.

Anyway, I honor what you call your "grand conclusion." You are never a nuisance, Ernest, but no, you cannot have a degree. Your mind still has some miles to travel before you will be eligible.

———————

Ernest has not given up yet. He tries one more time in a letter dated Nov. 3, 1995. He is now off on the question of whether society is going to fall apart, and he suggests that the university is a place of control, to assure that this does not happen. This conjecture leads him to the conclusion that we make decisions based on fear. *"We are afraid,"* he says, *"that the gold we have stashed away may be reduced to nothing."* So we all need to play *"the game."* It is a *"Dear Joe,"* letter again, and it begins once more with *"What's up Joe?"* The conclusion is a familiar one:

Oh and could I have my degree now? ... And why do I still want my, degree?, because like it or not I have to get into the game ... I too have a bunch of the biasedly accumulated schemas or beliefs and also have a trunk full of gold that is worthless to me away from the game ...

———————

One last time, I provide Ernest with an answer.

November 16, 1995

Dear Ernest:

Thanks for your latest. In all candor, you lost me with this one. I have no recollection of making the argument you impute to me. Of course our society, any society, has the potential to fall apart. And, just now, our own society is a troubled one. And, of course, universities have an obligation to help. After that, I don't recognize my views in your putative recapitulation of them. Control? Fear? I don't know what you're talking about. As for the existence and pursuit of truth, well, that is a notion you have surrounded with bizarre logic that allows you to come down , as the occasion requires, on either side (or all sides) of the question. At times, you take refuge in tautology—always a safe haven of sorts but not a port from which any proud ship of the line would sail.

Let me offer you a proposition: Let us change slightly your favorite expression; let us change "biasedly accumulated schemas" into "biasedlyaccumulated schemas"—two words instead of three. Let us then convey this notion acronymically. That would be: "BS". Ah, there's truth in that acronym!

No degree. Sorry.

I do not hear from him again.

Chapter Eight

~

Issues

CAMPUSES PROVIDE A WELCOMING AND COMMODIOUS ENVIRONMENT for the raising of challenging questions and the discussion of significant (or, for that matter, insignificant) issues. Obviously, that is as it should be. Such questions abound in classrooms and laboratories, and in the councils of administration, also. The discussion of issues is another constant of academic life. Presidents perforce get involved, though they are well-advised to choose carefully the occasions and dimensions of their involvement. There are many matters on which presidents ought not weigh in, with regard to which, indeed, they carry little or no weight. There are many questions that will be answered well with no help from the central administration. There are many issues that, left to play themselves out, will get resolved by others. Presidents—if they are to be effective—will recognize that they only get so many choices.

Making choices, nevertheless, is a major presidential responsibility. A problem will arise, or a letter will arrive, that demands the president's attention. Speaking on, or writing about (or both), these matters is part of the job. It may be that clarification is required, or information desired, that a stand be taken, a line drawn, some teaching done, or leadership in some other way be demonstrated. And it may be, too, that some self-administered succor for the president, a little exorcising of demons, can be built into the response.

I have selected six issues for inclusion in this chapter, again as a representative sample of a much larger universe. All six are covered by way of letters from me, two of which respond to letters from others. I wrote another two in reaction to newspaper columns and two more simply to address critical concerns in a timely fashion. Image is one subject of attention here, and a second, relatedly, is the consequential matter of the university's name. It would be difficult to claim that these letters are representative without having one on athletics, so I have included one below. A long-running policy debate on the question of freedom of information versus a student's right to privacy is the focus of a communication to a newspaper editor. Academic planning is the business at hand in a letter to a colleague. Freedom of speech is an ever-present source of controversy for universities, and a notable example is illustrated here in a letter to a Faculty Senate chairman. Not included below—to conserve space and because the emphasis is on the issues—is the correspondence or newspaper columns to which some of my letters respond.

$\sim$

Image

The rise of college guides and rankings in the late 20th century, the competition for students and the desire to be better understood, has led institutions across the land to be much more mindful of the need to market themselves. Sustaining and advancing the university image has become a continuing preoccupation. Parents and students have developed a consuming interest in what a college or university can deliver in the form of jobs for graduates, quality of programs, and that elusive consideration called prestige. We have dealt with all these matters at the University of Nevada, Reno, and also with the challenge of being, for a large percentage of the student body, the hometown institution.

———

Ms. Genevieve M. writes to me wondering what we are doing to build our image, whether the assessments of our reputation she is hearing from friends (and her daughter from her friends) are valid, and if I would be willing to promise her—she is a geography major—and her daughter a good education.

———

Dec. 18, 1990

Dear President Crowley:

I am a 44 year old, single parent with two children, and also a sophomore at the university. I attended the university originally in 1964-65 after I graduated from high school, but was not able to return until 25 years later. I always wanted to return but couldn't because of raising children, working, etc. I was very excited when the PACE program was offered, because it suited my needs. I have now switched my major to geography, and my ultimate goal is a B.S. in geography.

This information is important because it forms the basis of this letter. Getting a college education has become a top priority for me, because I waited so long for it, but I am constantly defending the university to colleagues, other parents, etc. I hear, almost on a daily basis, that UNR is a "podunk" school, that it has nothing to offer, that the degrees are worthless, and that employers don't like to hire anyone who has graduated from UNR because they don't feel that they have learned anything. The bottom line is that UNR has a bad image in this town, and I am not sure why. I personally feel that it has a lot to offer, but there are a lot of people who do not feel that way.

UNR has tried in the last year or so to introduce it's faculty to the community, and I think that this is a very good idea for PR. However, I think that the community needs to know what the university can do for the students. Many students, including my own daughter who will graduate from McQueen High School next June, plan to attend UNR, and I feel that they need to know that they will receive a quality, worthwhile education. That information can come only from the university.

In a town that is constantly struggling with it's image, a top-rated university would be a wonderful claim to fame. I am very proud of UNR's second-place football berth, but football shouldn't be the only thing that puts us on the map!

From someone who loves school and loves learning, and who loves the university, I implore you to do whatever you can to promote a positive image for the University of Nevada, Reno, and the sooner, the better!

Sincerely,
Genevieve M.

Dec. 31, 1990

Dear Ms. M.:

Thanks very much for your thoughtful letter of Dec. 18. The "image" issue, to which your letter refers, is an old and sensitive one for the university. Believe me, we spend a lot of time, effort and money on this issue. Viewing it from the perspective of someone who has spent 25 years at this institution, I think we have made a great deal of progress. We work on image-building not simply through our advertising campaign, but through high-quality publications, the dissemination of information about the university, a wide variety of programs involving people from the community in the life of the university, and an ambitious effort to relate to Nevada's high schools and their students. It's a slow process, but it's working.

It is important to remember that we are discussing image here, not substance. Our image has suffered, in my opinion, for three principal reasons. One is the fact that we are the university in your back yard, the hometown school whose warts are more visible than those of other institutions (and they all have them). Secondly, for a long period of time ... the university and the community were busy building barriers instead of bridges. We became estranged from the public that is our source of support and major constituency. Assuredly, that harmed our image. Thirdly, our admission policy is essentially an open-door one. Every guide to colleges and universities includes, as a major consideration, the institutions' admission standards. In my opinion, there is no relationship of consequence between such standards and the quality of instruction. Students who should not be here are gone within a semester, or a year at the most. Courses and curricula are largely unaffected. What suffers is the institution's prestige, not its programs. As you may know, we have proposed, on a variety of grounds, higher standards of admission for UNR. The regents are looking seriously at this matter. I suspect our standards will be raised in the reasonably near future. When that happens, our prestige will grow, our stock will rise, our image will improve, and our programs will change hardly a whit. We will be the same institution, by and large. But the public perception will be altered.

There is not much we can do about our location. Notwithstanding, we will continue to enroll the majority of our students (currently 58 percent) from Washoe County. When all is said and done, and the prestige game is played out, and parents reckon with the costs of sending children on to college, and the truth (as opposed to the fiction you hear from others about podunk schools, worthless degrees, and unhired graduates) gets to be a little clearer, Washoe County students always arrive here in large numbers. And they enjoy their time here; the good students do anyway. Interestingly, when we talk with students and their parents in Clark County, or elsewhere out in the state, the podunk and related concerns seldom arise. We are a well-regarded university in Las Vegas and in rural Nevada. That's how important the location factor is in the image business.

I suggest you ask your colleagues (and your daughter can ask hers) a few questions when they talk to you about the university. Ask them for specific information. Ask them to give you details on the quality of, say, UNR's geography program (or any other). Ask them to compare it with that of other universities. Ask them to give you statistics on employers who won't hire UNR graduates. They won't be able to answer these questions because these negative assessments are mythical. They have no foundation.

Or, you might ask your colleagues what the following people have in common: Senator Richard Bryan; former Governor Grant Sawyer; Ted Sanders, Assistant Secretary, U.S. Department of Education; Patricia Miltenberger, UNR vice president; Marvin Moss, former Washoe County Superintendent of Schools; Myrna Matranga, Associate Superintendent of Schools, Washoe County; Dorothy Nyswander, noted public health educator at the University of California, Berkeley; Joann Elston, Washoe County teacher of the year; John Flynn, Principal, McQueen High School; Bill Raggio, majority leader, Nevada State Senate; Frank Fahrenkopf, former national chairman of the Republican Party; Sig Rogich, Assistant to the President of the United States; Frankie Sue Del Papa, Secretary of State and Attorney General-elect, State of Nevada; Dorothy Gallagher, Chairwoman, University of Nevada Board of Regents; Frank McCulloch, executive editor, San Francisco *Examiner;* Rollan Melton, former president, Speidel newspapers, member of the Gannett Company board of directors and local columnist; Warren Lerude, Pulitzer Prize winner; the late Cliff Segerblom, noted western artist; Robert Laxalt, novelist; Bill Helming, president of Helming Group, Inc., the largest agricultural consulting company in the world; Bill Nicholsen and Jim O'Shaugnessy, presidents of major national corporations;

Procter Hug, Sr., former Washoe County Superintendent of Schools; Procter Hug, Jr., member judge, Ninth U.S. Circuit Court of Appeals; Procter Hug III, local attorney, and Dr. Cheryl Hug-English, Reno physician; Bruce Thompson, U.S. District Court judge; Charles Springer, Chief Justice, Nevada Supreme Court; bank presidents like Ernie Martinelli; heads of stock brokerage offices like Bill Kottinger and Mark Elston; Army generals like Sinclair Melner, Eugene Salet, and George Baxter; Lynn Atcheson, vice president, Harrah's; Andrea Pelter, Chief Executive Officer, Reno Iron Works; thousands of successful doctors, lawyers, nurses, engineers, artists, educators, veterinarians, businessmen, civil servants and others. These people have in common the fact that they are graduates of the University of Nevada, Reno.

There are many names to be added to this list. I could add those of hundreds of my own former students who have gone on to prestigious graduate and professional schools and successful careers. I could add those of my children—one a speech pathologist, a second a business executive, a third who is just finishing law school (There is a fourth, still a student at UNR, who is majoring in geography.). They are all delighted that they attended this university.

You suggested that your daughter and many of her classmates at McQueen need to know they will receive "a quality, worthwhile education." The university can only guarantee them the opportunity for such an education. We are happy to offer that opportunity. As always, it is up to the students whether they take advantage of it. University officials regularly visit McQueen and other Nevada high schools. Your daughter and her friends can, if they prefer, visit the campus, take a tour, raise questions in person or by telephone ...

We are working hard on our image in the expectation that some day it will approximate the reality. The reality is that this is a fine university; one that continues to get better; one that cares alike for students like your daughter (soon to be a high school graduate) and ... yourself (returning to college after a quarter of a century); one whose quality is best bespoken by its graduates.

Thanks again for writing. We will continue our efforts to make this institution one that you can be proud of, and your daughter as well.

Best wishes for the new year.

∾

What's in a Name?

For most of the history of the state of Nevada, there was but one institution of higher education within its borders. The University of Nevada was born in the state's 1864 Constitution, established in Elko in 1874, moved to Reno in 1885-86, and developed thereafter as a state-wide institution with assorted branches and degree levels. As the state grew in the last half of the 20th century, the university expanded, locating a branch in Las Vegas, installing two-year degree programs in its home curriculum, and founding a research institute as one of its divisions. Eventually, the Desert Research Institute became a separate entity. Community colleges were created around the state, as part of a growing system of higher education. And the branch campus in Clark County became an independent university.

By the end of the 1970s there were seven autonomous institutions in what was known first as the University of Nevada System and later as the University and Community College System of Nevada. As each of these entities took their separate places in the system, they were given an opportunity to create their own names. Two of the community colleges were afforded more than one such opportunity, as they sought a more descriptive nomenclature. The branch campus in Clark County became the Nevada Southern University and then, in a critical decision by the Board of Regents in 1969 (when the University of Nevada System was formally established), chose for itself (with regents' approval) the name University of Nevada, Las Vegas. That having been done, the regents decided at the same meeting that the University of Nevada needed renaming. In a stroke, with no opportunity to offer meaningful comment, we found ourselves with "Reno" added to our name and a controversy that would never die. That controversy is the subject of my following 1994 letter to then UCCSN chancellor Richard Jarvis and UNLV's acting president (and later, governor of Nevada), Kenny Guinn.

––––––––––

Dec. 13, 1994

Dear Richard and Kenny:

I thought it would be helpful to give you my view on the name question that became a major issue at a regents meeting a couple of years ago. The issue, then as now, is based on a strong concern by UNLV alumni and others in the UNLV community about this university's use of "Nevada" as a shorthand name. This usage has been in effect for a century, notwithstanding the decision by the Board of Regents—without prior consultation, indeed, without discussion—to add "Reno" to our name back in 1969.

There are very passionate feelings about this matter in the south. I understand these feelings, and we have tried to be sensitive and accommodative to them. I'm not sure I have made it clear that there are very passionate feelings in the north as well, born of that decision almost 26 years ago, born of a later decision to rename part of the university the University of Nevada School of Medicine (no Reno here), born of great frustrations over the confusion the institution has experienced on the name question. It is difficult for people in the north to understand why we got a "Reno" after our name because the university in the south needed renaming; why we had to take the "Reno" off our name for the School of Medicine because of southern sensitivities; why our Clark County cooperative extension office needs to be called the Nevada Cooperative Extension (again, no "Reno") because of southern sensitivities; why, if our football team is playing in Las Vegas, we better make sure to have that "Reno" affixed firmly to our name. It is difficult for people here to understand why we are the only institution in the system not consulted as to the nature of its formal name and the only one required to defend its shorthand name. It is difficult for people here to understand why folks associated with UNLV, a secure shorthand name known across the nation and highly valued on campus and in the Las Vegas community, would want to deny this university—especially in view of what has happened to us these last 26 years— the same opportunity. That is why, in brief, there is great passion in the north on the name question.

My understanding is that the objection to our use of "Nevada" is based in part on the opinion that it is illegal for us to do so but, more importantly, that this usage represents an attempt to appropriate for ourselves the name of the state and in that way seek to put the university in a superior (and UNLV in an inferior) position. I don't believe there is a legal issue here ... There is no dispute that we are the University of Nevada, Reno, as the law describes us. We are, again, employing a shorthand name we have used for a century, and we are following a practice in that regard experienced in *every* state in which the original public university has given its name to campuses developed later. So, I doubt that there is a legal problem.

I can appreciate why some feel we are trying to steal a march on UNLV with the "Nevada" usage. I can only say that we are not, that such is not our intention, that we have sought to give fresh emphasis to a name we have had forever so as, again, to provide us that same secure and accepted identification that our sister institution already possesses.

The name question seems to come down to three alternative possibilities:

1.*UNR*. We use this name freely and will continue to do so, just as the University of Nebraska, Lincoln uses UNL and the University of Tennessee, Knoxville uses UTK. But in our case, as in the others, the acronym has essentially no recognition beyond state borders. We tried to gain acceptance for UNR outside the state for years, but it simply is not possible. Only a handful of institutions (UNLV among them) have this kind of acronymic recognition.

2.*Nevada-Reno*. This is a name that was utilized around the country for several years to identify our institution. It has no standing on the campus and precious little in the community. It is a media invention, and very unpopular in these parts. Would it not be ironic, in light of all that has happened, if we were required to use this unacceptable name because, in effect, southern Nevada chose it for us?

3.*Nevada*. The logic, I think, speaks for itself [as it does for UNL (*Nebraska*), UTK (*Tennessee*), and the original public university in a dozen or so other states that have shared our experience]. We can see no other choice.

In sum, we have strong feelings north and south about this question. I have attempted to damp down the fires here, resisting the idea of a regents discussion of the issue in the north because it would only exacerbate a tense situation. I don't believe further discussion in regents meetings anywhere will solve our problem. The small group, face-to-face meeting(s) suggested by the chancellor [could be helpful]. I'll be happy to do what I can to explore possibilities and keep peace in the land.

∾

Athletics

The name controversy subsided during the late 1990s, thanks in part to efforts and goodwill on all sides, and in part to the circumstances that the two universities no longer shared membership in the same athletic conference. Sports competition continued, but on a smaller scale. It was this kind of competition that had escalated the controversy in the first place. It is a fact of life: college athletics produce controversy.

During the 1990-91 school year, the university community debated the question of whether to change conferences (from the Big Sky to the Big West) and NCAA classifications (moving up to IA from IAA). The views expressed around campus and in the community were generally, but not universally, positive. One person expressing opposition was Louis N., who wrote two newspaper columns on the subject. Louis was an influential student leader and a young man with whom I had a friendly, if sometimes disputatious, relationship. In his columns, he offered some of the classic arguments—financial drain, inappropriate priorities, academic sensitivities, alumni interference, adverse publicity—brought to bear over the decades by critics of college athletic programs. I joined the debate, though only, in this case, by way of a letter intended as a teaching opportunity.

———————

March 13, 1991

Dear Louis:

I have read with interest your two recent columns on athletics. Your prejudices do show, as does your honesty in admitting them. You make a well-considered case, though I thought it got beyond the bounds a bit with the comment about [athletics as] the "university leech." You are more convincing when you use reason, rather than visceral appeal, as a basis for criticism ...

No one here that I know of makes the case that our athletics program is "self-supporting." The language is budget office language, not that of the athletic department. That department's self-supporting budget covers only a part of its revenues and expenditures. This budget is lumped in with lots of others, of varying description, under a label that should be loosely interpreted. It is neither accurate nor fair to imply that the university tries to deceive the public on this matter. The athletics budget is not self-supporting here, when considered in its totality. Very few budgets of significance in a university are ... No academic department, school or college is self-supporting. Neither is my office, or most others ... Public universities, as a matter of general principle, are not intended to be self-supporting. In my view, it is hardly shocking, or immoral, that athletics is not a self-supporting department. Still, if one insists that it must be or otherwise it's a leech, you win the argument hands down. It's an easy victory over no competition.

Your second article was much more interesting, I thought. It seems to me, even so, that one must do more than simply claim that our program is a detriment to academics. That argument, in our case, is as loose as the one on the other side, that suggests that athletics brings "the almighty dollar" to the institution to assist in academic advancement. We have not made such a claim, or I have not, in any case. The evidence is very strong that athletic success, or failure, bears very little relationship to success or failure in fund-raising for academic programs. So you are correct on that point, but we are not claiming such a relationship here ...

Then there is the old canard about "the alumni." This bit of bashing is as old as athletics programs at universities, the presumption being, as you put it, that alumni "love to give to athletics and would hate it if we cut their budget." Have we said such a thing here? I hope not. The alumni are the folks who used to be students. When they were students, they either liked athletics, or disliked athletics or— most of them, probably—did not care much one way or the other. The students who graduate become alumni, right? You will be one soon. Your feelings are unlikely to change. This business about the alumni commitment to, and pressure on behalf of, their alma mater's athletic endeavors is one of the grand media fictions. No argument here ...

We are left then, as far as your arguments are concerned, with prestige and visibility. You do not spend any time on these issues, so I cannot tell why you make the claim. I would be willing to debate this part with you. I believe prestige is involved, or can be, and visibility, as well. I believe, too, that there is a point to be made about the obligations we have, as a public institution, to the community we serve. I believe athletics, done the right way, provide a source of pride and identity that cannot be quantified. You can't count it, Louis, but let me tell you, when we played for a national championship, you could feel that pride, that identification out there in the community, and you could sense that visibility out there around the country.

The key, of course, is doing it the right way. That means keeping strong institutional control over the program. College athletics can create terrible problems. The big dollars associated with big-time programs can reverse the pride, visibility, prestige. They can lead institutions to ignore their responsibility to control, to ignore the cheating that is all too common, to ignore the academic priority that ought to underlie college athletics. Those are the real issues. I believe we have maintained control here; that we operate a financially modest program, comparatively speaking; that we are vigilant against cheating; that we insist on an academic emphasis.

It is appropriate to raise questions about the financial implications of a move to IA, the Big West, or any other significant change in our athletic programs ... We will have a full, free, and fair discussion of any possible change of this type. I suspect you will still be opposed, and that will be fine. It seems to me that reasonable opposition ought to be based on the case that is made on behalf of a change. The university has not made and, with few exceptions, would not make the case you deftly defeated in your columns.

No need to respond. This isn't intended as a stern uncle kind of letter, but just to provide a little friendly food for thought, that's all.

∼

Rights in Conflict

For a number of years in the 1980s and '90s, two conflicting initiatives of the federal government created considerable discord on college and university campuses. The government mandated by statute the public dissemination of campus crime information. An earlier statute, known familiarly as the "Buckley Amendment," had been passed to assure the privacy of student records and assorted personal data. Campus newspapers argued vigorously that the crime-reporting legislation entitled them to have the names and attendant records of students charged with campus crimes provided directly and immediately by the university. The U.S. Department of Education, however, had ruled that this information was protected by the Buckley Amendment, and that its release would subject the offending institutions to forfeiture of all federal funding assistance, including student financial aid and research and development grants. In this situation, the colleges and universities, on the basis of insistent advice from their attorneys, had adhered to the Department of Education position. Campus journalists disagreed, often passionately.

At Nevada, we pursued a legal middle road by way of which the student newspaper, with a simple telephone call, could get the names of arrested students from the local police jurisdiction instead of from the campus blotter. Very little extra effort was thus required by reporters, but that was not the point. A sacred right to freedom of information was the point here, they argued. We held our ground. Eventually, to our great relief, the courts ruled against the Department of Education position, but not before the relationship between campus authorities and campus newspapers became seriously strained. My letter to Rachael Conlin (her real name), news editor of our campus paper, is instructive on this thorny issue.

Jan. 14, 1992

Dear Rachael:

Thank you for sending me a copy of your recent correspondence with [university counsel]. I was particularly interested in the communication to you from Mike Hiestand, Esq., of the Student Press Law Center. Mr. Hiestand's letter is long on fustian, foolishness and error. He is adept at the overwrought rhetoric that turns a complex legal and policy question into a struggle between the forces of light and the forces of darkness (he being on the former side, naturally). He is curiously short on facts.

Mr. Hiestand suggests that the threatened loss of federal funding was "a convenient excuse in the past" to withhold campus crime information. He questions "whether the Buckley Amendment was ever really anything more than a pretext" on this campus since, as he puts it, we have refused to provide "information regarding the campus crimes of non-students" as well as of students. I am probably old-fashioned, but it seems to me that the possible loss of millions of dollars in loans, grants, jobs and services for students would be a matter of concern to people working for a student-oriented organization. I do not sense that concern on Mr. Hiestand's part, more's the pity. I do sense a very nearly complete lack of understanding of the situation on this campus.

If the millions of dollars possibly lost to our students were mere pretext, so that we could keep campus crime secret, why would we go out of our way to assure that *Sagebrush* received expeditiously our campus police blotter information detailing the times and natures of any crime? Why would we arrange a process whereby *Sagebrush* reporters, through one extra phone call, could get the names of arrested students from the Washoe County Sheriff's Department? And what does Mr. Hiestand have in mind when he reports that we have withheld crime information on non-students when we have routinely provided it? If our real motive was to keep campus crime a secret and thus foist upon the public a false image of our "peaceful little world," we have done a dreadful job of it.

Ah well, overwrought rhetoric is never a substitute for truth. The truth is that, apart from routinely confidential information on ongoing investigations, there is *no* campus crime information, names included, to which *Sagebrush* lacks access.

Let us review the factual record that takes us from the Nov. 21 federal district court decision to the present.

Shortly after the decision was announced, a *Sagebrush* reporter called to ask if the university would now release student names. I responded that it seemed to me prudent, given the stakes involved, to seek advice from [our] General Counsel. Next day, I called [him]. He advised me to await clarification of the Department of Education's response to the district court decision. Meantime, your newspaper quoted you to the effect that, if the university persisted in its policy, "We'll sue their asses."

Despite this eloquently articulated threat, we decided to wait. A few weeks later (Dec. 11), *The Chronicle of Higher Education* reported that campuses were reacting differently to the court decision. Some were releasing student law enforcement records, others were not. I asked our [counsel] to review the matter and again advise me how to deal with the central issue. [One of our attorneys] has been in contact with a Department of Education attorney since the Missouri case last summer. Indeed, by now he has been in touch with her, or her office, several times. No clarification has been forthcoming. [His] view is that the department is precluded by the court's preliminary injunction from taking overt legal action against the university, though he can make no promises regarding other approaches the department might employ. He concludes, in a letter of Jan. 8, that "if the campus should decide to release [student law enforcement] reports, it would not place its federal funding in jeopardy."

For whatever it's worth, I have long held the view that the Buckley Amendment ought not apply in matters of campus crime. That view is generally shared by key campus administrators, which is why we have worked with your predecessors to assure *Sagebrush* can get the information it needs. Given the clear stand of the Department of Education to the contrary, however, I have not been willing to take any action that would jeopardize our federal funding. Any other policy on our part would have been irresponsible. Mr. Hiestand's agitated speculations notwithstanding, there is not a scintilla of evidence that this university's real motivation was to hide some awful truth. We have done what we could, instead, to make the truth available. The documentary record of our actions in this regard is available, should anyone wish to review it.

Henceforward, given the conclusion of [university counsel] as noted above, the information previously accessible to *Sagebrush* through the placement of one additional phone call will be available directly from the University Police Department.

Thanks again for keeping me advised of your interest in this matter. I am pleased to put the issue behind us.

∼

Planning

Given the rapidity with which higher education has grown in Nevada—at a rate that has consistently produced the highest or near-highest enrollment increase rates in the nation—it is not surprising that statewide academic planning has taken a back seat to meeting urgent needs. Other factors, including differing growth rates among the institutions and the regional character of Board of Regents membership, have contributed to this situation. In the early 1990s, some regents sought to remedy the absence of serious planning by bringing in external consultants. Resultant discussion produced tensions among the institutions. A case in point was the different responses to the regents' initiative emanating from the two universities. Ours was rather more positive, and that position was taken by some at UNLV as interference with that institution's programmatic development. UNLV president Robert Maxson and I had worked hard, and often successfully, to maintain a collaborative relationship. The strains resulting from the planning discussions led me to put on paper, in a confidential letter for president Maxson's consideration, my candid views on the situation.

It is worth noting, as a postscript, that the planning efforts yielded little fruit in the end and that now, in the new millennium, the need for substantive academic planning, for clear mission differentiation, for new consultants to provide guidance, is once again a Board of Regents priority.

Feb. 5, 1991

Dear Bob:

I would like to keep this letter principally between the two of us ...

The subject is one you and I have never discussed in any depth. Perhaps we should have, before the current spate of academic planning began. It seemed to me that, at the recent meeting between the presidents and planning consultants, you and I were engaged in a little verbal sparring. Perhaps that is inevitable. However, I think it wise for me to set down on paper—so that my position is clear to you—my views on academic planning in our system. I am of two minds about it, as will be suggested by what follows here.

I agree with the consultants that we have no real system of statewide academic planning or planning process in Nevada. The evidence is overwhelming on that point, I believe. The absence of planning is not altogether a minus. That absence has given us great institutional flexibility which, on the whole, has been a decided plus. We have been able to do things, good things, that we would have been constrained from doing were we locked up in a system controlled from the system office and governed by a plan enforced by that office. This is a freedom I would not lightly trade away.

And yet a part of me has always believed that something like the kind of planning suggested by the consultants would one day become necessary. We have had seven institutions exercising that considerable freedom. Inevitably, we will get in one another's way—the two universities, the community colleges, community colleges and universities, universities and [the Desert Research Institute]. And inevitably, we will reach a point where funding problems threaten us, especially in the high-growth situation we are all facing ... It may be, even so, that we will be unable to mount a successful planning effort and so will proceed with business as usual. I am certainly prepared for that result.

When asked about serious academic planning by regents, I have responded with skepticism. I am skeptical, certainly, that the current effort will lead to anything significant. That could only happen if our regents were prepared to take the bit by the teeth, to agree to accept the unavoidably painful consequences of effective planning. Given that our regents are elected, that there are difficult regional implications of planning, that we have an unusual geography, and that there is a whole lot of history and momentum behind that institutional freedom we have enjoyed, the likelihood of our board staying with it for the duration may well be slim. So, I am not a zealot for planning. I believe that, objectively, the time has probably arrived when we should be thinking about planning as a serious enterprise. But I am not convinced that, in our current situation, it is doable ...

I hope that any support I may offer to the argument on behalf of planning will not be taken as portending opposition on my part to the future UNLV seeks to achieve. Such support would be offered with the clear understanding that serious planning will operate to constrain UNR's options as well as UNLV's, as well as those of the other institutions. Those other institutions have some pretty fancy designs on the future that can cause problems among themselves and for the two universities. I suppose it is also unavoidable that the issue of growth enters the planning picture at some point ... No doubt we disagree at least in some measure on the growth issue. That's OK, as long as my position is not misconstrued as an attack on you or UNLV. UNR and UNLV are different institutions, as you have pointed out. UNLV may well have a greater ability, given all the givens, to absorb high growth rates. It is not my business to speculate on that matter. It is my business to point out that UNR does not have that kind of ability. Thus it is necessary for me to seek a place in the system sun for a university that does not want to grow the way others are growing. In that regard, it is a nice irony that occasionally UNR is referred to, at least implicitly, as an institution that is simply not getting the job done in terms of keeping up with its neighbors growth-wise when, in fact, we are growing at a rate which we have sought and which I believe is what we need.

I raise the growth issue for several reasons. One is that I want you to understand that my position is based on an honest appreciation of what growth can do generally and of what it would do particularly to UNR. Second, it seems almost certain that growth will become a central focus of any significant systemwide planning effort. Finally, the question of growth is one of the many distinguishing characteristics of our two institutions. With or without planning, I believe it necessary that UNR and UNLV be understood as different institutions. Too often we are treated as though we are just two peas in the system pod. Little has been done to clearly and meaningfully define and differentiate us. From my perspective, that is the central point made by the consultants: the need for definition and differentiation among all the institutions in the system.

I will argue for that need, planning or no planning. Again, I have a responsibility to do so. It would be good if such argument is not taken as an assault on UNLV or any other institution, or as an attempt to stop program development anywhere.

∾

Free Speech

If there is one issue that has most particularly and emphatically been a source of conflict on college campuses over the years (indeed, over the centuries), it would be this one. It has kindled the passions like no other issue. It has thrown campuses into disarray. It has aligned faculty against administration, or against one another, involved students in demonstrations, aroused public criticism, produced fires and firing, and, on occasion, ruined lives. It has been productive of interesting ironies, as those who have championed freedom of speech in one set of circumstances oppose it in another. It is a big, big issue. It is an issue that has been known, one way or another, to bring great grief to university presidents. Although some room to maneuver is essential because of the wildly variable circumstances in which the issue can come to the fore, I have taken the position that the president's role is to defend the principle of campus freedom of speech to the point of assuring maximum tolerance. Past that point is the ascertainable threat of violence. This side of it, irrespective of point of view, is protection of the speaker(s).

In spring 1995, the federal building in Oklahoma City was blown up, with catastrophic loss of life. In the wake of that tragedy, a radio personality and convicted felon (because of his involvement in the Watergate scandal of the Nixon era) named G. Gordon Liddy was alleged to have said he would shoot first and ask questions later if a federal official came knocking at his door. As fate would have it, Mr. Liddy was scheduled to appear a short time later at a Reno hotel. The hotel opted out, and sought to move Liddy's venue to a campus facility, for the day following our spring Commencement ceremony.

I received lots of mail. And telephone calls. And a few threats. Many ordinarily tolerant campus voices spoke up in favor of barring Mr. Liddy's appearance. Timing was a major concern, with respect to both Commencement and the Oklahoma City bombing. The Faculty Senate held a lengthy debate, and recommended against Liddy's appearance. In the aftermath of my response to that recommendation, set forth below, I received a number of very reproachful communications, and also congratulatory calls and messages from people who heretofore had not bothered to tell me of their commitment to freedom of speech.

Here is my letter to Scott Casper, a very fine young historian who was then Faculty Senate chair, and whose difficult job it was to carry the message of senate opposition to Liddy's speaking engagement:

May 15, 1995

Dear Scott:

I write in response to your memorandum of May 9, requesting the administration to act on a motion by the Faculty Senate at its May 4 meeting. The subject of the motion was Mr. G. Gordon Liddy's speech scheduled at Lawlor Events Center on May 21. The motion suggested that, while the right of free speech is recognized, the timing of Mr. Liddy's appearance is problematical in relation to both Commencement (May 20) and the recent tragedy in Oklahoma City. The administration was asked to withdraw its consent, set forth in an agreement with the sponsor... to the use of Lawlor for Liddy's speech.

I appreciate the senate's significant attention to this question, and its sensitivity to the university's role with regard to freedom of speech. I understand the concern about timing. However, I must respectfully decline to take the requested action. Liddy's appearance here has given rise to an outpouring of written and telephonic messages to my office from people on both sides of the issue. They share, however, a considerable passion on the subject. I offer here a summary of the views expressed by those who, in one degree or another, [agree with] the senate's position. My reaction to these views is also noted below.

As your memorandum observes, the question came to the senate out of a faculty member's concern about "hate speech," Liddy's comments in that connection, and the propriety of providing a campus venue for speech of this kind. Others have expressed to me a similar concern. While such speech is to be deplored, the university ought not place itself in the position of censoring it. Several years ago (1990), as you know, the [faculty] senate rejected a proposal to ban so-called "fighting words," an appropriate action I believe. Later (1992), it passed an anti-harassment policy, taking care in the process to state that:

> the university is a place to think the unthinkable, to challenge themunchallengeable and even utter the unspeakable in support of one's ideas.*

I concur. The senate's position here is similar to that taken by the Supreme Court of the United States in the case of *Terminiello V. Chicago* (1949):

> A function of free speech ... is to invite dispute. It may indeed bestserve its high purpose when it induces a condition of unrest, creates dissatisfaction with conditions as they are, or even stirs people to anger.

It is in this light that the university has traditionally understood the First Amendment's application to the campus. Further, of all social institutions, the university should be most friendly toward and protective of the right of free expression. We agree on that, I'm sure. In my opinion, Mr. Liddy's speech falls within the spirit of the senate's 1992 statement and within the wide boundaries set by *Terminiello*. I

---

* ......From a Senate "Request for Action" dated June 16, 1992.

should note that at least one of my correspondents argued that Liddy crosses the line established by the court in another case —the well-known limitation against yelling "fire" in a crowded theater. I can only respectfully disagree. Another person wrote from a conviction that Liddy should be refused a venue here because "he fosters the ideal of murder." Addressing me, the writer added (with a touch of unintended irony): "May you suffer damning consequences and be destroyed by your assistance to [Mr. Liddy]." I must respectfully disagree with this sentiment, as well.

Several individuals have suggested that Liddy could be prohibited from speaking here because he is an ex-felon. I have not heard this rationale before. Certainly, the university has not employed it as a basis for denying a speaker a campus venue. During the current academic year, for example, David Hilliard, an ex-felon and former member of the Black Panther Party, spoke at an event sponsored by a campus organization. There have been other examples. Indeed, Mr. Liddy has appeared here once before, in 1992, and then on the same program as another ex-felon (Timothy Leary). Perhaps those who hold to this view believe that only certain kinds of felonies would give just cause for limiting speech on campus, though making such determinations would be, I think, an inappropriate exercise for a university.

Another point made by callers and writers on the subject is that, by offering Liddy a campus venue, the university is saying, in effect, that it endorses his views. This is a puzzling observation. The university offers a forum to dozens of speakers every year, representing a great diversity of political, academic and other points of view. To offer a forum, of course, is not to endorse the views expressed, not in the Liddy case nor in those dozens of others.

The matter of timing, as a basis for refusing a forum, may be the most compelling argument. It may be that Commencement will lose for some something of its luster as a result of Liddy's appearance the day after the ceremony. I doubt that this will be a major concern for many. Of greater weight is the temporal relationship to Oklahoma City. Given Mr. Liddy's remarks in the aftermath of the bombing, we could wish his speech were scheduled at some distant date. It is also true that the time, place, and manner of expression are proper objects of university involvement. However, in this instance, we are accommodating a request from an external agency for a time already established. Moreover, one understands that it is precisely timing that often makes speech controversial, and thus gives greater consequence to the need to tend to the obligations of the First Amendment and of long-standing academic tradition. Such is the case, I believe, with the matter at hand.

The administration's first response to the request for Mr. Liddy to use Lawlor was to raise questions about public safety. We presented demanding and expensive conditions to the sponsoring agency, which agreed to meet every one of them. Once that was done, it seemed to me that freedom of speech became the issue. No reason advanced thus far for inhibiting that freedom in the Liddy case has been persuasive. I understand the care and concern people bring to the issue and, again, I respect the position taken by the senate. Notwithstanding, and for the reasons outlined above, Mr. Liddy's appearance will continue as scheduled.

∿

Chapter Nine

∾

A Bit of Whimsy

FINALLY, there is this need I have now and again to indulge a penchant toward inelegant wit, to tickle a funnybone (my own included), to deploy puns across a page of paper in unseemly large numbers. Once the act is done, the page cries out for an audience, since for a punster the reward is to know that those on the receiving end are groaning. Amid the cares and worries of the workday, these efforts can provide relief. As I have noted, they have a certain therapeutic value. In the interest of telling the whole story, of showing something of the soft underbelly of one president's letter-writing routine, I have taken the liberty of choosing—from an embarrassingly large collection—a mercifully small number of specimens. They can be found below. Not all dwell in the realm of low humor. Some that do are stimulated by letters from like-minded friends. Others cover topics such as an unusual gift, a dress code, an overdue book, and the proper translation (or, as my friend John would say, "Apodictic interpretation,") of a cautionary Latin phrase. Remembering that, as the late poet and critic Mark Van Doren said, "Wit is the only wall between us and the dark," the unusual gift would be a good place to begin.

∾

JoAnn

When to everyone's surprise, my own in particular, I managed to complete a decade of service as president, the regents threw a party for me. Some unconventional presents were given to me on this occasion, including one from our loyal alumni council. I am frequently called upon to speak at council meetings. There are those members (probably a tiny minority) who seem to think that my comments are often (a few might say *always*) rather more circumlocutory than the situation demands. Accordingly, the chair of the council presented me with a clock to commemorate my anniversary. It is, however, a three-minute clock, intended to set a time limit on my council speeches. The chair was JoAnn, and I must say that she was quite enthusiastic in giving me this gift. Of course, I write a thank-you letter.

March 1, 1988

Dear JoAnn:

Thanks so much for the presentation at my 10th anniversary reception. I will be sure to bring this thoughtful gift with me to future meetings of the Alumni Council. Further, I will attempt to contain my remarks within the three minutes the speech timer allows, though it is discomfiting to consider that it takes longer than that to boil an egg. Given that, my next speech to the council may be a little raw (but then, I know you and the members can take a yolk).

∾

Tricia

For two years (1993-95) I had the honor to serve as president of the National Collegiate Athletic Association. This was something like having a second (though unpaid) full-time job. It involved, among other responsibilities, a good deal of flying around the country, attending many meetings and chairing a number of committees. I had been active in the association for six years prior to becoming president, and had observed that the dress at many NCAA gatherings was a bit too starchy to suit my taste. Now that I held the reins of power (well, not a whole lot of power), I was determined to change this, at least in a measure. I served as chair of the Executive Committee—at that time, the NCAA's final decision-making authority—and of a search committee for a new executive director (the CEO position for the association).

Thus emboldened, I write a letter to my good friend, Tricia Bork, a senior NCAA executive and the key staffer to these two committees. I enclose a Gumpertz cartoon showing a male figure dressed to the nines and then, in states of increasing dishabille, to the sevens, fives, threes, twos and ones. The cartoon is intended to provide guidance on future meeting dress, as in the event it really did. I am told that this is the greatest legacy of my tenure as NCAA president.

June 11, 1993

Dear Tricia:

Enclosed is a dress-code chart to be employed for meetings of the Executive Committee and the Executive Director Search Committee. I regret that the chart is not gender equitable, but I believe that members of the unrepresented gender, being generally smarter than members of the represented gender, will be able to use the chart to make the right choice of attire.

Perhaps you could send the chart to the members of the aforementioned committees so that, at future meetings, they are not in peril of appearing in improper apparel. When the meeting notice is sent, it can simply say: "Dress code three," or whatever. We shall try to avoid nines and to keep in mind that, in some jurisdictions, you can be arrested for a dress code one.

Many thanks.

∼

Herb (and Mark)

Herb is Herb Caen, for decades a celebrated columnist for the *San Francisco Chronicle*. The late Mr. Caen had written a best-selling book 40 years earlier about his adopted city. One of the university's graduates had borrowed it from our library. It took him awhile to return it. It seems to me the story is worth Caen's attention, so I tell him about it.

Oct. 23, 1991

Dear Herb:

I recently received a book, a letter, and a check from a well-known and much-loved local publicist named Mark Curtis. I thought you might be interested.

The book is familiar to you, since you wrote it: *Don't Call It Frisco.* Mark checked it out of the university library in 1953. He returned it this week. In his accompanying letter, he observes:

> I figure the book is about 13,870 days overdue. Today's fine is 10 cents a day. My wife informs me that the book fine in the early '50s was three cents a day. So I have taken the average: 13 cents divided by two is 6.5 cents. Six and a half cents times 13,870 days is $901.55

Just to round it off, and probably because he enjoyed the book so much and so long, he settled at a figure of $1,000 and enclosed a check for that amount with his letter.

The university is in your debt for providing Mark with a thousand dollars (and 38 years) worth of entertainment.

∼

Dave

Professor David Seibert is the longtime chair of the theatre department at the university. He is a man with a fine, and sometimes wicked, sense of humor. I had referred to him over the years a number of the peculiar letters I received, which the better part of valor suggested I ought not answer. He was asked to compose responses that would never leave the university, but which the two of us might share with a small, selected audience. Dave always accepted this fanciful charge, and produced in time a quaintly jolly record of unmailed messages.

I had written him a letter, for some forgotten reason, offering him (in jest) three new faculty members, individuals who had come to be numbered among my least favorite citizens of the university. Dave is inspired to write back, expressing his gratitude and (as he often did) requesting permission to use a certain lethal device in the performance of a play. I respond in what might be called a disjointed fashion.

June 8, 1994

Dear Joe:

Green, Gray, and Brown all in my department! What can I say? I figured we'd get a new position ... but I never dreamed we'd get three! And the positions are already filled! ... Joe, I don't know how to thank you. I hope you don't get hassled about cronyism for this one. This is the nicest thing you've done for me ...

New subject: The regents' firearm policy requires your permission to bring guns to campus, and you've always been gracious about approving whatever mayhem we've wanted to undertake in the name of theater. But we've got a special problem for Jim Bernardi's upcoming production of *Scarlet Pimpernel*. We need a working guillotine. Have to lop off a couple of heads right smartly in the first scene. The Regents Handbook is silent on guillotines. So we don't need permission or anything.

It is more blessed to ask forgiveness than permission, but ... I thought it best to implicate you in whatever might go wrong.

We can't afford to rent or buy a real guillotine, so we're making one out of scrap materials. It will take a lot of trial and error to get the thing working properly, but we've got plenty of time and the show has a huge cast.

So, just thought you'd like to know what's coming off over here.

Again, thanks a million for the new positions.

Sincerely yours,
Dave

June 13, 1994

Dear Dave:

Thanks for your letter of glowing appreciation and imminent dismemberment.

Is there any connection (or, for that matter, disconnection) between the reference to your three new professors in the first paragraph and the lopping requirement noted in paragraph two?   If so, the university will provide severance pay. It will be a shear pleasure to do so.

I hope the *Scarlet Pimpernel* production will not have a negative impact on our head count enrollment. Do those who lose their heads get top billing?

By the way, do you suppose the guillotine is the source of the term "splitting headache"?

I apologize. No more cutting remarks. If the show is a success, I'll buy drinks for the cast. Separators all around.

~

Jack

Jack is another of my good friends with an antic sense of humor. He writes from time to time to offer droll observations on matters of interest to him. I try to respond in kind. He works at Carnegie Mellon University, an institution founded a century ago by Andrew Carnegie and to which he imparted his motto: "My Heart is in the Work." That motto arises in the following correspondence, which begins with a letter from John commenting on a book of mine.

Sept. 7, 1994

Dear Dr. Crowley:

Your recent book, *No Equal in the World*, has changed my life. After the first reading, I found that I no longer suffered the nightly effects of sonorem tremens, a rare African malady which I contracted while fighting Ennui during the Boer War. By the second time through, I was being visited frequently by a large and rather virile Cajun tigress, Bertha deBleuse, who seemed intrigued by the Metaphors and Chapter Notes which I read to her in a lilting voice as we shared croppers.

In my third and most recent reading, a fortnight ago, I found that Ennui had returned, by the night train from Pretoria, my eyelids fluttered uncontrollably (a further attraction to Bertha) and the Cuban boat-people seem to have invaded Pittsburgh by the Monongahela river.

As you will no doubt understand, therefore, I eagerly await your next tome ... to see what further dimensions and dementians it may form in my life.

Sincerely,
An Aphid Reader

Dec. 9, 1994

Dear Jack:

Well, your letter of Sept. 7 finally showed up. (It came by knight train from Malta.) This is the one about my book, *No Iguana in the Whirl*. I was disturbed to learn about your sonorem tremens but relieved that the malady was contracted in the Boer War, since I previously understood it to be an ailment suffered by soldiers in the Mexican War of 1848 (specifically those involved in that well known engagement, The Tremendous Battle of Sonora). But I didn't believe you could be that old. Now 1898, that's believable.

The Tremendous Battle of Sonora, as you may recall, was waged on the other side by large lizards, several of whom became prisoners of war and subsequently married an American woman named Elizabeth Taylor, who later made a movie about her experience called *Nine of the Iguanas*. My book, of course, is about one who did not make it to the altar with Liz but instead became a ... college president and died in a boating accident when caught in an eddy named Nelson. It's true, to be sure, that he did intervene, as *tertius gaudens*, in one of the troubled marriages, from which Liz extracted herself to pursue a small but devilishly handsome gecko. You will remember that the original Tertius was a Roman soldier who stood guard at the time Cleopatra and Antony got together and who was so moved by the courtship that he made a movie about it (released through Twentieth Centurion Fox) with Liz in the starring role, and wrote a book on the subject as well, entitled, I think, *Keep the Asp-idistra Flying*. Or, well, it could have been ... by George! it was ... some other bloke that wrote the book. Richard Burton, possibly, who played opposite Liz in the Cleopatra film, appeared later as ... a well-sauced iguana in search of eddyfication, served as British consul at an Adriatic port city (writing there his famous *Bonjour Trieste*), and—with a chap named Speke to whom he eventually stopped speaking— tried to find the source of the Nile, a subject that had intrigued him ever since his dalliance with Cleo downstream from the Aswan Dam (which, by the way, was designed by a faro dealer from Reno, who in later life was arrested—by Keystone Cheops—for conducting a pyramid scheme and, on facing a firing squad for this offense, asked for one last ziggurat).

As for Ms. Taylor, she has been known occasionally to take on the personality of a virile Cajun tigress named Bertha de Bleuse, of whom it is related that she never metaphor she didn't like, who is said to have lost considerable weight since she went on an exclusive diet of Carnegie melons, and whose mantra is "My Heart is in the Work," though previously she left it (her heart, not her mantra) in San Francisco, where she had a fling with the great detective, Sam Spade, after encountering him at a football game between the Forty-Niners and the Maltese Falcons.

Regards.

∽

Ted

For a few years in the early 1990s I exchanged notes and letters with my friend Ted, who possessed a mordant wit and a writing ability to go with it. At one point, we fell into a long-distance written conversation regarding the origins and meaning of certain expressions—the "off ox," for example, and "hog on ice," and "in a pig's eye." I asked him to do some research on these matters, and also on a football player made famous by James Thurber. Ted writes in response to that request.

———————

July 25, 1993

Dear Joe:

I apologize for the delay in responding to the research challenge that you extended to me in your July 12 letter. While it is true, as you proffer, that good research always leads to more questions, it is equally true that research—good, bad or, in this case, inane—takes time. But enough rationale: on to your questions.

First, if the driver changed positions, would the off ox be the one on the left? Perhaps only in England, you suggest. Well, in England, the ox is haute cuisine, of course, along with tripe and Yorkshire pudding and various recipes for boiled cardboard. And consider the poor ox if the driver changes only to the center of the wagon, causing the ox to lurch determinedly from ditch to ditch, much as our nation does as its [leaders] change from left to right, and then pretend to sit in the center...

Of course, as Washington Irving wrote, "There is a certain relief in change, even though it be from bad to worse, as I have found in traveling in a stagecoach, that it is often a comfort to shift one's position and be bruised in a new place." I can find no indication that Mr. Irving gave a passing thought to the ox, off or otherwise.

Second, you ask if Thurber's Ohio State football player could be called an oxymoron, which, of course, he could, thus making his name indistinguishable from so many others who take up that sport. Actually, his name was distinguishable. It was Bolenciecwcz, a Thurberesque study in misplaced vowels...

> One day when we were on the subject [in economics class] of transportation and distraction, it came Bolenciecwcz's turn to answer a question. "Name one means of transportation," the professor said to him. No light came into the big tackle's eyes. "Just any means of transportation," said the professor. Bolenciecwcz sat staring at him. "That is," pursued the professor, "any medium, agency or method of going from one place to another." Bolenciecwcz had the look of a man who is being led into a trap. "You may choose among steam, horse-drawn or electrically propelled vehicles," said the instructor. "I might suggest the one which we commonly take in making long journeys across land." There was a profound silence in which everybody stirred uneasily, including Bolenciecwcz and [professor] Bassum. Mr. Bassum abruptly broke this silence in an amazing manner. "Choo-choo-choo," he said, in a low voice, and turned instantly scarlet. He glanced appealingly around the room. All of us, of course, shared Mr.

Bassum's desire that Bolenciecwcz should stay abreast of the class in economics, for the Illinois game, one of the hardest and most important of the season, was only a week off. "Too, too, toooooot!" some student with a deep voice moaned, and we all looked encouragingly at Bolenciecwcz. Somebody else gave a fine imitation of a locomotive letting off steam. Mr. Bassum himself rounded off the little show. "Ding, dong, ding, dong," he said, hopefully. Bolenciecwcz was staring at the floor now, trying to think ...

"How did you come to college this year?" asked the professor...

"M' father sent me," said the football player.

"What on?" asked Bassum...

"Train," said Bolenciecwcz.

"Quite right," said the professor.[*]

Third, I already have provided the requested explanation of "a hog on ice," knowing that your peace, spelled as you wish, of mind depended on it. The problem is your request for the meaning of "in a pig's eye." The derivation is difficult to discover... I focused on it ferociously, though. "I'd give my eye tooth for the answer," I asserted. "I can do this; I used to date acuity. Just give me rheum." To the naked eye, I've always been a good pupil, so I should have a 20-20 chance. And if I'm wrong, I can always issue a refraction. But ... you have backed me into a cornea, put me into orbit. You have a lot of nerve, obviously optic. I have a blind spot. I could try to make a joke, but it would be vitreous humor. I wouldn't want to be superciliary. I have a fixation on this, but I just can't find a palpebral solution, let alone optical. I find myself bleary-eyed, stymied, as it were. Walleye just don't know. We'll just have to facet. Iris my case. Myopia is now yours.

"Some men there are love not a gaping pig," said Shakespeare in "The Merchant of Venice." I'm certainly one of them.

Sincerely,
Ted

---

[*] Thurber, James, from the short story, "University Days," in *Thurber Carnival*. New York: The Modern Library, 1957, pp. 223-225.

Aug. 2, 1993

Dear Ted:

Your letter ... provided many chuckles, but this is no surprise when one remembers that among the bovid brothers of the ox is the yak. Likewise, the water buffalo. That young man at Penn might have done better to refer to the raucous celebrants outside his dormitory window as oxen or yaks, or even as ruminants.

I am puzzled by this, though: Can you explain to me why standing is often given to the term "ruminant scholars"? Perhaps this term, like Mr. Bolenciecwcz, is an oxymoron. On the other hand, maybe it is simply redundant one way or the other. I'll expect an answer.

Exception is hereby taken to your critique of Yorkshire pudding; also, by implication, of oxtail soup, a wondrous dish. I developed a taste for the local cuisine while on leave in England a few years back. At Oxford, of course.

I'll be honest with you. At first glance, your paragraph on porcine acuity aroused in me a favorable reaction. "Hey," I said, "the eyes-man cometh." When I read it again, however, I could only grunt, "Get outta my sight!" The only thing you omitted was an old saw or two. Such excessive punning, as you should know, is punishable: An eye for an eye, after all. Forty lashes, maybe. Or you could see some prism time. I have a detachment of lawyers on retina. One of them will be in contacts with you. Don't cross him or you'll be winking at a strabismal fate. You need to understand that you've made a spectacle of yourself and you'll carry astigma forever. You cannot duct it, not even if you shed tears of contrition and seek forgiveness on bended pince-nez.

For the moment, my advice to you is to take a few days off. Hang a sign on your door that says, "Gone vision." While you are away, consider that the clue to the pig's eye may lie in the sty. Ruminate on that awhile. And remember, things cud be worse.

Finally, I saw a gaping pig last weekend and loved him, indeed squealed in delight at the sight of him. He is of the pot-bellied persuasion and he belongs to my brother. His name is Hamilton Lardner Crowley.

I thought it was Sir Francis Bacon who wrote about gaping pigs. Thus, your quotation from Shakespeare was a real loining experience for me.

∼

John

Finally, there is that business of the Latin phrase, and the exchange of correspondence it generated. It started in the summer of 1982, when an associate of mine (let's call her Betty), who was leaving the university, wrote me a farewell letter. The letter ended as follows: *Ab illegitimis ne vexeris!* I knew some Latin, having once served as an altar boy, and I thought I understood what Betty was telling me. Just to be sure, though, I turned for help to my good friend, John Marschall. John, a former Roman Catholic priest and later a professor of religious history at the university, was serving at the time as an assistant to me. Our exchange begins innocently enough, but then, as the reader will discern, gets out of hand:

———————

Dear John:
    Translation, please.

———————

Dear Joe:
    "Don't be bugged (vexed) by the bastards."

———————

John:
    Is this roughly the same as *"Illigitimis non carborundum?"* (Don't let the bastards get you down.)

———————

Joe:
    Yes, or *Nil Illegitimis carborundum* (depending on whether you are in the "vocative" of "hortatory" mood!)

———————

John:

Probably hortatory. I don't recall that I have ever been in a vocative mood, although there are some things, I'm sure, that my mother never told me. If I am hortatory, am I *nil* or *non?*

Joe:

I would say you are generally ahortative, which is not to say you are *un/nil/non* or *prohortative*. Sometimes you have demonstrated cohortativeness (Irish Mafia syndrome), which has hort you.

It would probably be best to return the letter to Betty for an apodictic interpretation, translation or exegesis.

John:

I think the matter is not of sufficient imphort to refer to Betty, though given what you have accused me of, I may refer it to my lawyer. Seems to me to be a clear case of hort tort, for which you should be held accountable. Of course, you may have fallen into a vocative mood when you made these accusations, and that would be an extenuating circumstance. I'm sure, in any case, that your hort was in the right place.

Joe:

Before I abhort this rethort to your last rephort, I should explain that I've had a short snhort.

In view of recent epistles and other communications (which may not be gospel) concerning effhorts by some to exthort power, it is incumbent on me to confess that the original latinism—i.e., *illegitimis*— was ablative plural. That is to say the original correspondent (Betty) was attempting to identify more than one *persona illigitima* of dubious purpose. *Il faut que nous parler tout de suite.*

John:

We are enjoined by the Good Book—whether in epistles or the gospels, I'm not sure—to love our enemies, to turn the other cheek. Or, if not enjoined, we are surely exhorted, to accept our fellows, whorts and all. It may not be rechorted as a mhortal sin to do otherwise, but I take this as an horter from Higher Authority. Acchortingly, it makes no difference to me whether it is ablative singular or ablative plural. These *personae illegitimae* are not *personae non gratae* to me. I open my arms to them, and my cheeks as well, and I say (or sing):

"Let Me Call You Suitehort!"

∾

Chapter Ten

~

The Last Word: A Brief Memoir

"And now, here for a few brief remarks is the president."

HOW OFTEN IN THE COURSE OF 23 YEARS OF SERVICE I have heard that introduction. And how often I have ignored it. I am a person for whom long-windedness is the stuff of legend. It was only natural for those experienced in my deportment at the podium to suggest, when they introduced me, that my remarks ought to be brief and— adding to the admonition—that they be few as well. I tend to be a stream-of-consciousness kind of speaker, one thought leading to another and thence to another, so that, if I am not careful, I can turn a welcome into a treatise or an answer into a dissertation. There are those who believe that I have kissed the Blarney Stone too often (in truth, only twice), or that perhaps public loquaciousness is the other side of the coin of a reserved private temperament. I have always simply (and maybe smugly) maintained that, because I am the president of a great and growing university, I just have a lot to talk about.

In any case, I have talked a lot these 20-plus years. I hope that, in some meaningful measure, what I have had to say has contributed to the campus conversation. This book, of course, has focused not so much on what I have said but on what I have written, entries I have passed along on paper to the continuing discourse of the university. There is no place quite like an academic institution for conducting a lengthy discussion. The comments, written or verbal, can be mean: I remember the story of two sixth-century rhetoricians who argued for 15 days and nights about the vocative case of a particular Latin word and who—the argument not being resolved—thereafter attacked one another with weapons. More often, I like to think, the conversation is as Alexander Pope would have it: a "sweeter banquet of the mind." While not partaking of every course, and finding some partaken of distasteful, I have nevertheless been grateful to have a seat at the banquet table. When one happens to have the good fortune to serve as president, that seat offers special opportunities. It affords certain speaking prerogatives, yes, but better yet for me has been the license I have had to write and to submit what I have written to the conversation. That is a perquisite I will miss.

The speeches and the essays and the letters, most of them anyway, grew out of experiences I have had in a job that has been immensely rewarding. The time comes, of course, when last words are spoken and written. One recalls being invited, on previous occasions, to imagine what those last words might be.

Back in 1987, I was asked to participate in a program of last lectures at the university. In an earlier era, such programs were popular on college campuses, and this was an attempt to resurrect them for the pleasure of a later generation. Mine was to be, in last lecture theory, a farewell address. It was an opportunity to reflect on my nine years as the institution's president, to consider the highs and lows, and to convey some sense of the values I had brought to the task. So I prepared carefully, gave meticulous attention to the requirements of splendid oratory, and looked forward to the night I would address the assembled multitudes.

The multitudes, however, did not assemble. My wife and children were there that night, perforce. And some friends, dragooned into service as listeners. And a couple of drifters seeking warmth on a cold January evening. Seventeen people in all. And a photographer for the student newspaper, which, next morning, ran a front page picture showing me giving my last lecture to row after row after row of empty seats. I took comfort in the anticipated exaltation of those who have humbled themselves.

The following year, I published a book of essays and speeches that included, as a penultimate piece, a retrospective of my first decade in office. I wrote about the job as a learning experience, about its limited powers and its seductive invitation to don the emperor's new clothes. I described what an essential place of freedom a university campus must be, and observed that the responsibility of leadership in such a place is "to align all that freedom behind a common vision, to forge from a diversity of people and programs a unity of purpose." I offered thanks to the cast of thousands with whom I had shared the institution for what I characterized as "one hell of a grand time." I remember wondering, as I penned those lines, what kind of emotions I would be feeling if this piece was, in effect, my *real* farewell speech. But that day, I thought, would still be a little while in coming.

Well, it's here! We are not dealing with a theoretical last lecture at this point, or a decade's retrospective. The age of farewells has arrived, although it has taken more than a little while to make the trip. From the time I conjectured about those final day feelings, it has taken nearly 13 years.

There's that number again: 13. It's my lucky number, and I have bored people to tears writing and talking about it; about becoming the university's 13th president in the 13th month of interim service in the position, the interim job having come my way during my 13th year at Nevada, whose main campus is at Exit 13 of Interstate 80. On several auspicious presidential occasions, when I counted the slices in my daily grapefruit, the number was...13!

Don't ask why I count grapefruit slices. It's just a whimsical little habit of mine, a way to put my mind in idle while preparing to take on the challenges of a truly daunting day. A day like the one that now dawns... a farewell kind of day; a day for memories.

I remember when a new decade made landfall in 1980. It was difficult then to find reasons to argue that there might be a bright time ahead for the university. I gave my first State of the University address that September, and I spoke of hope. The analysts of higher education's future carried a different message. They wrote of declining prestige and priority for American universities and colleges. They recited a litany of something close to despair. In the years that followed, it began to look as though those analysts were right. The university came to know hard times. The Nevada economy went sour. In Carson City, we found ourselves on the defensive. We lacked credibility. We had little clout. We were a ready target for criticism.

Yet, somehow, we put all that behind us. We maintained hope. We grew bolder. We built credibility. We talked realistically about a brighter future. We had a very successful legislative session in 1985, and then again in 1987 and 1989. We could see the outlines of a new and promising era for the university. It would not have been appropriate in 1980 to entertain a vision of greatness. We were a good, solid institution then, but there was so much to do and so little with which to do it. By the end of the '80s, however, we could say we were ready to take on that vision. And the decade that followed proved that we were.

The 1990s saw a reawakened commitment to undergraduate education, a new core curriculum and honors program, significant growth in graduate studies, a remarkable expansion of research, a rededication to our land grant charter and its attendant outreach obligations, the completion of the most successful fund-raising campaign in the history of Nevada, outstanding new faculty members arriving every year, new university buildings abounding, and enrollment increases that carried us by the year 2000 to a student population exceeding 13,000 (and there's that number again!). In the same year—this year—we reached the top echelon of American universities in the Carnegie classification, the most prestigious form of recognition in the business.

These were busy decades, the '80s and '90s, full of adventure and accomplishment, and of memories. But one doesn't just remember the era; one remembers the years, particular years. There was 1979, for example, before those decades got underway, when it appeared that my tenure as president would be a brief one. A campus search committee, for understandable reasons, did not believe I had the qualifications to turn the interim presidency into the real thing. It would be impossible to forget the ensuing controversy, the daily headlines, the anger and elation of those months. Or the anxious hours of closed debate among the regents one March day, that ended with a 6-2 vote in my favor. That was 1979.

I was back in trouble in 1983, and, indeed, went to bed after the first day of a Board of Regents meeting that spring expecting to be fired the next morning. The issue was the hiring of a vice president, played out against a background of intense debate over dicey systemwide policy questions. Guardian angels intervened that night. I was allowed to keep the job. So was the new vice president, and he is in office still, 17 years after both of us were nearly shown the door.

And there was 1989, when a powerful legislator declared publicly that my time had run its course and the regents should damn-well remove me from the president's chair forthwith. This was headline stuff again, and cause for weeks of speculation. I was not worried about keeping my job, since I had strong support from the board, other legislators, and faculty leaders. However, the incident helped convince me that 11 years was long enough in a position that wears away one's passion for the work. The fire in my belly had gone out, and I so informed the regents. Instead of accepting this verifiable conclusion, however, they awarded me a leave and told me to get out of town for a semester. I went away that fall, far away, to Oxford, and lived the scholar's life. I came back reinvigorated, the intestinal fire alight once more, ready for the next 11 years, for that decade of success that was the 1990s.

I remember other years, the ones I spent laboring in the NCAA vineyards, pursuing the cause of athletics reform. This service culminated in my election as president of that large, complex, and troubled organization. People would ask me how someone like me—a guy from Nevada, of all places—ended up as NCAA president. I didn't have a rich background in athletic administration. I had not been a college athlete, or much of an athlete at all. I couldn't make it as a boxer, Mike Feld having bested me in a three round split-decision at the Knights of Columbus hall when I was in the second grade. (Mike was in first grade.) As for baseball, "good field, no hit" was a phrase that fit me perfectly, emphasis on the "no." My football career, as a blocking back in the old single-wing formation, resulted in a badly broken finger, a paralyzing pinching of a shoulder nerve, a severe and prolonged attack of what we used to call water on the knee, a nose that was relocated to another part of my face, and a decision that I was better suited for other duties.

And then there was basketball. In those long ago days, if you were 6 feet tall, the coach made you the center. I was 6 feet tall. The coach said to me, "You're the center, until you prove otherwise."

I proved otherwise.

So, I don't know how it came to pass that I was asked to lead the NCAA for two years. As with other significant occurrences in my life, this was something that just seemed to fall out of a tree and land on my head. Maybe Calvin said it best (that would be the great philosopher from the comic strip, *Calvin and Hobbes*): "It's not so much being in the right place at the right time. It's getting to the right place and hanging around for awhile." I hung around the NCAA for 10 years, and those years are still ripe with fine memories.

So is that portion of each odd-numbered year, covering the late winter and spring, a season when the governor and legislature forge the state's future in Carson City.

The American people are inclined to think ill of their elected officials, members of a despised tribe known as politicians. We don't stop to consider that these officials, to be successful, must practice in public what the rest of us routinely do in private: the art of compromise. I had developed a pretty good understanding of the public political life by the time 1978 rolled around. I was a teacher of government and politics, had been an active volunteer in election campaigns, and had seen frequent duty as an observer of the legislative process. It is fair to say, as well, that I had standing as a campus politician. None of these experiences qualified me for service as a university president, of course. Still, when my predecessor in this position was summarily fired by the Board of Regents in February, 1978, it was precisely this background that led a large campus committee to propose my name for the interim presidency. The university—Nevada higher education in general—was at that time held in low esteem in Carson City. The committee suggested a 16 month appointment for me—never imagining, given my lack of administrative qualifications, that I might somehow stay longer—in the interest of having me on the scene for the 1979 legislative session. That's how it all began.

I joined the system chancellor, the chairman of the Board of Regents, and other presidents at a hearing of the Assembly Ways and Means Committee one year later. This was my first visit to the legislature as the president. It was a memorable one. Within five minutes, the lot of us had been ejected from the hearing by the committee chair (the same gentleman who, as it turned out, demanded ten years later that the regents eject me from the presidency). The system budget request had been prepared in the wrong format, reason enough for the chair to cast us into the outer darkness. This was a commentary on the low state of our credibility, as well as on the committee chairman's dislike for the chancellor. Bob Cashell, who then presided over the Board of Regents and who was not accustomed to life in the outer darkness, asked me to go forth and repair the damage.

That assignment took six years, until we had that great legislative victory in the 1985 session. But then again, it was a task never completed, because you don't simply one day arrive at a point where you have access and influence and stay there forever. You have to maintain that position. Given the growing, complicated, and contentious system of higher education in Nevada, this can be hard duty. That system has managed from time to time to follow faulty legislative strategies, raise legislative eyebrows about assorted policies, make enemies of people one needs to have as friends, or find new ways to shoot off its toes. Indeed, as recently as 1999, we showed a remarkable capacity for taking pistol practice on our pedal digits. We survived it, though, maintained our standing, even prospered a bit as we relearned the ancient lesson that a united front can see us through.

I have fought the good fight for 11 biennial sessions of the legislature now, and stored up remembrances of each of them. Most of all, I'll remember the people with whom I worked: Lobbyists like the formidable fellow in whose company—plus that of a tough committee chairman—I had a drink one evening in 1979. The lobbyist did not stop at one; by my awe-struck actual count, he had 24 martinis. I was seeking support from the chairman for an important budget item. At the end of his martini marathon, the lobbyist observed that he had to work on a bill draft, raised his ample bulk to a steady standing position, turned to the legislator and said in a voice as sober as if he had consumed nary a drop, "Mr. Chairman, be sure to give Crowley what he wants tomorrow." He turned out early the next day, with his bill draft done. The chairman found the money for my budget item.

I'll remember the governors, too, all of whom treated me well: Mike O'Callaghan, a good friend from my days in partisan politics; Bob List, whose bad luck it was to serve during Nevada's first recession in half-a-century; Dick Bryan, a former student body president at Nevada; Bob Miller, a strong supporter of higher education and a man who wasn't sure he wanted to be governor but held the office longer than anyone ever had; and Kenny Guinn, another old friend and, for a year, a fellow university president.

And the legislators, certainly, a raft of them. That would include the late Jim Gibson, a senator from Clark County, a man of quiet resolve who—once the biennial battles had played themselves out—could step in, get the conflicts settled, and close down a legislative session as though he had been born to the work. And the late assemblyman, Marvin Sedway, who chaired the Ways and Means Committee for several sessions, was an advocate for higher education, put his views on the table without dressing them up for popular consumption, and refused to go gently into that good night. And Joe Dini, the long-standing Speaker of the Assembly, who was always ready to lend an ear and find a way to get done what needed doing. Much of the expansion of higher education's resources in Nevada carries his mark. Senator Ray Rawson and the late assemblywoman Jan Evans shared a generosity of spirit and perspective that embraced a multitude of worthy causes and an undeviating willingness to assist a struggling university president. Assembly Majority Leader Richard Perkins, Lynn Hettrick, the Assembly Minority Leader, Morse Arberry, another chair of Ways and Means, John Marvel, a long-time member of that committee, Assemblywoman Barbara Cegavske, and Senator Bernice Martin-Mathews were ever available for an audience and sage advice. Sue Wagner, who had a distinguished career in both legislative houses, and as lieutenant governor, offered wise counsel on many an occasion. And there were other helpful legislators, whose number, through those 11 sessions, is legion.

And there was Bill Raggio. It's a wonder he ever forgave me. In 1970, he ran for United States Senator against the incumbent, Howard Cannon. Those were difficult days, when the university was caught up in the turmoil of war in Vietnam, marching in the streets, and students demanding certain privileges not previously considered appropriate for them to exercise. The campus became a campaign issue, and, thinking Mr. Raggio was on the wrong side of that issue, I wrote a critical letter to the editor of the local newspaper. The paper, not friendly to the Raggio campaign, published it as an editorial. It was a humorous, though pointed, letter. It could not have pleased candidate Raggio, who lost that election. My letter had little to do with the loss, but it seemed to me likely to be something that would stick in the craw. A few years later, Raggio was elected to the Nevada State Senate. A few years after that, I became president of the university. Would that stick-in-the-craw letter of mine, I wondered, now become a bone of contention?

In the event, Senator Raggio, a gracious man, did not mention the letter until 20 more years had passed. We were having lunch one day in Carson City, during a legislative session. He was then the Senate majority leader, as well as chairman of the Finance Committee. We had become good friends. My long-ago letter, he suddenly observed, had not been a friendly one. That was it. I bought lunch.

Senator Raggio is a masterful legislator. Over the years, no one could surpass his ability to shroud his hole card(s) in a veil of secrecy for months on end. No one could play the card(s) with greater skill when the end game arrived in Carson City. Higher education has always been a major priority for him. So it has been my good fortune, despite that nervy letter of mine 30 years ago, to often have a seat of sorts at the table (or at least in the anteroom) when that game was in progress. A large part of such success as I have had in the legislature is due to Bill Raggio's steadfast support for the Nevada university and community college system, and his willingness (except for one tiny reminder) to let a sleeping letter lie.

I'll remember legislative incidents as well, such as the recitation by an unfriendly committee member of the extensive travel habits of a particular university administrator. The legislator had detailed information on the many trips the administrator had taken, this information having been provided, in the grand Nevada tradition, by a faculty member who wasn't traveling much at all. The recitation occurred at a time when *Naked City* was among the nation's favored television programs, one that always opened with a New York detective saying, against a background of the Manhattan skyline, "There are 8 million stories in the naked city."

When the legislator completed his recital, he fixed me with a scornful stare and said, "Dr. Crowley, I want an explanation of this man's wasteful spending practices." I assumed as best I could the look of that television detective, called to mind the approximate number of campus citizens we then had, and replied, "Well, Senator, there are 8 thousand stories in the naked university." Riotous laughter ensued from the committee members (probably, you had to be there), and I only needed to add that the administrator's story was but one of the eight thousand. The rest of them were happy stories, and would the committee be interested in hearing some of them? No, not really. This was one of those bullet dodging moments that the mind's eye can picture forever.

Likewise an infamous 60 seconds early on in my lobbying career when a trip to the hallway cost the university $1.5 million. Toward the end of the session at that time, when the Senate Finance and Assembly Ways and Means committees met to try to iron out their differences in an atmosphere of intense hostility between the two committee chairs, one wanted to maintain a constant vigil lest a carefully nurtured project suddenly became trade bait. For some reason, on this particular morning, I was feeling secure, and so—when summoned outside the chamber for a quick conversation—I complied. I was back in one minute. When I returned, that one-and-a-half million I had guarded with my life for five months was gone, traded away by the two chairs. The money was intended for an addition to our fine arts building. At that moment, I envisioned myself—a very different picture in the mind's eye—hanging in effigy, or maybe in the flesh, from a rafter in that building, and I thought I ought to provide the rope.

The story had a happy ending: A few years later, with the legislature's blessing, we managed to find nearly $9 million for that expansion project and we built something bigger and better than the original appropriation would have allowed. Even so, I didn't receive flowers from the fine arts faculty.

Well, there are eras—the decade of the 1980s was one such for me. The '90s were another. And there are particularly memorable years. Years during which I nearly lost my job, or served in a second one (like the NCAA presidency), or certain legislative years when the bacon was brought home (or wasn't). And there are days, special days to recall: That day—night actually—when vice president Bob Gorrell called to give me the shocking news that I was to be recommended to the regents as interim president. The day 13 months later when the regents gave me the job for real, and the campus carillon chimed for the first time in a long time. The day in October 1979, when I was inaugurated, and old friends—doubtless just as surprised as I was—came from far and near to help me celebrate. The day in June 1985, when the legislature passed the authorization and appropriation bill and seven years of hard labor finally bore fruit. The day in New Orleans, in January 1993, when 2,000 convention delegates elected me NCAA president (and the one two years later, in San Diego, following a series of perilous adventures, when I passed the gavel to my successor). The day (night, again) in September 1995, when Dixie May took a deep breath in front of 800 people at the annual Foundation Banquet and pledged the $1 million that took us over the top in our five-year capital campaign. The day Bill Raggio mentioned that letter.

Oh, and there is that other kind of day. This is the one (and I have known quite a few of them) planned well in advance, carefully nurtured and fiercely protected by the office staff, who have erected clever,

impenetrable defenses against those determined to ruin it, fill it up
with their need for counsel, money, therapy, mere conversation, or the
chance to inveigh against a parking ticket.

This is a day with a completely empty calendar, offering an opportunity to catch up on overdue correspondence, to read, reflect, un-
wind, sleep in a little later, perhaps, and take your secretaries to lunch.
It stretches out before you in all its beckoning loveliness. You wake up,
and you want to sing, "Zipadee do dah!" And then, in a trice, it's
gone, the victim of an instant crisis, irate drop-in trade, unannounced
visits from old friends or itinerant celebrities, a scandal in the department of whatsis, a thousand different things that were not in the
plan, not even on the horizon, things that have never happened before on any campus, anywhere, all of them requiring immediate attention, inquiry, decision.

On these days, life is not lived at a leisurely pace. This is life at the
vortex. This is the president taking on the role, as one observer has
described it, of master of the unforeseen. There are no courses to teach
you how to handle such days. You just remember that lesson from
baseball—the one about crossing the white lines onto the playing field
every day, no matter how long you have been in the game, knowing,
that you are going to see something you've never seen before. You
manage, in these situations, by instinct.

One remembers these days, too. And Commencement days. And
big victory days on the athletic field or court. And days—20 of them—
when I gave the annual State of the University Address. If you laid
those addresses end to end, they would probably take up a whole day
of their own; 24 hours. Some would argue for a higher number.

And that day, finally, the one that's dawning now, when I leave the
Clark Administration building for the last time as president, glancing
to my left as the door closes behind me. There, between the building
and Manzanita Lake, is a red oak tree, donated in my honor in the late
1970s, by friends, to commemorate my appointment. I will want to
walk back around the building, to the south door. Etched in marble
above this door are the words, *Library of the University of Nevada, Erected
1926* (The library moved into new quarters in 1962.). I will want to call
to mind again that augury I experienced in 1958, when I was an undergraduate student at the University of Iowa. I saw a motion picture
then called "Five Against the House." It was an eminently forgettable

movie, but somehow one scene stayed with me down through the years. Brian Keith (the lead actor in the film) and fellow students were gathered on the steps of a building on a pretty college campus, plotting a robbery at a Reno casino. Etched in marble above the door just behind them were the words, *Library of the University of Nevada, Erected 1926.*

I have arrived at that point when people—knowing I am leaving soon for labor in other vineyards—ask me what advice I would have for my successor. In this matter, I side with Ambrose Bierce, who defined advice as the smallest current coin. I might want to advise the next president to offer *no* advice when he or she is asked the same question some years down the road. Times, events, circumstances, pressures, personalities—these doubtless will be different for the next person in this job. It seems presumptuous to suggest to this person how the job should be done.

Still, I could be tempted to say, "Remember those fours Ps. Be patient. Be persistent. Know that pain will be a frequent companion. Maintain that sense of humor that comes with having a broad perspective, the kind that makes room for both human heterodoxy and human genius, and allows you to laugh at yourself." I might add that, on those inevitable occasions when you are inclined to give a high estimate of your own genius, when you are ready to launch a bold venture on the basis of no one's counsel but your own, you consider this little piece of possible wisdom: "There is only a vowel's worth of difference between deft and daft." Perhaps I would want to say as well how important it is to keep in mind that those quantum leaps for which higher education is famous are usually preceded by inches of torturous progress. And that, as I opined at that last lecture long ago, "the university should be an institution that nurtures both the inches and the leaps."

Oh, and I suppose it could be appropriate to remind my successor, who probably already knows it, that maybe the most fundamental requirement of success in the job is to hire (and retain) good people. The good people you hire will hire good people, who, in turn, will hire good people. That's how you move an institution.

It is a common criticism of those who hold positions of authority that they are wont to hire yes-persons. I have heard that criticism myself; it seems to go with the territory. The fact is that the president who finds comfort only with yes-persons sends himself (or herself) on a fool's errand. He (or she) will not be gone long. If those around you are there to tell you how wonderful you are, how great your ideas are, and how clever your decisions, you should go out to spread this message to the real world. On this trip, too, you won't be gone long. If you are a practical person, possessed of an iota or two of common sense, you make it your chief business to hire good people. Then you get out of their way.

The analysts are out in force again now, trying to make sense of a new century, trying to project a future wrought from further technological advances. This time, unlike their forebears from the early 1980s, they don't often offer a litany of despair for higher education. Their prognoses for the decades ahead tell of eminently accessible instructional programs, of open gateways to constantly increasing quantities of information, of a world where one can get a college education without leaving the house. Some imagine a future in which university campuses are almost solely virtual, the real ones having become, like the Pyramids, vestiges of an earlier civilization.

"Imagine" may be the key word here. These analytical visions of higher education's destiny are interesting, inventive, provocative. But they leave out the leaveners. The future will not develop simply out of the deterministic influences of technology or economy. *People* will create the future, partially out of raw material yet to be discovered, partially out of the will to build. Their determination, rather than some theory of determinism, will be the essential ingredient.

Just so at the University of Nevada. We did not accept here in 1980 those portents of dire days to come. Instead, lots of people got together—those good people who hire good people—and continued the work of erecting a cathedral. The pundits of 20 years ago would not have predicted what was to transpire here in the decades between then and now. But then, pundits do not build cathedrals. As for me, well, I have been privileged to be among the stonemasons. This is not a future I foresaw for myself—not when I became a college dropout in the 1950s, nor when I returned to the University of Iowa five years later. Not when I started graduate work at Fresno State and later at the University of Washington, nor when I arrived in Reno 35 years ago with a wife and three kids, and one more to come (our only native Neva-dan!), happy to have a job that paid $3500 for a one-semester fill-in appointment. Not even when I took that peculiar journey to the president's office in February of 1978, ill-prepared to assume the position and never supposing I might still be in it 23 years later.

And, speaking of stonemasons, certainly not when I was called upon for the first time to help dedicate a new campus building. It has long been a tradition of the university to invite the local Masonic Temple to participate in the ceremonies, and such was the case with this one. Among my duties that day was to assist the regent in attendance in whose honor the building had been named—in applying fresh mortar to the cornerstone. I was to hand her the trowel with the mortar on it, which I did. In the process, I managed to transport the mortar earth-ward, its passage ending on top of the regent's new shoes. "I'm sorry," I said. "We call this the trowel and error system."

I survived that experience, and the many errors that followed. Service as a university president is a privilege accorded to few. I have loved doing this job, and I am thankful to all those who have made it possible for me to do it for so long. Francis Wayland, the great 19th century president of Brown, wrote of the relief and freedom he felt when he heard the university bell ring to open the 1855 college year. To hear that bell, he observed was "to know, for the first time in nearly 29 years, that it calls me to no duty." I'll let you know how it feels to me when I hear the campus carillon chime in the Fall of 2001.

End of conversation.

∾

Colophon

Designed by Robert E. Blesse at the Black Rock Press, University of Nevada, Reno Library. The typefaces are Stone Serif for the text and Oxford and Myriad for the cover. Printed and bound by Sheridan Books, Ann Arbor, Michigan. Special thanks to Maggie Eirenschmalz who assisted with the production of this book.